COGNITIVE SCIENCE and its APPLICATIONS for HUMAN-COMPUTER INTERACTION

COGNITIVE SCIENCE
and its APPLICATIONS
for HUMAN-COMPUTER
INTERACTION

Edited by

Raymonde Guindon
Microelectronics and
Computer Technology Corporation

LEA LAWRENCE ERLBAUM ASSOCIATES, PUBLISHERS
1988 Hillsdale, New Jersey   Hove and London

Lawrence Erlbaum Associates, Inc., Publishers
365 Broadway
Hillsdale, New Jersey 07642

Library of Congress Cataloging-in-Publication Data

Cognitive science and its applications for human-computer
interaction.

Includes indexes.
1. Interactive computer systems.   2. System design.
3. Cognition.   I. Guindon, Raymonde.
QA76.9.I58C63   1988   004'.33   87-36523
ISBN 0-89859-884-2

Printed in the United States of America
10   9   8   7   6   5   4   3   2

Contents

Contributors

Kim M. Fairchild

Microelectronics and Computer
    Technology Corporation
3500 West Balcones Center Drive
Austin, Texas 78759

Gerhard Fischer

Computer Science Department
University of Colorado
Boulder, Colorado 80309

Barbara Fox

Linguistics Department
University of Colorado
Boulder, Colorado 80309

George W. Furnas

Bell Communications Research
435 South Street, Room 2M 397
Morristown, New Jersey 07960

Raymonde Guindon

Microelectronics and Computer
    Technology Corporation
3500 West Balcones Center Drive
Austin, Texas 78759

William P. Jones

Microelectronics and Computer
    Technology Corporation
3500 West Balcones Center Drive
Austin, Texas 78759

Roger King

Computer Science Department
University of Colorado
Boulder, Colorado 80309

Andreas C. Lemke

Computer Science Department
University of Colorado
Boulder, Colorado 80309

Clayton Lewis

Computer Science Department
University of Colorado
Boulder, Colorado 80309

James E. McDonald

Computing Research Laboratory
New Mexico State University
Las Cruces, New Mexico 88003

Peter G. Polson

Department of Psychology
University of Colorado
Boulder, Colorado 80309

Steven E. Poltrock

Microelectronics and Computer
    Technology Corporation
3500 West Balcones Center Drive
Austin, Texas 78759

Roger W. Schvaneveldt

Computing Research Laboratory
New Mexico State University
Las Cruces, New Mexico 88003

Paul Smolensky

Computer Science Department
University of Colorado
Boulder, Colorado 80309

Preface

Breaking the communication barriers between experts in different disciplines requires overcoming differences in jargon, and more importantly, profound differences in paradigms. Being an expert in more than one technical area is a rare achievement. The field of human-computer interaction is striving to provide the conceptual foundations for designing computer tools and the environment needed to perform increasingly more complex and specialized tasks. To achieve this goal, human-computer interaction must rely on the meeting of specialized, expert minds. Each of the research projects presented in this book investigate some critical question on the path of progress in human-computer interaction. These projects would not have been feasible without the multidisciplinarity of the research team or of the researchers themselves.

This book is composed of chapters organized around the theme of multidisciplinary research and the contribution of cognitive science to the research projects. Interestingly, we find instances of research projects overlapping in goals, but using widely diverse methodologies. We also find research projects using the same or similar methodologies to answer quite different questions. These methodologies and techniques come from such diverse fields as scaling and measurement, computer science, experimental psychology, and linguistics. The applications of these varied methodologies and techniques act in synergy to solve the problems posed by human-computer interaction.

Why say in many words what an annotated diagram can explain more concisely and directly? Some of the interconnections between the research projects presented in this book are depicted in the figure on the next page. The dotted links point to the concepts, techniques, and models underlying the research projects, while the solid links point to the goals of the projects.

The goal of Fischer and Lemke, in the first chapter, is to provide maximal access to the rich functionality available in current computer systems to

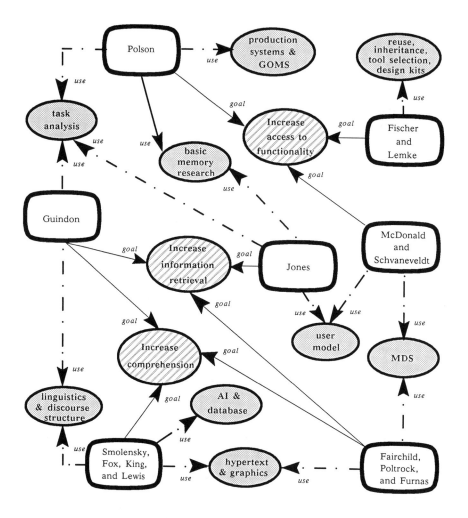

Figure 1: Overlap in goals and techniques between chapters

casual and intermediate users. They present an analysis of these users' needs based on previous research and their own observations. They found that casual and intermediate users are rarely willing or capable of spending the time necessary to acquire the detailed knowledge needed to make adequate use of the available functionality. They have developed a computer environment supporting constrained design processes as a step towards convivial computer systems. These processes allow the novice and intermediate users to access rich functionality without extensive initial learning, while allowing expert users to reuse already developed and tested components. The described constrained design processes are achieved through selection, combination, and instantiation of general tools, and design kits.

In the second chapter, Polson also concerns himself with maximizing the use of available functionality. His strategy is to empirically determine the conditions favoring skills transfer between interfaces. He describes in detail the notion of consistent interfaces in terms of the GOMS model. He builds and validates a model of the transfer process between consistent interfaces based on the cognitive complexity theory. He shows that basic findings from early research in psychology on human memory is relevant to understanding the transfer of skills between computer systems and the phenomenon of interference between interfaces.

Smolensky, Fox, King, and Lewis describe an environment to support reasoning and decision-making. This environment provides for the representation of complex arguments with semi-structured forms. The argumentation language, ARL, captures the formal aspects of the argument, while the user provides the informal components in natural language. The environment, EUCLID, provides some processability of the semi-structured arguments by testing, for example, their well-formedness. It also provides already built-in schemas or templates for many types of arguments. Moreover, users can examine the content and structure of an argument with graphical or tabular displays. EUCLID is expected to increase the logical reasoning skills of users, both in the generation and in the comprehension of arguments and proofs. This research project is based on linguistics research in argumentative discourse structure, artificial intelligence, database technology, and cognitive psychology.

Turning to my chapter, I compare the structure of user-advisor dialogues in their most frequent form, spoken face-to-face between two humans, to the structure of typed dialogues between a user and a computerized advisory system. The purpose of the study is to gather data about users' dialogues to guide the design of natural language front-ends to advisory systems. It is hoped that determining the structure of users' dialogues will help natural language interfaces perform anaphora resolution. The study uses findings and methods from linguistic discourse analysis and experimental psychology to answer a question in human-computer interaction. In the study, a task analysis based on the GOMS model is completed and a corresponding task structure is derived. The task structure seems to have more influence on the structure of spoken face-to-face dialogues than on the structure of typed dialogues. Typed user-advisor dialogues resemble independent queries more than cohesive discourse. Implications for the design of natural languages interfaces are generated.

Contending with information overload, SemNet is a 3-D graphical interface for large knowledge bases. Designed by Fairchild, Poltrock, and Furnas, SemNet allows easy retrieval of information from and exploration of large knowledge bases. The user "travels through" the knowledge base with a choice of many navigation techniques. The knowledge base information is also selectively displayed through FishEye views specified by the user. The positioning and the selection of elements to be displayed is based on techniques such as multidimensional scaling and the centroid heuristic. SemNet has been used and empirically evaluated as an interface to a large knowledge base of Prolog rules to perform morphological analysis.

Also struggling with information overload, Jones' Memory Extender system provides for context based retrieval of files from large filing systems. In the ME system, files and context are represented in an associative network of weighted term links. Three processes underly the adaptive and contextually sensitive retrieval: an exchange of representational information, a decay mechanism, and a spreading activation matching algorithm. The ME system is founded on a task analysis of information retrieval and, as in Polson's model, on basic research on the properties and mechanisms of human memory. By designing a system with good fit to both the task and the user's capabilities, ME provides a computational extension to the user's memory. Jones' research reveals a mutually beneficial interplay between basic research in human information processing and applied efforts to build more usable computer systems.

McDonald and Schvaneveldt share the goal of Fischer and Lemke and of Polson: maximal access to the functionality of computer systems to casual and intermediate users. They propose an interface design methodology which they are testing. The methodology involves uncovering the conceptual models of a computer system from experienced users. These models are uncovered through the use of hierarchical cluster analysis, multidimensional scaling, and the Pathfinder algorithm. They have applied the methodology to the design of an interactive Unix documentation system, Superman II. They present a review of several applications that illustrate key aspects of their methodology.

This book grew from presentations at a regional meeting of the American Association for the Advancement of Sciences, held at the University of Colorado, Boulder. I was asked to help organize a session at the Psychological Sciences section of the conference by Dr. Jesse Purdy. Strong interest was expressed by the conference organizers in the topics of cognitive science and of human-computer interaction. I felt that these topics were quite close to each other in the sense that the development of cognitive science had provided many of the empirical methodologies and conceptual models used in the field of human-computer interaction. So I selected as the theme of the session the contribution of the different disciplines composing cognitive science to the study of human-computer interaction. I also emphasized the multidisciplinarity required of the researchers or teams of researchers working in the area of human-computer interaction. The University of Colorado was an especially appropriate site for the conference because of its excellent Institute for Cognitive Science and multidisciplinary work in human-computer interaction. Moreover, this conference gave me an opportunity to describe some the work in progress in human-computer interaction at the Microelectronics and Computer Technology Corporation.

I wish to thank the many colleagues who reviewed one or more chapters of this book and who significantly helped increase their quality: Ernest Chang, Jeff Conklin, Joyce Conner, Nancy Cooke, Jonathan Grudin, Will Hill, Patrick Lincoln, Gale Martin, Jim Miller, Don Norman, Ken Paap, Nancy Pennington, and Elaine Rich. And thanks to all the contributors who also reviewed each other's chapters and thus, helped produce a more integrated book. Also, this book would have never appeared without Bill Curtis' encouragement and support throughout.   Finally, Joyce Conner performed excellent editorial supervision, accomplished the feat of producing the camera-ready version of this book, keeping track of chapters in various stages of completion, designing the layout of the chapters, ensuring uniformity of style throughout the book, improving the writing style, and much more.

Raymonde Guindon

1
Constrained Design Processes: Steps Towards Convivial Computing

GERHARD FISCHER
ANDREAS C. LEMKE

Our goal is to construct components of *convivial computer systems* which give people who use them the greatest opportunity to enrich their environments with the fruits of *their* vision. *Constrained design processes* are a means of resolving the conflict between the generality, power, and rich functionality of modern computer systems, and the limited time and effort which casual and intermediate users want to spend to solve their problems without becoming computer experts. Intelligent support systems are components which make it less difficult to learn and use complex computer systems. We have constructed a variety of *design kits* as instances of intelligent user support systems which allow users to carry out constrained design processes and give them control over their environment. Our experience in building and using these design kits will be described.

1. Introduction

Most computer users experience computer systems as unfriendly, uncooperative and requiring too much time and effort to get something done. Users find themselves dependent on specialists, they notice that *software is not soft* (i.e., the behavior of a system can not be changed without reprogramming it substantially), they have to relearn a system after they have not used it for some time, and they spend more time fighting the computer than solving their problem.

In this chapter we will discuss what design kits can contribute to the goal of convivial computing systems. From a different perspective, design kits also contribute to two other major goals of our research: to construct intelligent support systems (Fischer, 1986) and to enhance incremental learning processes with knowledge-based systems (Fischer, 1987). In

Section 2 we will briefly describe what we mean by convivial systems. One way of making (especially functionality-rich) systems more convivial is to provide intelligent support systems (Section 3). In Section 4 we argue that for certain classes of users and tasks there is a need for constrained design processes. In Section 5 we present methodologies and systems which support constrained design processes. In Section 6 we describe in detail some of the tools and the systems which we have built to support constrained design processes:

1. WLISPRC is a tool to customize WLISP (a window-based user-interface toolkit, based on LISP, developed by our research group over the last 6 years (Fabian & Lemke, 1985; Boecker, Fabian, Lemke, 1985; Fabian, 1986)).

2. WIDES, a window design kit for WLISP, allows designers to build window-based systems at a high level of abstraction and it generates the programs for this application in the background.

3. TRIKIT is a design kit for TRISTAN. TRISTAN (Nieper, 1985) is a generic tool for generating graphical representations for general graph structures. TRIKIT uses a form-based approach to allow the designer to combine application specific semantics with the generic tool.

In Section 7 we briefly describe our experience with using these systems. Section 8 relates our systems to other work in this area, and the last section discusses a few conclusions drawn from this work.

2. Convivial Computer Systems

Illich (1973) has introduced the notion of "convivial tools" which he defines as follows:

> Tools are intrinsic to social relationships. An individual relates himself in action to his society through the use of tools which he actively masters, or by which he is passively acted upon. To the degree that he masters his tools, he can invest the world with his meaning; to the degree that he is mastered by his tools, the shape of the tool determines his own self-image. Convivial tools are those which give each person who uses them the greatest opportunity to enrich the environment with the fruits of his or her vision.
>
> Tools foster conviviality to the extent to which they can be easily used,

by anybody, as often or as seldom as desired, for the accomplishment of a purpose chosen by the user.

Illich's thinking is very broad and he tries to show alternatives for future technology-based developments and their integration into society. We have applied his thoughts to information processing technologies and systems (Fischer, 1981) and believe that conviviality is a dimension which sets computers apart from other communication technologies. All other communication and information technologies (e.g., television, videodiscs, interactive videotex) are passive, i.e., users have little influence to shape them to their own taste and their own tasks. They have some selective power but there is no way that they can extend system capabilities in ways which the designer of those systems did not directly foresee.

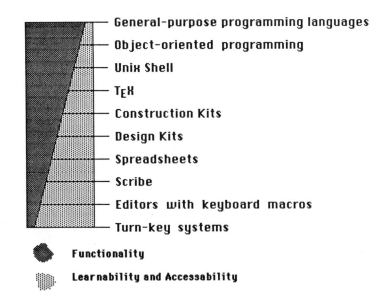

Figure 2-1: The spectrum of conviviality

We do not claim that currently existing computer systems are convivial. Most systems belong to one of the extremes of the spectrum of conviviality (Figure 2-1):

1. **General purpose programming languages:** They are powerful, but they are hard to learn, they are often too far away from the conceptual structure of the problem, and it takes too long to get a task done or a problem solved. This class of systems can be adequately described by the Turing tar-pit (defined by Alan Perlis; see Hutchins, Hollan, & Norman (1986)):

   Beware the Turing tar-pit, in which everything is possible but nothing of interest is easy.

2. **Turn-key systems:** They are easy to use, no special training is required, but they can not be modified by the user. This class of systems can be adequately described by the converse of the Turing tar-pit:

   Beware the over-specialized system where operations are easy, but little of interest is possible.

Starting from both ends, there are promising ways to make systems more convivial. Coming from the "general purpose programming languages" end of the spectrum, object-oriented programming (in SmallTalk (Goldberg, 1981) or ObjTalk (Rathke, 1986)), user interface management systems, programming environments and command languages like the UNIX shell are efforts to make systems more accessible and usable. Coming from the other end, good turn-key systems contain features which make them modifiable by the user without having to change the internal structures. Editors allow users to define their own keys ("keyboard macros") and modern user interfaces allow users to create and manipulate windows, menus, icons etc., at an easy to learn level.

Turn-key systems appear as a monolithic block (Figure 2-2). The user can choose to use them if their functionality is appropriate. But they become obsolete if they cannot meet a specific requirement.

The user should have control over a tool on multiple levels. Figure 2-3 shows the levels of control for the EMACS editor (Stallman, 1981; Gosling, 1982). The keystroke level together with its special purpose extensions (lisp mode, etc.) is most frequently and most easily used. The lower

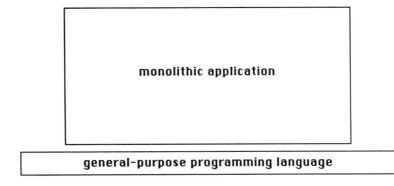

Figure 2-2: Turn-key systems

levels gradually provide more functionality but require more knowledge about the implementation of the editor. Due to this structure, EMACS is perceived as a convivial tool that can be extended and adapted to many different needs.

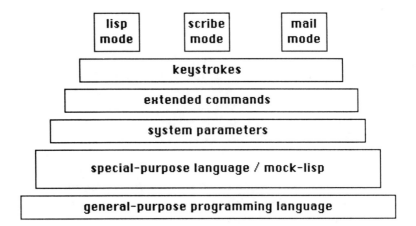

Figure 2-3: Levels of control over the EMACS editor

Despite our goal of making computer systems more convivial, i.e., giving more control to the user, we *do not believe that more control is always better.* Many general advances in our society (e.g., automatic transmission in automobiles) and those specifically in computing are due to the automation of tasks which before had to be done by hand. Assemblers freed us from keeping track of memory management, high level languages and compilers eliminated the need to take specific hardware architectures into account, and document production systems allow us to put our emphasis on content instead of form of written documents.

The last domain illustrates that the right amount of user control is not a fixed constant, but depends on the users and their tasks. Truly convivial tools should give the user any desired control, but they should not require that it be exercised. In this sense, the text formatting systems T_EX and Scribe (Furuta, Scofield, & Shaw, 1982), show the following differences (see also Figure 2-1):

1. The T_EX user is viewed as being an author who wants to position objects exactly on the printed page, producing a document with the finest possible appearance. The user has to exercise a rather large amount of control. The emphasis is on power and expressiveness of the formatting language.

2. The Scribe user is viewed as an author who is more interested in easily specifying the abstract objects within the document, leaving the details of the appearance of objects to an expert who establishes definitions that map the author's objects to the printed page. The Scribe user usually exercises little control. Although Scribe offers substantial control over the appearance of a document, it does not allow to specify everything that is possible with T_EX. Scribe's emphasis is on the simplicity of its input language and on support by writer's workbench tools.

The development of convivial tools will break down an old distinction: *there will be no sharp border line between programming and using programs* -- a distinction which has been a major obstacle for the usefulness of computers. Convivial tools will remove from the "meta-designers" (i.e., the persons who design design-tools for other people) the impossible task of anticipating all possible uses of a tool and all people's needs. Convivial tools encourage users to be actively engaged and to generate creative extensions to the artifacts given to them. Their use and availability should not be restricted to a few highly educated people. Convivial tools require to replace "Human Computer

Communication" by "Human Problem-Domain Communication". Human Problem-Domain Communication is an important step forward, because users can operate within the semantics of their domain of expertise and the formal descriptions closely match the structures of the problem domain.

Convivial tools raise a number of interesting questions, which we will investigate in our future research: Should systems be *adaptive* (i.e., the system itself changes its behavior based on a model of the user and the task (Fischer, Lemke, & Schwab, 1985)) or should systems *be adaptable by the user*? Should systems be composed of simple or intelligent tools (Norman, 1986)? *Simple tools* can have problems, because they require too much skill, time and effort from the user. It is, for example, far from easy to construct an interesting model using a sophisticated technical construction kit (Fischer & Boecker, 1983). *Intelligent tools* can have problems because many of them fail to give any indication of how they operate and what they are doing; the user feels like an observer, watching while unexplained operations take place. This mode of operation results in a lack of control over events and does not achieve any conviviality.

3. Intelligent Support Systems

The "intelligence" of a complex computer system must contribute to its ease of use. Truly intelligent and knowledgeable human communicators, such as good teachers, use a substantial part of their knowledge to explain their expertise to others. In the same way, the "intelligence" of a computer should be applied to providing effective communication. Equipping modern computer systems with more and more computational power and functionality will be of little use unless we are able to assist the user in taking advantage of them. Empirical investigations (Fischer, Lemke, & Schwab, 1985) have shown that on the average only a small fraction of the functionality of complex systems such as UNIX, EMACS, or Lisp is used. In Figure 3-1 we give an indication of the complexity (in number of objects, tools, and amount of written documentation) of modern computer systems.

Number of Computational Objects in Systems

EMACS:
- 170 function keys and 462 commands

UNIX:
- more than 700 commands and a large number of embedded systems

LISP-Systems:
- FRANZ-LISP: 685 functions
- WLISP: 2590 LISP functions and 200 ObjTalk classes
- SYMBOLICS LISP MACHINES: 19000 functions and 2300 flavors

Amount of Written Documentation

Symbolics LISP Machines:
- 10 books with 3000 pages
- does not include any application programs

SUN workstations:
- 15 books with 4600 pages
- additional Beginner's Guides: 8 books totaling 800 pages

Figure 3-1: Quantitative analysis of some systems

In our research work we have used the computational power of modern computer systems to construct a variety of *intelligent support systems* (see Figure 3-2). These support systems are called *intelligent*, because they have knowledge about the task, knowledge about the user, and they support communication capabilities which allow the user to interact with them in a more "natural" way. Some of the components (e.g., for explanation and visualization) are specifically constructed to overcome some of the negative aspects of intelligent tools as mentioned above (e.g., the user should not be limited to be an observer, but should be able to understand what is going on).

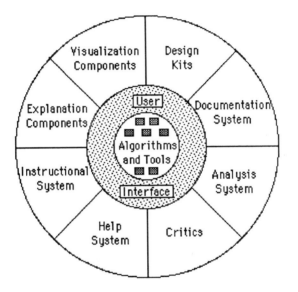

Figure 3-2: The architecture of intelligent support systems

By constructing these intelligent support systems we hope to increase the conviviality of systems. Some of our prototypical developments are described in the following papers:
- documentation systems in (Fischer & Schneider, 1984),
- help systems in (Fischer, Lemke, & Schwab, 1985),
- critics in (Fischer, 1987),
- visualization tools in (Boecker, Fischer, & Nieper, 1986) and
- design kits in Section 6 of this chapter.

4. The Need for Constrained Design Processes

Alan Kay (1984) considers the computer as the first *metamedium* with degrees of freedom for representation and expression never before encountered and as yet barely investigated. This large design space makes design processes very difficult. Much experience and knowledge is needed if this space is to be successfully used. Especially for those who use the computer only as a tool, this space is overwhelming and can prevent any attempts at making the computer convivial. Constraining the design space in a user- and domain-dependent way can make more design processes tractable, even for non-computer experts.

With these research goals in mind, we encounter a difficulty in terminology: our users should not just be consumers but also designers. Therefore, we have to introduce the notion of meta-designer for the group of people who build design tools for other people. For simplicity, we will use the pair "designer and user" instead of "meta-designer and designer". Having pointed out this distinction, a "user" is still not a clearly defined concept. In some cases he/she may be the domain expert (i.e., a person who knows little about computers but much about a certain application domain), in other cases he/she may be a system designer who uses a knowledge representation formalism or a user interface toolkit. Most of the design kits described in Section 6 build a bridge between these two levels.

The following objectives generate a need for constrained design processes:

1. *to enhance incremental learning of complex systems* and to delimit useful microworlds -- inexperienced users should be able to get started and do useful work when they know only a small part of the system (Fischer, 1987);

2. *to increase subjective computability* (e.g., by eliminating prerequisite knowledge and skills and by raising the level of abstraction);

3. *to make experts more efficient* (e.g., they can reuse tested building blocks and they do not have to worry about details);

4. *to guide users in the relevant context* so they can choose the next steps (e.g., WIDES (see Section 6.2) provides in the code window the corresponding ObjTalk definition of what users would have to do if the WIDES were not available);

5. *to lead the user from "chaos to order"* (e.g., the primitives of a programming language or the basic elements of a technical construction kit give little guidance on how to construct a complex artifact to achieve a certain purpose).

4.1 User Modifiability and User Control

Why is there a need for user modifiability and user control? The specification process of what a program should do is more complex and evolutionary than previously believed. This is especially true for ill-structured problems like those which arise in areas like Artificial Intelligence and Human-Computer Communication. Computer systems in these areas are *open systems*, their requirements cannot be defined in detail at program writing time but will arise dynamically at program run time. Programs have to cope with "action at a distance." Many non-expert users who used the computer mostly to support them in carrying out routine cognitive skills like text processing are now more and more requiring individualized support for increasingly demanding cognitive skills like information retrieval, visualization support in understanding complex systems, explanations, help, and instruction.

The goal of making tools modifiable by the user does not imply transferring the responsibility of good tool design to the user. It is probably safe to assume that normal users will never build tools of the quality a professional designer would. But this is not the goal of convivial systems. Only if the tool does not satisfy the needs and the taste of the users (which they know best themselves) then should they carry out a constrained design process to adapt it. The strongest test of a system with respect to user modifiability and user control is not how well its features conform to anticipated needs but how well it performs when one wants to do something the designer did not specifically foresee although it is in the system's global domain of application.

Pre-designed systems are too encapsulated for problems whose nature and specifications change and evolve. A useful system must accommodate these changing needs. The user must have some amount of control over the system. Suppose we design an expert system to help lawyers. As a lawyer uses this system, the system should be able to adjust to his or her particular needs which cannot be foreseen because they may be almost unique among the user population. Furthermore, in many cases this adjustment cannot be done by sending in a request for modification to the original system developers, because they may have problems understanding the nature of the request. The users should be able to make the required modifications in the system themselves.

4.2 Support for the Casual and Intermediate Users

The rich functionality of modern computer systems made two classes of users predominant: *casual* and *intermediate* users. The demands made on users' memory and learning ability are illustrated by a quantitative analysis of the systems used in our research (Figure 3-1).

Even if users are experts in *some* systems, there will be many more systems available to them where they are at best casual users. *Casual users* need in many cases more control and more variability than turn-key systems are able to offer, but at the same time it should not be necessary to know a system completely before anything can be done. Another issue is also crucial for casual users: the time to relearn a system after not having used it for some time. It seems a safe assumption that a system which was easy to learn the first time should not be too difficult to relearn at a later time.

In order to successfully exploit the capabilities of most complex computer systems, users must have reached an *intermediate* level of skills and knowledge. Incremental learning processes (Fischer, 1987), which extend over months and years, are required to make the transition from a novice to an expert. One intrinsic conflict in designing systems is caused by the demand that these systems should have *no threshold and no ceiling*. There should be entry points which make it easy to get started and the limitations of the systems should not be reached soon after. Constrained design processes are one way to partially resolve this design conflict. Our window design kit (see Section 6.2) has exactly this goal: to serve as an entry point to the full generality of our user interface construction kit. The code for various types of windows can be created automatically by making selections from a suggestion menu. If more complex windows are desired, one can modify the generated code. Under this perspective it serves as a *transient object*: if someone knows the underlying formalisms well enough, then there is no need any more to use the design kit.

4.3 Support for Rapid Prototyping

Constrained design processes are *not* only useful to produce transient objects. Experts can also take advantage of them if the functionality required is within the scope of the constrained design processes. The advantages of restricting ourselves to the limits of constrained design processes are: the human effort is smaller (e.g., less code to write), the process is less error-prone (because we can reuse tested building blocks), and users have to know less to succeed (e.g., no worries about low-level details). These advantages are especially important for a rapid prototyping methodology where several experimental systems have to be constructed quickly.

4.4 From Design to Redesign

We argued before that complex systems can never be completely predesigned, because their applications cannot be precisely foreseen, and requirements are often modified as the design and the implementation proceed. Therefore, real systems must be continuously *redesigned* (Fischer & Kintsch, 1986). *Reuse* of existing components is an important part of this process. Just as one relies on already established theorems in a new mathematical proof, new systems should be built as much as possible using existing parts. In order to do so, the functioning of these parts must be understood. An important question concerns the level of understanding that is necessary for successful redesign: exactly how much does the user have to understand? Our methodologies (differential programming and programming by specialization based on our object-oriented language ObjTalk) and our tools are one step in the direction of making it easier to modify an existing system than to create a new one.

5. Methodologies and Systems to Support Constrained Design Processes

Informal experiments (Fischer, 1987) indicate that the following problems prevent users from successfully exploiting the potential of high functionality systems:

- users do not know about the existence of tools,
- users do not know how to access tools,
- users do not know when to use these tools,
- users do not understand the results which are produced by the tools,
- users cannot combine, adapt, and modify a tool to their specific needs.

In this section we describe how constrained design processes, based on different methods and systems, can overcome some of these problems.

5.1 Selection

Selection of tools from a set of tools seems to be the least demanding method to carry out a constrained design process. But in realistic situations, it is far from being trivial. Different from a Swiss army knife, which has at most 15 different tools (Figure 5-1), we may have hundreds or thousands (Figure 3-1) of tools in a high functionality computer system.

The CATALOG, a tool which we recently built to access the many tools and application systems in our WLISP system, simplifies the selection process. The iconic representations help users to see what is there and it provides clues about systems they might be interested in.

Selection systems can be made more versatile by giving the user the possibility to make adjustments or set parameters (like specifying options to commands). They require that most work be done by the designer in anticipation of the needs of the user. This strategy leads to systems containing a large number of tools many of which may never be used and which are, consequently, unnecessarily complex.

Figure 5-1: Selection of tools: the Swiss army knife

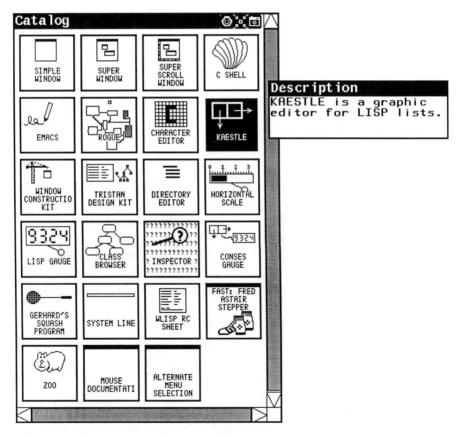

Figure 5-2: The CATALOG: a tool to simplify selection processes

Are selection type systems all that we need? We do not think so and agree with Alan Kay (1984) who notes:

> *Does this mean that what might be called a driver-education to com-*
> *puter literacy is all most people will ever need - that one need only*
> *learn how to "drive" applications programs and need never learn to*
> *program? Certainly not. Users must be able to tailor a system to their*
> *wants. Anything less would be as absurd as requiring essays to be*
> *formed out of paragraphs that have already been written.*

5.2 Simple Combination

Believing in recursive function theory, we know that we can compute anything with a set of very simple functions and powerful ways of combination like function definition and recursion. But the more interesting combinations are too complicated and require too many intermediate levels to get to the level of abstraction the user can operate at.

A good example of a simple combination process is illustrated with the electric drill in Figure 5-3 (the basic design of TRIKIT in Section 6.3 is very similar).

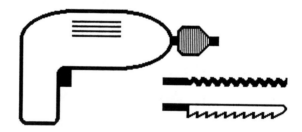

Figure 5-3:   Simple combination of tools: the electric drill

Other simple combination processes allow the user to define keyboard macros in extensible editors. The combination method, in this case, is just a simple sequencing operation. Another example is the concept of a pipe in UNIX which allows to use the output of one tool as the input to another tool. Direct manipulation styles of human-computer interaction are also based on a simple combination process: any output which appears on the screen can be used as an input (a concept called "interreferential I/O" by Norman and Draper (1986)).

Combination processes become more difficult if there are many building blocks to work with, if the number of links necessary to build a connection increases and if compatibility between parts is not obvious.

5.3 Instantiation

Instantiation is another methodology to carry out constrained design processes. The adjustable wrench (Figure 5-4) can be thought of (in the terminology of object-oriented programming) as being the class of all wrenches which is instantiated through an adjustment process to fit a specific bolt. A restricted form of programming, in an object-oriented formalism like ObjTalk, can be done by creating instances of existing classes. Classes provide a set of abstract descriptions. If enough classes exist, we can generate a broad range of behavior. In KBEmacs (Waters, 1985), instantiation is used to turn abstract cliches into program code.

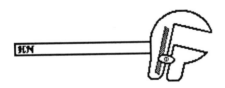

Figure 5-4:   Instantiation: the adjustable end wrench

5.4 Design Kits

Computer-supported design kits, as we try to envision and construct them, should not be restricted to providing the building blocks for a design, but they should support the process of composing interesting systems within the application domain. The building blocks should have self-knowledge and they should be more like active agents than like passive objects.

Design kits can be differentiated from:

1. *construction kits:* the elements of construction kits (e.g., the mixins and the general classes in WLISP (Figures 6-1 and 6-2); the parts in a technical construction system) are not particularly interesting by themselves but serve as building blocks for larger structures. Examples of excellent construction kits can be found in the software of Electronic Arts (e.g., the PinBall and the Music construction kits), in technical areas (e.g., FischerTechnik (Fischer & Boecker, 1983)), and in the toy world (e.g., LEGO).

2. *tool kits:* tool kits provide tools which serve specific purposes (e.g., the more specific classes in WLISP (Figure 6-1) or the entries in the catalog (Figure 5-2)); but a tool kit itself provides no guidance on how to exploit it's power to achieve a certain task. Contrary to components of construction kits, tools do not become part of the system constructed.

Design kits are *intelligent support systems* (Figure 3-2), which we see as integral parts of future computer systems. We believe that each system which allows user modifiability should have an associated design kit. Design kits can contribute towards the achievement of the following goals: to resolve, at least partially, the basic design conflict of generality and power versus ease of use; to make the computer behind a system invisible; to allow the users to deal primarily with the abstractions of the problem domain (human problem-domain communication); and, finally, to protect the user from error messages and from attempting illegal operations.

Design kits provide prototypical solutions and examples which can be modified and extended to achieve a new goal instead of starting from scratch; they support a "copy&edit" methodology for constructing systems through reuse and redesign of existing components (Fischer, Lemke, & Rathke, 1987).

5.5 Object-Oriented Programming

Objects encapsulate procedures and data and are the basic building blocks of object-oriented programming. Objects are grouped into classes and classes are combined in an inheritance hierarchy (Figure

6-2). This inheritance hierarchy supports differential description (object y is like object x *except for* u,v,...). Object-oriented formalisms (Lemke, 1985; Rathke, 1986) support constrained design processes through instantiation of existing classes (see Section 5.3) and through the creation of subclasses which can inherit large amounts of information from their superclasses. Many tasks can be achieved before one has to use the full generality of the formalism by defining new classes. New programming methodologies like differential programming and programming by specialization are supported.

6. Examples of Design Kits

The design kits described in this section have been implemented within the WLISP environment (Fabian & Lemke, 1985). Figure 6-1 shows an example screen. WLISP is an object-oriented user interface toolkit and programming environment implemented in FranzLisp and ObjTalk (Rathke, 1986), an object-oriented extension to Lisp.

The object-oriented nature of the system provides a good framework to represent the entities of the toolkit (windows, menus, push buttons, etc.). Figure 6-2 shows an ObjTalk inheritance hierarchy of some simple window classes. In the following sections, we will see how design kits can help build new applications from the building blocks of this hierarchy.

6.1 WLISPRC[1]

Characterization of the Problem Situation: Like many large systems, WLISP has several configuration parameters that make it adaptable to various uses:

- A *programmer* may want to have a debugger immediately available and see system resource statistics,

---

[1]The name WLISPRC has been chosen because it creates a system initialization file for WLISP. In Unix jargon the names of these files are commonly composed of the system name and the letters 'rc'.

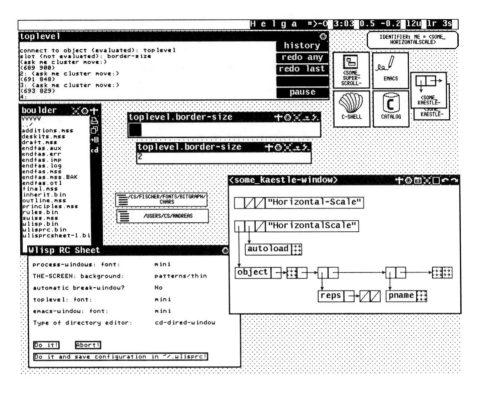

Figure 6-1: The WLISP programming environment

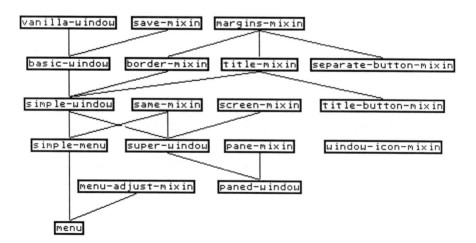

Figure 6-2: The inheritance hierarchy of windows

- whereas if the system is used for text processing, a text editor, a directory editor, and a text formatter should be in close reach.

Many of these parameters are not easy to access; their names are hard to remember; the user may not even know of their existence. A second problem is that most of them live in the dynamic environment of the executing system only and are reset to their default values when the system is rebooted. For this reason, a mechanism must be provided to save these parameters for future sessions.

Approach: A system configuration sheet has been built which shows certain system parameters. It allows their values to be edited in a constrained way and to permanently store the state of the system (Figure 6-3).

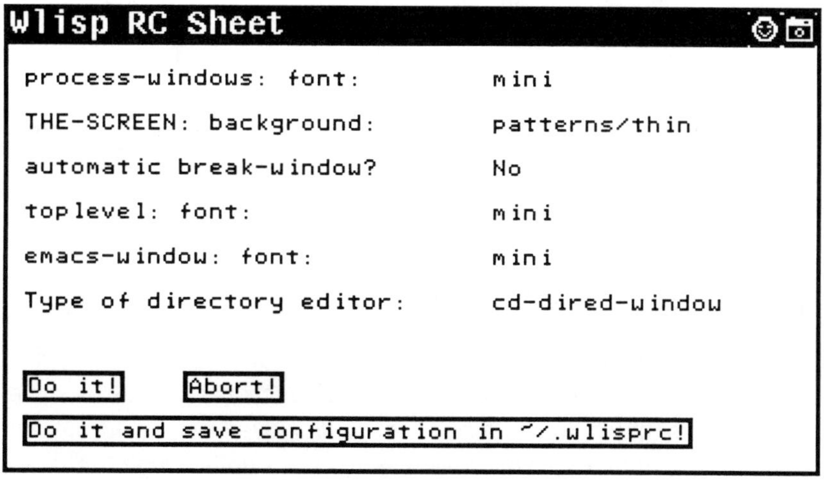

```
Wlisp RC Sheet                                        ☺ 📷

   process-windows: font:              mini

   THE-SCREEN: background:             patterns/thin

   automatic break-window?             No

   toplevel: font:                     mini

   emacs-window: font:                 mini

   Type of directory editor:           cd-dired-window


   Do it!     Abort!
   Do it and save configuration in ~/.wlisprc!
```

Figure 6-3: The WLISPRC sheet

6.1.1 Description of WLISPRC

We have considered two basic approaches to customize the WLISP programming environment:

1. Some systems have a configuration file, possibly with a specific editor which helps to fill in correct parameters, and

2. the user modifies the state of the system while using it through means provided inside the system (e.g., manipulation of the screen display with the mouse), and the system stores those settings immediately or at the end of the session in permanent memory (disk file).

WLISPRC is a system configuration sheet with two functions:

1. Setting certain system parameters (e.g., fonts of certain windows) which are shown in the sheet and which are otherwise only accessible through the LISP interpreter. At the same time, it makes sure that only legal values are entered (constrained editing). This is done using menu selection and choice fields which cycle through a set of values (Yes/No toggles are a special type of them).

2. Saving the system configuration for later use.

In addition to the parameters shown in the sheet, the configuration includes the current size and location of system windows on the screen and some information pertaining to currently loaded applications.

Figure 6-4 shows a system initialization file as generated by WLISPRC. Some of its entries have been commented for illustration purposes. The file contains Lisp and ObjTalk code.

6.1.2 Evaluation

Although system initialization files that can contain arbitrary program code provide the same, basically unbounded functionality, WLISPRC gives to most users much more *subjective control* over screen layout and many other parameters. Note that WLISPRC does not exclude the use of a regular initialization file.

WLISPRC is an example of the *reduce learning principle*. It can be easily seen that considerable knowledge would be necessary to write this file directly. The user would have to know the names of fonts, the names of the objects, and the slots where the parameters are to be stored.

In the case of the size and position of a window (screenregion), the numeric coordinates do not say much about the overall appearance on

```
;; The font of the toplevel window. Ask is the form to send a
;; message to an object (here the toplevel window).
(ask toplevel font = mini)

;; Size and position of the toplevel window.
(ask toplevel screenregion = (1 884 542 120))

;; Font default for process windows is mini.
(setq process-window-font 'mini)

(ask THE-SCREEN background = patterns/thin)

;; Do not pop up the break window automatically.
(setq automatic-break-window 'nil)

(ask emacs-window repslot: font (default process-window-font))

(setq directory-window cd-dired-window)

;; Load the sysline window and set its size, position, and mode.
(load-if-needed 'sysline window:dir)
(ask sysline-window-1 set:
     (screenregion = (0 1006 768 18))
     (flags = ""))

;; Load the catalog.
(load-if-needed 'catalog/system-catalog window:dir)
(ask Catalog move: 1 561)
(ask Catalog size = 283 283)

;; Load the directory editor and create an instance.
(load-if-needed 'directory-editor window:dir)
(setq current-directory (path:pwd))
(ask ,(ask ,directory-window instantiate:
            (screenregion = (616 534 146 260)))
     totop: nil)

;; Load the window identifier.
(load-if-needed 'identify window:dir)
(ask identifier move: 608 972)
```

Figure 6-4: The system initialization file generated by WLISPRC

the screen. If users see the real screen layout then they can tell immediately whether it is satisfying.

Instead of using a low level language, WLISPRC lets users make these specifications by directly moving windows to desired places, selecting fonts from menus, etc. The mode of interaction can be characterized as selection and direct editing and manipulation.

There are some problems which are not sufficiently addressed yet:

- It is not easy to know what the system's idea of its state is. The sheet shows only those parameters that can be modified using the sheet. Layout parameters which are affected through direct manipulation with the mouse are not reflected. What is a good way to do that?

- The meaning of some parameters (e.g., `automatic break window`) may be obscure to beginners because they may not even have encountered a situation where they are relevant. A user model could help to control whether this parameter should be listed and, if yes, in which way.

- It is not a priori clear which parameters of a system are part of its state and which of them are only relevant for the current context. Since WLISPRC has a set of permanent parameters that it stores in a disc file, it provides WLisp with some knowledge about this problem. For a parameter like the font of the toplevel window, however, this decision cannot be made generally. The reason for choosing a particular small font may be to be temporarily able to see a complete listing of some particular large data, but it may also be that the original font does not have a certain character that frequently occurs in outputs to this window.

- The classification of parameters may also change with the uses of the system and when it is being modified. It may be necessary to extend the system's notion of its state (e.g., "The following files should be loaded automatically"). How can the system be told to save more states? Currently there is only a programming language level interface for this purpose.

- Why not simply save everything and avoid worrying about the systems state? If the system is in some erroneous state or contains a lot of "garbage", it is certainly necessary to either suppress automatic state saving or to be able to go back to an earlier version.

6.2 WIDES: A Window Design Kit

Characterization of the Problem Situation: Window systems and user interface tool kits have a rich functionality. There are text windows and graphic windows that may have controls like menus and push buttons associated with them. There are various text, graphic, and network editors that may be adapted for particular applications.

Currently, the use of these components requires a considerable expertise which may only be acquired through an extended learning and experimentation period. The goal of WIDES is:

1. to reduce the knowledge required to use the components,
2. to support this learning process, and
3. to provide guidelines to structure a toolkit in such a way that useful work can be done when only a small part of it is known.

Approach: Building design kits is a way to address these goals. WIDES provides a safe learning environment in which no fatal errors are possible and in which enough information is provided in each situation to make sure that there is always a way to proceed. The design kit allows users to create simple window types for their applications.

6.2.1 Description of WIDES

The initial state of the system is shown in Figure 6-5. It is a window with four panes:

- a *code* pane that displays the current definition of the window type,
- a menu of *suggestions* for enhancements of the window type,
- a history list, and
- a menu of general *operations*.

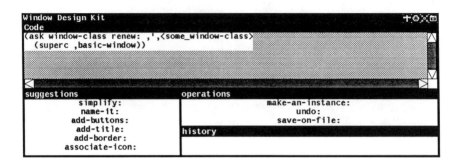

Figure 6-5: Initial state of WIDES

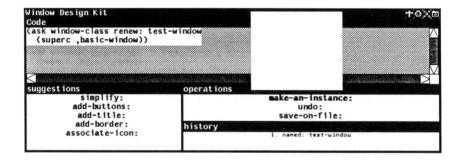

Figure 6-6: An instance of the current window definition
has been created

Selection of the "name-it:" entry of the suggestions menu makes the
system ask for a name the user wants to call the window type to be built.
Selection of the "make-an-instance:" item of the operations menu
creates a window (an *instance* of the type) that corresponds to the
current definition in the code pane. This definition describes a very basic
type of window (Figure 6-6); there is no border, no title bar yet; just a
rectangular white area. Nevertheless, this window has a set of
properties which are inherited from its superclass basic-window. It
reacts on mouse clicks by showing the window-menu, a menu with
operations like move, reshape, etc.

Selection of "add-title:" and "add-border:" produces the state of
Figure 6-7. Two superclasses (border-mixin, title-mixin) have
been added to the definition and a new instance shows a default title
(<some_test-window>) and a default border size of two pixels.

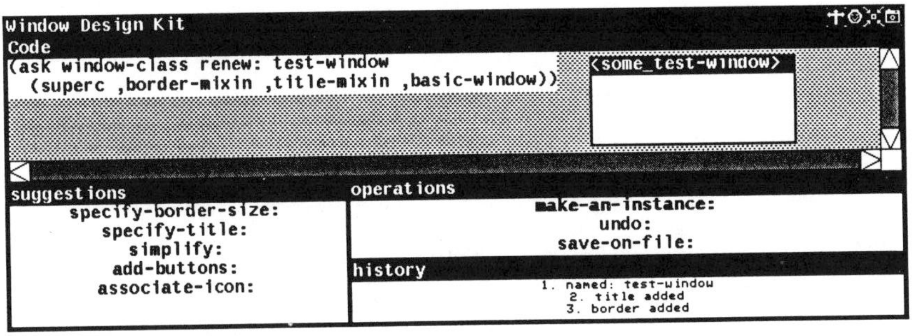

```
Window Design Kit                                              +O×回
Code
(ask window-class renew: test-window          <some_test-window>
    (superc ,border-mixin ,title-mixin ,basic-window))

suggestions                    operations
      specify-border-size:                ■ake-an-instance:
         specify-title:                        undo:
            simplify:                       save-on-file:
          add-buttons:            history
        associate-icon:                       1. named: test-uindow
                                              2. title added
                                              3. border added
```

Figure 6-7: Title and border have been added to the window type

The suggestions menu changes its contents. If, for instance, "add-title:" has been executed, it is replaced by "specify-title" which would not have been meaningful before having a title. The system, in giving its suggestions, adheres to a tree-like regime. Once a key decision (like having a title) has been made, its menu item is replaced by suggestions for more detailed descriptions. This provides the user with some guidance about reasonable next steps, eliminates illegal operations, and reduces the information overload.

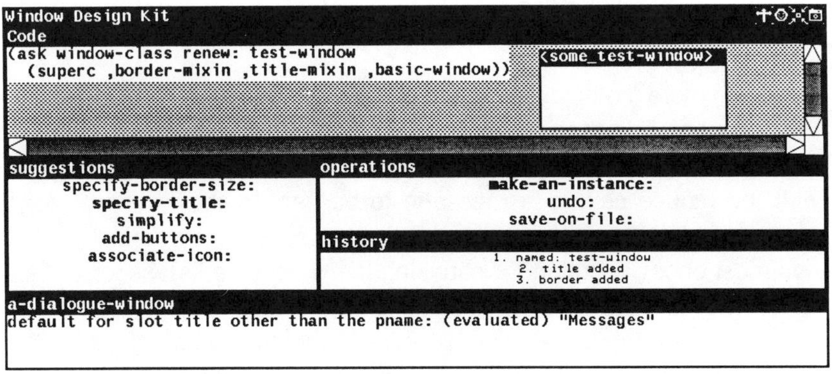

```
Window Design Kit                                              +O×回
Code
(ask window-class renew: test-window          <some_test-window>
    (superc ,border-mixin ,title-mixin ,basic-window))

suggestions                    operations
      specify-border-size:                ■ake-an-instance:
         specify-title:                        undo:
            simplify:                       save-on-file:
          add-buttons:            history
        associate-icon:                       1. named: test-uindow
                                              2. title added
                                              3. border added
a-dialogue-window
default for slot title other than the pname: (evaluated) "Messages"
```

Figure 6-8: Specification of the title

Figure 6-8 shows a modification that requires user input. Selection of "specify-title:" causes a dialogue window to pop up which prompts the user for an expression to be used as the title of the window.

Figure 6-9 shows that the input has been added as a default for the title slot.

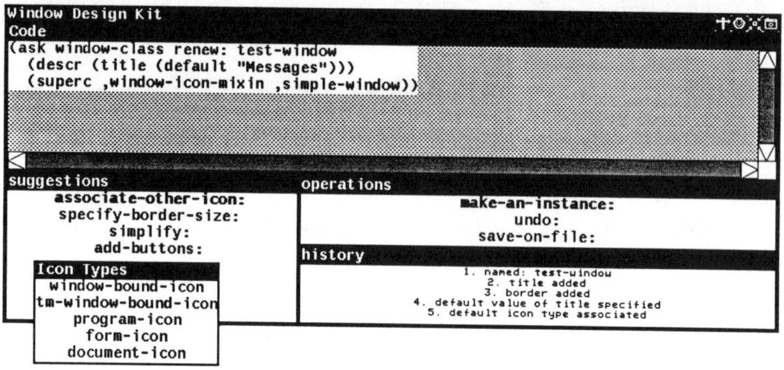

Figure 6-9:   Association of a different icon to the window

If specific inputs are required, we cannot expect the user to know what the legal inputs are. Therefore, as in Figure 6-9 where the user associates the window with an icon, a menu of alternatives is displayed (see the pop-up menu at the bottom). Figure 6-10 shows a window and an icon of the selected type.

An even more complex modification is demonstrated in Figure 6-11. Windows can be associated with push buttons such as those in the upper right corner of the window design kit window. Clicking the button with the mouse causes a message to be sent to the window. As an extension of the push buttons in the title bar supplied by default (the two rightmost ones), a button for shrinking the window to its associated icon is to be added. After selecting from the suggestions menu "add-more-buttons-to-title-bar:", the user is asked to choose a button icon and a message from two menus. The shrink button appears as the leftmost button in the instance of test-window in Figure 6-11.

The "save-on-file:" operation may be used to save the final definition for later use.

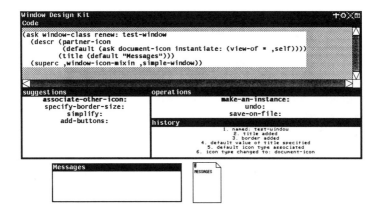

Figure 6-10:   The window and its associated icon

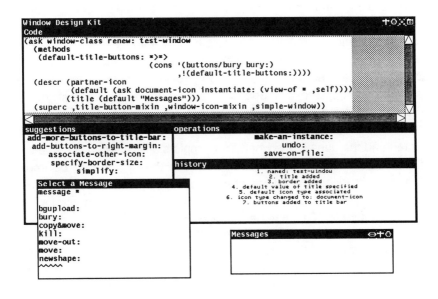

Figure 6-11:   Adding a button to the title bar

6.2.2 Evaluation

Although not much code is being generated by the system because it can use many high level building blocks (see the Code panes in the various stages of the design process), having WIDES represents a significant advantage for the user. In order to construct a new window type, it is no longer necessary to know what building blocks exist (*superclasses*: e.g., title-mixin), what their names are, and how they are applied. It is no longer necessary to know that new superclasses have to be added to the superc description of a class. Also, WIDES determines their correct order. The system knows what types of icons are available, how an icon is associated with a window, etc.

User interface techniques like prompting and menus make it easy to experiment in the domain of window construction. The system makes sure that errors are "impossible". This does not mean that these techniques make sure that users always *understand* what they are doing. A test person, for example, could not tell the difference between the "add-title:" and "specify-title:" suggestions before actually trying them. Similarly, the pop-up menu of available icon types does not show what the icons look like (it should be replaced by a pictorial type of menu). On the other hand, we claim that it is not appropriate to invest too much to make sure that a satisfactory result is achieved with the first try. Rather, the system is intended to support an experimental style. The "undo:" operation should make it easy to step back and retract a decision and to proceed differently. So far, the UNDO feature is not implemented and the question is whether a simple stack oriented scheme or a selective UNDO of operations further back in the history can be implemented. To support the full use of an UNDO, the system needs a network to take care of dependencies: removing the title bars of a window implies that the buttons have to be removed too.

A previous version of the system required the user to know which button icons and which messages are available for adding to the title bar, and they had to be specified by name. The current version with the "Select a Message" menu (Figure 6-11) shows some choices from which to select. It also allows to type in the name of a message that is not displayed, possibly because it is some "internal" message or because it is a new message that the user is going to define later. This method gives users some guidance but does not prevent them from entering unforeseen values.

Methods like this can quite easily be applied in well-structured domains like the present one. However, there are two problems that need to be addressed. The first one is the understanding problem. Seeing an option in a menu does not imply that its significance is obvious. What does "`associate-icon:`" mean? What is the function of a window's icon? Another problem may be the sheer number of options. We did not look into this problem because it does not occur in this relatively small system, but future systems may offer hundreds of choice points. For these design kits, a system of reasonable defaults may provide some help if it is combined with a set of predefined samples that are already rather specific starting points.

With the current implementation it is not easy for a novice to see which modifications of the definition were caused by an action. Highlighting the modifications caused by the last action is a possibility. It should also be possible to point at pieces of the code and obtain an explanation of its function and which user action created it. Many questions are still open: How can these selections be done? What if the user selects a piece of code that does not correspond clearly to one feature?

Informal experiments with novices have shown that the abstraction gap "class - instance" constitutes a problem. The code window shows the window class, whereas the windows created by "`make-an-instance:`" are its instances. A modification of the class (e.g., a modification of a default) does not automatically affect them. Properties cannot be specified as immediate values but have to be specified as defaults or methods inherited by instances. If the user, experimenting with an instance of the window type, changed the local value of a parameter (e.g., the title) so that it no longer corresponds to the default, then a change of the default in the class has no consequences for existing instances.

The system in its current form is almost too small to be really used. The created window types do not have much functionality and represent only a framework which has to be augmented by more ObjTalk code. Still, users found it exciting that, with some menu selections, real code could be produced.

The system also achieves the goal of being a learning tool. Users can see how window types are constructed from predefined components. They learn that defining a new window type means creating a new class that inherits from some existing classes and is augmented with new defaults, slots, and methods. Therefore, the system provides a good starting point for learning about the concepts and structure of this domain.

6.3 TRIKIT

Characterization of the Problem Situation: A very common user inter-face problem is the display and modification of hierarchical and network structures. Application systems which deal with structures of databases, directory trees, or dependency graphs are examples.

Approach: For this purpose, a design kit for graph display/edit tools has been built. Figure 6-12 illustrates its usage. The application program-mer who is an expert for the application system, but not for building user interfaces, adjusts parameters of a generic tool - Tristan - and specifies the links between it and the application. The result of the design process is a new, application specific tool to display and edit the underlying data structure.

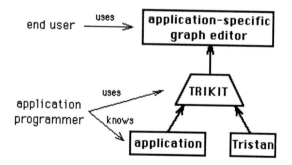

Figure 6-12: Usage of TRIKIT

6.3.1 Application Domain of TRIKIT

Many data structures of computer programs can be viewed as graphs. The nodes are data items which are interconnected with arcs representing a semantic relationship between them. In the following we will use the example of a hierarchical file system which may be displayed as in Figure 6-13. Here the nodes are directories and files, which are the leaf nodes. The arcs represent the membership relation between files and directories (which can themselves be members of other directories). Each one of the nodes is a data structure with properties like name, creation time, owner, protection, size. TRIKIT requires some access functions to these data structures. In this example there are functions for retrieving pieces of the graph (e.g., `list-directory`), and for creating and deleting nodes and arcs.

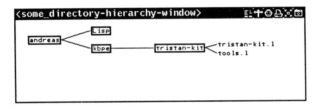

Figure 6-13: A hierarchical file system display

Also, there is a way to refer to particular nodes of the structure by a name relative to some "current directory" or by an absolute path name specifying the way from the/a root of the hierarchy, or by some other description. Conversely, a screen representation must be defined for the nodes. This might be just the name of the node or the name plus some of the properties such as owner or size. If there are multiple types of nodes, different representations may be desired.

6.3.2 The Generic Graph Display/Editor

TRIKIT is based upon Tristan (Nieper, 1985), a generic display and editing system for graph structures through direct manipulation on the screen. Tristan provides facilities for:

- selective display of parts of the graph: specified by name, immediate children or parents of a node, a whole subhierarchy of a node (possibly to a certain depth),
- automatic layout planning,
- manual layout modifications by constrained moving of nodes,
- highlighting of nodes, and
- editing the graph structure by creating/removing links and nodes.

Tristan is independent of the particular node representation. It only assumes it to be a subclass of a certain general window class.

6.3.3 Description of TRIKIT

TRIKIT presents itself to the user as an interaction sheet as shown in Figure 6-14 (top window). It is the place where the user specifies the interface to the application, chooses a graphical representation for the nodes, and controls the creation of the user interface.

The following types of fields may be found in the interaction sheet (some of them were also used in WLISPRC; see Section 6.1):

- edit fields   indicated by their dotted background; for entry and modification of names, numbers, program code, etc.; a mouse click on the field moves the cursor into it and allows editing of its contents.

- choice fields   if the number of possible values of a field is very small, this type of field is being used; mouse clicks circle through the set of values.

- menu fields   for a larger number of choices; a mouse click produces a pop-up menu.

- push buttons   low and long rectangles with a black frame; a mouse click activates their associated action.

- subform icons   large squares; a mouse click produces a subform.

The initial form is filled in with an example application (an ObjTalk inheritance hierarchy display system[2]; Figure 6-14: bottom window). This

---

[2]It was used to create Figure 6-2.

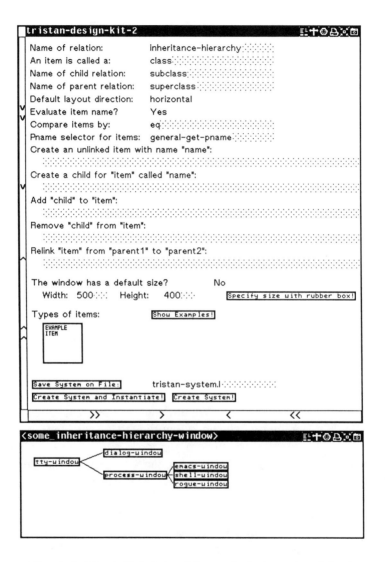

Figure 6-14: Initial state of the main form and an inheritance hierarchy window generated from it

allows the user to familiarize him/herself with it, to modify parameters and to find out about their significance.

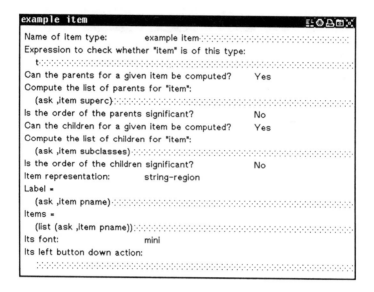

Figure 6-15: Initial state of the node form

Clicking the square representing the `example item` subform produces the form of Figure 6-15. While the main form is associated with the graph in general, the subforms describe the properties of its nodes.

Let us examine the use of the system with the example of building a directory editor like the one shown in Figure 6-13. A directory editor is a tool to view a hierarchical file system and to do operations on it such as creating/removing a directory, moving a file into another directory, and renaming files.

In Figure 6-16 the first four fields have been filled in to reflect the terms of the file system domain. They establish a common vocabulary for the user and the system. They describe the names of the relation to be displayed, of the items that are elements of the relation, and of the links to superordinate and subordinate nodes in the relation. The next field (`Evaluate item name?`) says that a name of a file or directory represents itself as opposed to being the name of a variable holding the actual item. `Equal` is used as a comparison function for directories. No other changes have been made to this form.

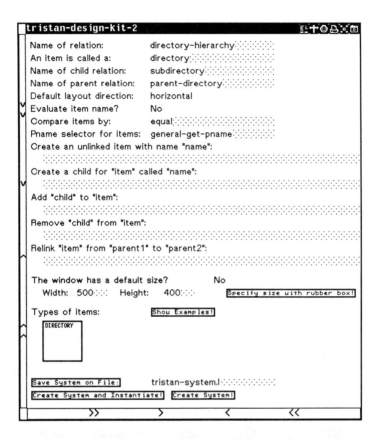

Figure 6-16: Main form, modified to describe a directory editor

The `example item` form has been renamed (Figure 6-17) and the most important fields have been adapted to the new application:

- the `de:parents` function computes the list of superdirectories;

- the `de:children` function computes the subdirectories, i.e., the contents of the directory; and

- the `de:pname` function in the label field computes a "print name", a label for the items, i.e., it strips off the leading pathname component and leaves the file name which is unique only locally within its directory.

```
┌─────────────────────────────────────────────────────────────────┐
│ directory                                              ▣⊙🔊🔟▨ │
│ Name of item type:          directory                           │
│ Expression to check whether "item" is of this type:             │
│   t                                                             │
│ Can the parents for a given item be computed?      Yes          │
│ Compute the list of parents for "item":                         │
│   (de:parents item)                                             │
│ Is the order of the parents significant?           No           │
│ Can the children for a given item be computed?     Yes          │
│ Compute the list of children for "item":                        │
│   (de:children item)                                            │
│ Is the order of the children significant?          No           │
│ Item representation:        string-region                       │
│ Label =                                                         │
│   (de:pname item)                                               │
│ Items =                                                         │
│                                                                 │
│ Its font:                   mini                                │
│ Its left button down action:                                   │
│                                                                 │
└─────────────────────────────────────────────────────────────────┘
```

Figure 6-17: Node form, modified to describe a directory node

Functions with a "de:" prefix (de:parents, de:children, de:pname) belong to the application domain. They are application specific and have to be supplied by the user (the application expert).

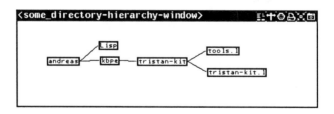

Figure 6-18: An example directory hierarchy window

The mentioned modifications are sufficient to produce a first, working version of the directory editor. A click on the "Create System and Instantiate!" push button compiles the forms into a Tristan system. Part of it is the directory-hierarchy window type which is being instantiated.

In Figure 6-18 this instance can be seen showing a directory hierarchy. There is a directory called `andreas` with two of its subdirectories (`Lisp` and `kbpe`). `kbpe` has further subdirectories. Note that it is not necessary to display the complete graph; the display may be limited to any subset of it.

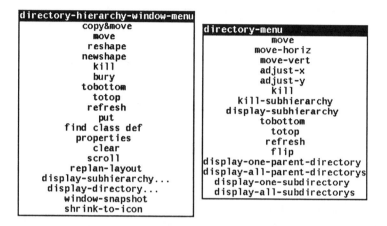

Figure 6-19: The main menus of the directory hierarchy window
and the directory node

Figure 6-19 shows on the left the main menu of directory hierarchy windows. In addition to generic window operations such as "`move`" or "`kill`", three application specific operations have been added automatically:

`replan-layout`
> supplied by the Tristan system: an operation to automatically rearrange the layout of the graph;

`display-subhierarchy...`
> also supplied by the Tristan system: display all the (recursively) subordinated nodes of a given node; and

`display-directory...`
> generated by TRIKIT: display a given directory (this is a renamed version of "`display-item...`" of Tristan).

The trailing triple points indicate that a name is going to be prompted for by the system.

The menu on the right of Figure 6-19 is associated with directory nodes. Again, some of the operations are general (like `move`), others are supplied by Tristan (`kill-subhierarchy`) and the display operations are generated by TRIKIT.

subdirectory-menu
```
          /cs/andreas/kbpe/tristan-kit/####THE-SCREEN-1.bin
/cs/andreas/kbpe/tristan-kit/####tristan-design-kit-11.bin
      /cs/andreas/kbpe/tristan-kit/#example item1.bin
      /cs/andreas/kbpe/tristan-kit/#list-directory.l
          /cs/andreas/kbpe/tristan-kit/#slug
  /cs/andreas/kbpe/tristan-kit/#tristan-design-kit-1-1.bin
  /cs/andreas/kbpe/tristan-kit/#tristan-design-kit-1-1.pkd
      /cs/andreas/kbpe/tristan-kit/#tristan-kit1.l
    /cs/andreas/kbpe/tristan-kit/all-the-classes.l
      /cs/andreas/kbpe/tristan-kit/de-wind.bin
  /cs/andreas/kbpe/tristan-kit/default-node.bin
 /cs/andreas/kbpe/tristan-kit/default-system.bin
    /cs/andreas/kbpe/tristan-kit/junk-system.l
      /cs/andreas/kbpe/tristan-kit/junk.l
      /cs/andreas/kbpe/tristan-kit/line-editor.l
    /cs/andreas/kbpe/tristan-kit/list-directory.l
      /cs/andreas/kbpe/tristan-kit/mod-node1.bin
    /cs/andreas/kbpe/tristan-kit/mod-system1.bin
      /cs/andreas/kbpe/tristan-kit/mod-wind1.bin
/cs/andreas/kbpe/tristan-kit/super-objtalk-inheritance.l
      /cs/andreas/kbpe/tristan-kit/tristan
  /cs/andreas/kbpe/tristan-kit/tristan-design-kit-3-1.bin
    /cs/andreas/kbpe/tristan-kit/tristan-incl.l
    /cs/andreas/kbpe/tristan-kit/tristan-kit.mss
    /cs/andreas/kbpe/tristan-kit/tristan-kit1.l
    /cs/andreas/kbpe/tristan-kit/tristan-output-2.l
    /cs/andreas/kbpe/tristan-kit/tristan-output.l
      /cs/andreas/kbpe/tristan-kit/tristan-system.l
```

Figure 6-20: The subdirectory menu

If, for example, the directory menu has been popped up on the node labeled `tristan-kit` and `display-one-subdirectory` has been selected, the menu in Figure 6-20 will pop up. Because the system knows how to compute all the subordinate nodes of a given node (Figure 6-17) it is able to determine what should go into this menu.

The directory hierarchy editor, as it is, has a number of shortcomings. One of them certainly is the large subdirectory menu. It would be nice to display the file names without the leading path names (`/cs/fischer/kbpe/tristan-kit/`). This can be achieved by specifying a special pname (print name) selector for the menus. In Figure 6-21 the pname selector field has been changed to `de:pname`.

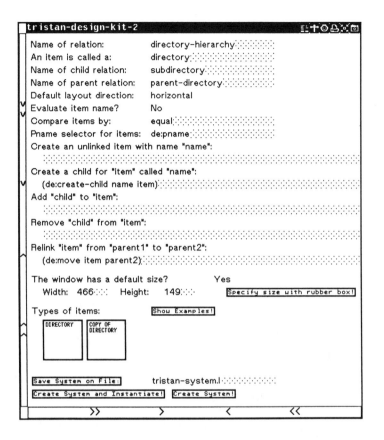

Figure 6-21: Extended description of the directory hierarchy window

Also, in order to make the system into a true editor it should be possible to create new nodes and to alter the graph structure. For this purpose, the meaning in terms of the application of creating a child (`de:create`) and of relinking a node from one parent to another (`de:move`) has been specified in the main form.

Also, there are actually two types of nodes in the application: directories and files. Therefore, the user creates a new subform (`Copy of Directory`, Figure 6-21) by cloning the existing one. Now, it is neces- sary to tell the system how to distinguish between the two node types. Consider Figure 6-22. The second field specifies the necessary predicate expression (`de:directoryp`). There has also been an action

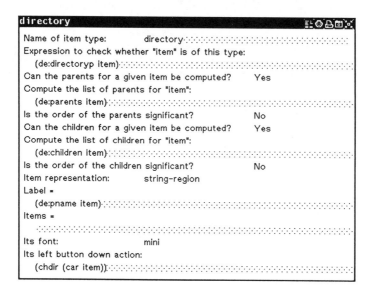

Figure 6-22: The directory node form

associated with the node: clicking the node will make the directory it is representing the current working directory.

This action is not appropriate for plain files (Figure 6-23). Instead an action to load the file into an editor has been specified. Since the nodes are different in their semantics it would be nice to display them differently. The `Item representation` field has been set to `label-region` which has no frame. Figure 6-24 shows a window created according to these modifications.

The directory menu of the modified system presented in Figure 6-25 shows the two new operations (`create-subdirectory...` and `relink-directory`) that have become possible through the modifications in the main form (Figure 6-21). Also, the subdirectory menu shows the file names without their paths as returned by the `de:pname` function.

```
file                                                    ≣⚆🖫🗗⚙
Name of item type:              file
Expression to check whether "item" is of this type:
   (de:filep item)
Can the parents for a given item be computed?        Yes
Compute the list of parents for "item":
   (de:parents item)
Is the order of the parents significant?             No
Can the children for a given item be computed?       Yes
Compute the list of children for "item":
   nil
Is the order of the children significant?            No
Item representation:         label-region
Label =
   (de:pname item)
Items =

Its font:              mini
Its left button down action:
   (emacs-file (car item))
```

Figure 6-23: The plain file node form

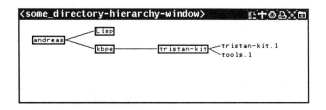
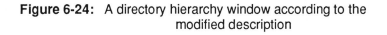

Figure 6-24: A directory hierarchy window according to the
modified description

In case this version of the system does not yet satisfy the requirements
of the user, he/she will have to descend one level and work on the system at the implementation level. The Save System on File operation in the main form creates a file containing the code of the directory
editor, which then may be used as a basis for further extensions (see the
appendix for more details).

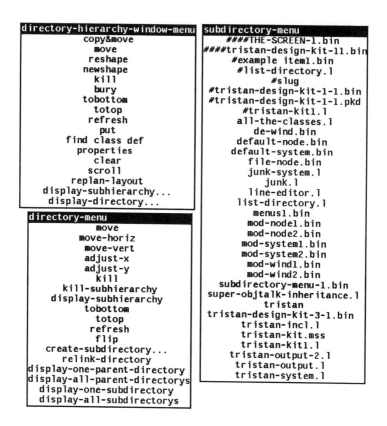

Figure 6-25:   The new menus of directory hierarchy window
and directory node

6.3.4 A Rule Dependency Display: Experiences with TRIKIT

This section describes the application of TRIKIT to the visualization of the
relationships of rules of an expert system. A rule would be displayed as
a small rectangle with the rule number in it and, on its left, the premises,
and on the right, the conclusions, both as larger rectangles with several
lines of text. See Figure 6-26.

Separate rules can share nodes within this network. For example, the
conclusion of one rule could be necessary for a clause of the premise of

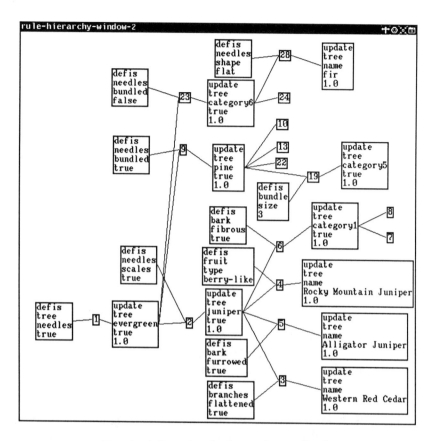

Figure 6-26: A rule dependency display

another rule to be true. This display was very helpful to have an over-view of and to debug a set of approximately 100 rules.

When using the system, problems with certain features and concepts became apparent which were not initially understood:

- The system can be: created, created and instantiated, and saved. The user needs to understand what is being created and what is saved (e.g., a definition of a hierarchy? the forms? his application? a specific picture?). Making the objects involved visible, can make the system easier to un-derstand.

- It is not obvious at first that one needs to use two types of "sheets" to define the relation.   The first relates to the hierarchy in general (Figure 6-21). The second one (Figure 6-15), which you get by "clicking" example node, defines the properties of different types of nodes in the system. The titles of the sheets should be changed to better reflect their purpose.

- The system also contains default values in the main hierarchy sheet. The user may not realize this.

- In the sheets, the two terms *item* and *name* are used. It did not become clear that *item* refers to the elements of the application relation as data structures, whereas *name* refers to their external representation through an identifier.

- Some parts of the system can be understood through experimentation only. An example is the item representation field of the node subform whose possible values (e.g., string-region, label-field) determine the overall appearance of the nodes.

The meaning of some fields (Pname selector for items) is not obvious. Also, users may not know whether a system supplied value of a field (general-get-pname) works with their application. Adding more knowledge about the applicability of defaults can solve this problem.

The use of the fields is not obvious. Some values of fields have functional purposes, for example, they specify how to compute the subdirectories; others just have label purposes such as to serve as the title of a menu.

6.3.5 Evaluation

TRIKIT may be used to construct useful systems without knowing details of the selected building blocks. Although the design space is limited by the available options in the forms, there is still the possibility of using this system to create a prototype which may be refined on a lower level.

The system has been used to build the following applications:
- ObjTalk inheritance hierarchy editor
- UNIX directory editor
- Subwindow hierarchy display

- A project team hierarchy
- Emycin rule dependency display (see Section 6.3.4)

A critical design decision was to not make the user explicitly aware of the fact that for each item in his or her relation a node object will be created that represents the item on the screen. When setting the font of the item, the user refers to the node object. When specifying how to compute the parents of an item, an element of the application relation is referred to. The system tries to conceal this ambiguity and present a simpler model of itself to the user. Initially this distinction was explicit and led to confusion. It is unclear if it will be necessary to reintroduce this distinction when more functionality is added to TRIKIT.

The design space of possible systems must be extended. This may be done, for example, by extending the forms with new fields and by providing new forms for other aspects or views of the system. The tool could be extended to:

- visualize dynamic processes by highlighting currently involved nodes (inferences in the rule display),
- allow to send output to nodes,
- support more than one type of links between nodes,
- be integrated with efforts to build a more general window design kit (see Section 6.2). This could give the application programmer more control over the behavior of the graph window as well as the individual nodes. The generated graph display/editor could be made part of a larger system.

7. Experiences with Methodologies and Systems to Support Constrained Design Processes

Advantages. We have used the design kits described in the previous section for some time and they have been useful in the following ways:

- They increase the control of the user over systems without making it necessary for the user to learn many details. This became apparent when casual users started using WLISPRC instead of relying on standard initialization files to tailor their systems manually.

- They acquaint users with new and complex system features (e.g., WIDES).
- Systems can be created more quickly, because one can rely on well-developed parts and one can take advantage of stable subassemblies (e.g., exploiting the rich inheritance network in the WLISP system). Simon (1981) demonstrates that this is a crucial aspect in the development of complex systems.

Who uses the design kits? Our experiences have shown that the use of design kits is not restricted to the inexperienced user: if the functionality offered by the design kit is sufficient, then there is no reason why the expert should not use it (see the use of TRIKIT to create the rule dependency display in the previous section).

Human-Computer Interaction. It is misleading to assume that knowing how to use a design kit would come for free and would not require a learning process at all. Learning processes are required at different levels in using design kits: users have to operate on different descriptive levels, they need to understand the domain concepts used in the kit and they must know how to use a specific kit for their purposes and goals.

It remains an open question whether we can succeed in considerably extending the functionality of the design kits to cover a substantial part of their domains while, at the same time, retaining or even improving the simplicity of use. WIDES is currently easy to use -- but will we be able to retain this when the system will cover more kinds of objects (e.g., menus, icons, gauges) and not only windows?

A difficult question has been to establish a shared vocabulary between the designer and the user to enable the user to understand the descriptions for the required inputs. The label `Pname selector for items` (Figure 6-21) is not obvious to someone who does not know this technical term of the menu system. To remedy some of the shortcomings, we have to solve the following problems:

- try to find a better conceptualization of the design task and use it to restructure the forms to make them easier to understand;
- use more carefully selected examples to convey a better

feeling of what needs to be done (by taking task structures and the user's knowledge into account);

- provide optional descriptions for all fields;
- allow alternate modes of specification; explore more direct forms of manipulation of prototypes; and
- prompt for information at the time it is needed: the information about creating a link between two nodes should be asked for only the first time this action is being executed.

Currently the interaction with the design kits is mostly a *monologue* by the user. The system does not actively act on user inputs. Our goal is to make *dialogues* possible in which the user and the system take turns with their actions, correct each other's errors and false assumptions. Small examples of this kind of interaction can be found in the current implementations:

- default values of fields represent initial assumptions of useful values;
- when the user creates a new type of node in TRIKIT, the system copies its properties from an existing node, because it assumes that it is going to be more like that one than like the original defaults.

Consistency. Once a system has been modified at the code level, it is no longer possible to use the design kits to make further modifications. A program analysis component could make it possible for the high level (form) description and the program code to coexist. In this way the user could use both languages alternately.

A set of issues needs to be further explored in connection with the conceptual distance between a description and what it describes. What happens to an existing object whose description has been changed? Should it be updated? This is not always desired or possible, because

- immediate updates may be computationally too expensive,
- the screen display may change to a degree that the user loses track of where things are,
- changes of descriptions of actions executed at the creation time of objects have no effect on already existing objects (e.g., initial size of a window), and
- in cases where properties are not visible, they can not be changed in a direct manipulation style.

Methodologies and Tools for the Designer of Design Kits. Regarding design kits as desirable components of computer systems, the question arises: what do we have to do to develop *kit-kits*, i.e., design kits for designers of design kits. What challenges and problems do designers face in developing design kits? Their design requires a qualitatively different description level (using many more abstractions) and they have to defer commitment so users are left with their share and influence on the design.

8. Comparison with other Systems

The problems addressed by our research are widespread and there exist a large number of research efforts to address them. We briefly describe some other work which is most closely related to our approach.

KBEmacs (Waters, 1985, 1986) is an effort to produce a prototype of the Programmer's Assistant (Rich & Shrobe, 1978). The system's goal is to make expert programmers superproductive by having the assistant carry out the mundane and repetitive parts of the programming task. KBEmacs contains a small library of algorithmic cliches (serving the same role as the classes in WIDES), which provide a vocabulary of relevant intermediate and high-level concepts and the system is able to deal with two representations of a program (a textual representation and a plan representation). Based on the currently small number of cliches, problems regarding their organization and how a programmer will find the right kind of cliche have not been relevant for this research effort.

Trillium (Henderson, 1986) is a computer-based design environment to support rapid prototyping of user interfaces to simple machines like copiers and printers. It provides a construction kit of elements to build interfaces quickly, so the designer can shift quickly between designing the interface and trying it out to evaluate the effects achieved. By restricting the problem domain, Trillium provides a powerful tool which is in widespread use. It remains to be seen how some of the ideas explored in this work (e.g., support for constrained design processes like composition and specialization) will carry over to other design environments.

User Interface Management Systems (Olsen et al., 1984; the COUSIN system by Hayes, Szekely, and Lerner, 1985) are based on the idea that the user interface portion of a program can be separated from the portion implementing its functionality. Limiting the information exchange between user interface and application system is a reasonable approach for some problems. Based on our architecture and on the kinds of problems we try to solve (building intelligent support systems such as help, documentation and explanation systems), we claim that a strong separation between interface and application is impossible because the user interface has to have extensive access to the state and actions of the application system. We regard and model a computational system as a collection of communicating objects or agents, each of them having an internal state and an external view, and we provide mechanisms, such as ObjTalk's constraints, to maintain their consistency.

All these systems have *in common* that they attempt to overcome the tediousness of programming, to take advantage of existing components, to speed up the design cycle, and to provide an escape mechanism to lower levels if the needed design abstractions are not contained in the construction kit. To provide this kind of assistance, all of these system are knowledge-based. The **uniqueness of our approach** is the development of a general framework for constrained design processes and the augmentation of construction kits with design kits. Design kits guide the designers when they create a new system; for construction kits with hundreds and thousands of elements, the existence of a design kit is not a luxury but a necessity, especially for designers which are not totally familiar with the construction kit. To make this approach viable, the system must have an understanding about the design space; it must indicate which opportunities and restrictions exist at a certain point in the design process. This is captured to some extent in the suggestion list of WIDES or in the goal browser of the PRIDE system (Bobrow, Mittal, & Stefik, 1986). Another specific feature of our approach is the effort to integrate design kits into the architecture of intelligent support systems (Figure 3-2). This architecture is a first step towards our long-range goal to regard programming not as writing code, but as representing knowledge about specific domains. Different system components (e.g., help, documentation, critics, design and visualization support) are then generated in a coherent way from the underlying knowledge base.

9. Conclusions

*Give humans some fish and they can eat for a day -- teach them
to fish and they have something to eat for their whole life!*
Asian Proverb

Our research is concerned with how computer systems can be made
more convivial. We would like to identify methods to give users the
amount of control over systems that they desire. This is especially important because the number of those systems increases where the *vision*
of the designer and the *real needs of the users* are dramatically different.
Some of these discrepancies can be reduced by having a heavy user
involvement and participation in all phases of the development process,
but they will not be eliminated: modifiability by users will be a necessity
to cope with new and unforeseen situations. Our research so far has
raised the interesting issue that systems which give control to the user
might be *less complicated*, because they do not have to anticipate all
possible futures (laws are complicated because they cannot be adapted
dynamically). We have tried to show some approaches that find new
middle roads between the full generality of programming languages and
the limitations of turn-key systems. Intelligent support systems that allow
the user to carry out constrained design processes are a promising step
towards the goal of making computer systems more convivial.

Acknowledgements

The research described here was supported by the University of
Colorado, the Office of Naval Research (contract number: N00014-85-
K-0842), Triumph Adler (Nuernberg, Germany), and the German Ministry
for Research and Technology. We wish to thank Jim Miller for his comments on an earlier version of this chapter.

References

Bobrow, D. G., Mittal, S., & Stefik, M. J. (1986). Expert systems: Perils and promise. *Communications of the ACM, 29*(9), 880-894.

Boecker, H. -D., Fabian, F., Jr., & Lemke, A. C. (1985). WLisp: A window based programming environment for FranzLisp. *Proceedings of the First Pan Pacific Computer Conference* (pp. 580-595). Melbourne, Australia: The Australian Computer Society.

Boecker, H. -D., Fischer, G., & Nieper, H. (1986). The enhancement of understanding through visual representations. *Human factors in computing systems, CHI'86 Conference Proceedings (Boston)* (pp. 44-50). New York, ACM.

Fabian, F. (1986). Fenster- und menuesysteme in der MCK. In G. Fischer & R. Gunzenhaeuser (Eds.), *Mensch- Computer - Kommunikation. Vol. 1: Methoden und werkzeuge zur gestaltung benutzergerechter computersysteme.* Berlin - New York: Walter de Gruyter.

Fabian, F., Jr., & Lemke, A. C. (1985). *Wlisp manual* (Tech. Rep. CU-CS-302A-85). Boulder: University of Colorado.

Fischer, G. (1981). Computer als konviviale werkzeuge. *Proceedings der Jahrestagung der Gesellschaft fuer Informatik (Muenchen)* (pp. 407-417). Berlin - Heidelberg - New York: Gesellschaft fuer Informatik, Springer-Verlag.

Fischer, G. (1986). From interactive to intelligent systems. In J. K. Skwirzynski (Ed.), *The challenge of advanced computing technology to system design methods (Proceedings of a NATO Advanced Study Institute, University of Durham).* Berlin - Heidelberg - New York: Springer-Verlag.

Fischer, G. (1987). Enhancing incremental learning processes with knowledge-based systems. In H. Mandl & A. Lesgold (Eds.), *Learning issues for intelligent tutoring systems.* Berlin - Heidelberg - New York: Springer-Verlag.

Fischer, G., & Boecker, H. -D. (1983). The nature of design processes and how computer systems can support them. In P. Degano & E. Sandewall (Eds.), *Integrated interactive computing systems* (pp. 73-88). European Conference on Integrated Interactive Computer Systems (ECICS 82), North Holland.

Fischer, G., & Kintsch, W. (1986). *Theories, methods and tools for the design of user-centered systems* (Tech. Rep.). Boulder: University of Colorado.

Fischer, G., & Schneider, M. (1984). Knowledge-based communication processes in software engineering. *Proceedings of the 7th International Conference on Software Engineering* (pp. 358-368). Orlando, Florida.

Fischer, G., Lemke, A. C., & Rathke, C. (1987). From design to redesign. *Proceedings of the 9th International Conference on Software Engineering* . Monterey, California.

Fischer, G., Lemke, A. C., & Schwab, T. (1985). Knowledge-based help systems. *Human factors in computing systems, CHI'85 Conference Proceedings (San Francisco)* (pp. 161-167). New York, ACM.

Furuta, R., Scofield, J., & Shaw, A. (1982). Document formatting systems: Survey, concepts and issues. *Communications of the ACM, 14*(3), 417-472.

Goldberg, A. (1981). Smalltalk. *BYTE (Special Issue),* Vol. *6*(8).

Gosling, J. (1982). *Unix Emacs.* Pittsburgh, PA: Carnegie-Mellon University.

Hayes, P. J., Szekely, P. A., & Lerner, R. A. (1985). Design alternatives for user interface managment systems based on experience with COUSIN. *Human factors in computing systems, CHI'85 Conference Proceedings (San Francisco)* (pp. 169-175). New York: CHI-85 Conference Proceedings, ACM.

Henderson, D. A. (1986). The Trillium user interface design environment. *Human factors in computing systems, CHI'86 Conference Proceedings (Boston)* (pp. 221-227). New York, ACM.

Hutchins, E. L., Hollan, J. D., & Norman, D. A. (1986). Direct manipulation interfaces. In D. A. Norman & S. W. Draper (Eds.), *User centered system design, New perspectives on human-computer interaction.* Hillsdale, NJ: Lawrence Erlbaum Associates, Inc.

Illich, I. (1973). *Tools for conviviality.* New York: Harper and Row.

Kay, A. (1984). Computer software. *Scientific American, 251*(3), 52-59.

Lemke, A. C. (1985). *ObjTalk84 reference manual* (Technical Report CU-CS-291-85). Boulder: University of Colorado.

Nieper, H. (1985). *TRISTAN: A generic display and editing system for hierarchical structures* (Tech. Rep.). Boulder: University of Colorado, Department of Computer Science.

Norman, D. A. (1986). Cognitive Engineering. In D. A. Norman & S. W. Draper (Eds.), *User centered system design, New perspectives on human-computer interaction.* Hillsdale, NJ: Lawrence Erlbaum Associates, Inc.

Norman, D. A., & Draper, S. W. (Eds.). (1986). *User centered system design, New perspectives on human-computer interaction.* Hillsdale, NJ: Lawrence Erlbaum Associates, Inc.

Olsen, D. R., Jr., Buxton, W., Ehrich, R., Kasik, D. J., Rhyne, J. R., & Sibert, J. (1984). A context for user interface management. *IEEE Computer Graphics and Applications,* pp. 33-42.

Rathke, C. (1986). *ObjTalk: Repraesentation von wissen in einer objektorientierten sprache.* Doctoral dissertation, Universitaet Stuttgart, Fakultaet fuer Mathematik und Informatik, Deutschland.

Rich, C., & Shrobe, H. E. (1978). Initial report on a Lisp programmer's apprentice. *IEEE Transactions on Software Engineering, SE-4*(6), 456-467.

Simon, H. A. (1981). *The sciences of the artificial.* Cambridge, MA: The MIT Press.

Stallman, R. M. (1981). EMACS, the extensible, customizable, self-documenting display editor. *ACM SIGOA Newsletter, 2*(1/2), 147-156.

Waters, R. C. (1985). The programmer's apprentice: A session with KBEmacs. *IEEE Transactions on Software Engineering, SE-11*(11), 1296-1320.

Waters, R. C. (1986). KBEmacs: Where's the AI? *AI Magazine, 7*(1), 47-56.

Appendix: Code Generated by TRIKIT

Compared to the other design kits, a considerably larger amount of code is being generated by TRIKIT. The following listing of the code generated for the directory editor application illustrates the way in which this is done:

1. Code templates are instantiated and filled in from the forms, and
2. specific code is generated for distinguishing between the different node types.

Most of the code is written in the object-oriented language ObjTalk and FranzLisp. It makes use of predefined objects and libraries of the WLisp system.

The comments in the following program code are put in manually and are not generated by TRIKIT. It would be straightforward, however, to generate the comments automatically since they do not use special domain knowledge. Underlined pieces of code are taken directly from the forms (Figures 6-21, 6-22, and 6-23).

```
;;; Load the Tristan library
(include-file 'tristan-incl '/cs/fischer/lib/system85/trikit/)

;;; The directory editor window type
(ask class renew: |file system-window|
  (methods
```

```
(get-item: ,?name => (progn (de:create-item name)))

;; find out type of item and create the right type of node
(create-node-for: ,?item =>
  (cond ((de:directoryp item)
         (ask directory instantiate:
           (item = ,item) (label = ,(de:pname item))))
        ((de:filep item)
         (ask file instantiate:
           (item = ,item) (label = ,(de:pname item))))
        (t (error '|file system-window:|
             "Don't know how to create a node for:" item))))

;; renamed method: items are files in this application
(display-file...: => (ask self display-item...:)))

(descr (top-menu (default |file system-window-menu|)) ;defined below
       (item-name (default 'file))
       (background (default nil))
       (layout-direction (default 'horizontal))
       (equality-operator (default 'equal)))
(superc window-repr-mixin
        window-util-mixin
        hierarchy-mixin
        scroll-hand-mixin
        super-scroll-window))

;;; Toplevel menu of the directory editor window
(ask pop-up-menu remake: |file system-window-menu| with:
  (pname-selector = lmenu:get-pname)
  (items = (;; general window operations
            copy&move move move-out reshape newshape kill bury
            tobottom totop
            refresh bgupload |find class def| shrink-to-icon
            window-snapshot
            clear scroll | |
            ;; operations provided by Tristan
            replan-layout display-subhierarchy...
            ;; operations generated by TRIKIT
            display-file...)))

;;; The node type for representing files
(ask class renew: file
  (methods
    (left-button-down: ,?rep =>=>
      (let ((item ,!item)) (emacs-file (car item))))
    (get-parents-items: =>
      (let* ((item ,!item)
             (parents (de:parents item)))
        (or (null parents) (dtpr parents)
            (error "The list of parents is required. "
                   "Check the \"Compute the parents\" field!"))
        parents))

    ;; renamed methods
    (display-one-parent-directory: => (ask self display-parent...:))
    (display-all-parent-directorys: => (ask self display-parents:))

    (get-children-items: =>
```

```
        (let* ((item ,!item)
               (children nil))
           (or (null children) (dtpr children)
               (error "The list of children is required. "
                      "Check the \"Compute the children\" field!"))
           children))

      ;; renamed methods
      (display-one-member: => (ask self display-child...:))
      (display-all-members: => (ask self display-children:)))

    (descr (top-menu (default file-menu))  ;defined below
           (parents-menu (init parent-directory-menu))
           (children-menu (init member-menu))
           (font (default 'mini)))
    (superc node-repr-mixin
            node-util-mixin
            node-mixin
            adaptive-text-region))

;;; Operations on file nodes
(ask pop-up-menu remake: file-menu with:
  (pname-selector = lmenu:get-pname)
  (items = (;; general window operations and operations
            ;; provided by Tristan
            move move-horiz move-vert adjust-x adjust-y kill
             kill-subhierarchy
            display-subhierarchy tobottom totop refresh
             insert-link-to-child
            remove-link-to-child flip | |
            ;; operations generated by TRIKIT
            create-member... relink-file
            display-one-parent-directory
            display-all-parent-directorys
            display-one-member display-all-members)))

;;; The node type for representing directories
(ask class renew: directory
  (methods
    (left-button-down: ,?rep =>=>
      (let ((item ,!item)) (de:make-current item)))

    (get-parents-items: =>
      (let* ((item ,!item)
             (parents (de:parents item)))
         (or (null parents) (dtpr parents)
             (error "The list of parents is required. "
                    "Check the \"Compute the parents\" field!"))
         parents))

    (display-one-parent-directory: => (ask self display-parent...:))
    (display-all-parent-directorys: => (ask self display-parents:))

    (get-children-items: =>
      (let* ((item ,!item)
             (children (de:children item)))
         (or (null children) (dtpr children)
             (error "The list of children is required. "
                    "Check the \"Compute the children\" field!"))
```

```
                children))

     (display-one-member: => (ask self display-child...:))
     (display-all-members: => (ask self display-children:))))

  (descr (top-menu (default directory-menu)) ; defined below
         (parents-menu (init parent-directory-menu))
         (children-menu (init member-menu))
         (font (default 'mini)))
  (superc node-repr-mixin
          node-util-mixin
          node-mixin
          adaptive-text-region-with-border))
```

```
;;; Operations on directory nodes
(ask pop-up-menu remake: directory-menu with:
  (pname-selector = lmenu:get-pname)
  (items = (;; general window operations and operations
            ;; provided by Tristan
            move move-horiz move-vert adjust-x adjust-y kill
            kill-subhierarchy
            display-subhierarchy tobottom totop refresh
            insert-link-to-child
            remove-link-to-child flip | |
            ;; operations generated by TRIKIT
            create-member... relink-file
            display-one-parent-directory
            display-all-parent-directorys
            display-one-member display-all-members)))
```

```
;;; Menu used to select a parent directory
(ask pop-up-menu remake: parent-directory-menu with:
  (pname-selector = de:pname)
  (items = nil))
```

```
;;; Menu used to select a directory member
(ask pop-up-menu remake: member-menu with:
  (pname-selector = de:pname)
  (items = nil))
```

```
;;; Make the directory editor known to the system
(ask window-types add: |file system-window|)
```

2
The Consequences of Consistent and Inconsistent User Interfaces

PETER G. POLSON

The acquisition, transfer, and retention of user skills are central issues in human-computer interaction. New users can experience serious difficulties learning typical applications. Skilled users also have problems learning and remembering how to use new tools. This chapter presents a theoretical analysis and supporting experimental results on the effects of consistent user interfaces on learning and transfer of user skills. These results show that consistency leads to large positive transfer effects. However, inconsistency is the rule in user interfaces; consistency is the exception. This chapter will also discuss the impact of inconsistencies on learning, transfer, and retention of user skills.

1. Introduction

The primary goal of this chapter is to present a theoretical analysis and empirical findings on the effects of consistent user interfaces on learning and transfer of user skills. An example of consistency is the common text editing methods used in almost all applications on the Apple Macintosh: the same sequence of user actions is required in all contexts to accomplish editing operations on text such as delete, insert, and move. Consistency both within and across applications is generally considered to be an important design goal (Rubenstein & Hersh, 1984; Smith & Mosier, 1986; Smith, Irby, Kimball, Verplank, & Harslem, 1982). This chapter summarizes experimental results which show that consistency within an application, between different versions of the same application, and across different applications lead to large positive transfer effects, that is, reductions in training time ranging from 100% to 300%.

However, in the world of user interfaces inconsistency is the rule; consistency is the exception. In many of the most popular application programs for a widely used personal computer, different sequences of user actions are required for the same editing operations. The actions required to edit a title of a graph, a heading or title in a spreadsheet, and a line of text in a manuscript can all be different and thus inconsistent. This chapter will also discuss the impact of such inconsistencies on learning, transfer, or retention of user skills. There is currently limited direct evidence on the effects of inconsistencies, but it will be shown that it is possible to extrapolate from the classical verbal learning literature on learning, transfer, and retention (Postman, 1971).

1.1 Central Issues

The acquisition, transfer, and retention of user skills are central issues in human-computer interaction. Carroll and Rosson (1987) summarize research demonstrating the incredible problems that new users can have in learning typical applications like word processors. Norman (1985) describes difficulties in the acquisition and retention of commands caused by basic features of the user interface of a widely used time-sharing system.

Nielsen, Mack, Bergendorff, and Grischkowsky (1986) have found underutilization of integrated software packages that incorporate spread-sheet, word processing, graphics, and other business applications. The typical skilled, discretionary user mastered one application in the system. The other applications directly relevant to a user's work were not utilized in part because of difficulties in learning and remembering how to use new tools. Difficulties in acquisition, transfer, and retention of necessary skills are fundamental limitations to both new and experienced users of complex, modern application programs and work stations (Fischer and Lemke, in this book).

1.2 The Cognitive Complexity Framework

Kieras and Polson (1985) assume that the **cognitive complexity** of a task determines the difficulties in acquisition, transfer, and retention of the skills necessary to perform the task using a given application. Cognitive complexity is a function of the **content, structure**, and **amount** of knowledge required to perform a task using a specific application program. Kieras and Polson proposed that application programs be designed by minimizing the cognitive complexity of tasks to be performed by the program. Consistency is a powerful tool for reducing cognitive complexity. Polson (1987) outlines a tentative design methodology employing the cognitive complexity framework. This chapter presents analyses of the impacts of consistent and inconsistent interfaces on acquisition, transfer, and retention using the cognitive complexity framework.

1.3 Outline Of Chapter

The chapter is organized into six major sections. Section 2 describes the theoretical basis of the analyses of consistency and inconsistency: the GOMS model (Card, Moran, & Newell, 1983) and the cognitive complexity theory (CCT) (Kieras & Polson, 1985). Sections 3 to 5 summarize three experiments demonstrating large positive transfer effects between various tasks within an application, between different versions of the same application, and between different applications. Section 6 describes how the cognitive complexity framework provides a common framework to understand the findings from the three experiments. Section 7 discusses the effects of inconsistencies on transfer and retention discussing experiments by Engelbeck (1987) and Polson, Muncher, and Kieras (1987). The final section summarizes these results and discusses possible implications for the design of user interfaces.

2. Theoretical Foundations

The theoretical foundations for the analyses of acquisition, transfer, and retention are the GOMS model (Card, Moran, & Newell, 1983) and CCT (Kieras & Polson, 1985). Both frameworks characterize the knowledge necessary to perform routine tasks like text editing. The GOMS formalism describes the content and structure of the knowledge underlying these skills. CCT represents this knowledge as production rules permitting quantification of the amount of knowledge. CCT incorporates all of the assumptions of the GOMS model. Quantitative predictions of training time, transfer of user skills, and performance can be derived from the production rule formalism (Polson & Kieras, 1985; Polson, Muncher, & Engelbeck, 1986; Polson, 1987). The frameworks are described in the next two sections.

2.1 The GOMS Model

2.1.1 Goals, Operations, Methods, And Selection Rules

The GOMS model represents a user's knowledge of how to carry out routine skills in terms of **goals, operations, methods**, and **selection rules**.

Goals represent a user's intention to perform a task, subtask, or single cognitive or physical operation. Goals are organized into structures of interrelated goals that sequence methods and operations. Examples of goals are edit manuscript, delete file, or set heading in italics.

Operations characterize elementary physical actions (e.g., pressing a function key or typing a string of characters) and cognitive operations not analyzed by the theory (e.g., perceptual operations, retrieving an item from memory, or reading a parameter and storing it in working memory).

A user's knowledge is organized into methods which are subroutines. Methods generate sequences of operations that accomplish specific goals or subgoals. The goal structure of a method characterizes its internal organization and control structure. Examples include methods for entering a parameter into a menu, moving from one menu to another, and deleting a word.

Selection rules specify the appropriate conditions for executing a method to effectively accomplish a goal in a given context. Selection rules are compiled pieces of problem-solving knowledge. They function by asserting the goal to execute a given method in the appropriate context.

2.1.2 Content And Structure Of A User's Knowledge

The GOMS model assumes that execution of a task involves decomposition of the task into a series of subtasks. A skilled user has effective methods for each subtask. Accomplishing a task involves executing the series of specialized methods that perform each subtask. There are several kinds of methods. High-level methods decompose the initial task into a sequence of subtasks. Intermediate-level methods describe the sequence of functions necessary to complete a subtask. Low-level methods generate the actual user actions necessary to perform a function.

A user's knowledge is a mixture of task-specific information, the high-level methods, and system-specific knowledge, the low-level methods. Intermediate-level methods can appear in many different contexts. Examples are the editing operations on the current line of input: a line of text being entered into a text editor, an operating system command, or labels for a graph or figure. Figure 2-1 shows parts of a GOMS model for text editing based on Card, Moran, and Newell (1983, Chapter 5). Panel (A) is the top-level control structure for text editing; panel (B) is the model for the delete method.

In summary, the GOMS model characterizes the user's knowledge as a collection of hierarchically organized methods and associated goal structures that sequence methods and operations. The knowledge captured in the GOMS representation describes both general knowledge of how the task is to be decomposed and specific information on how to execute methods required to complete the task on a given system.

2.2 Cognitive Complexity Theory

Kieras and Polson (1985) propose that the knowledge represented in a GOMS model be formalized as a production system. Selection of production systems as a vehicle for formalizing this knowledge is theoretically motivated. Newell and Simon (1972) argue that the architecture of the human information processing system can be characterized as a production system. Since then, production system models have been developed for various cognitive processes (problem solving:

(A) Top Level of Manuscript Editing Task

Goal: EDIT-MANUSCRIPT
    Goal: PERFORM-UNIT-TASKS
    (do until no more unit-task)
        Goal: ACQUIRE-UNIT-TASK
            Goal: LOOKUP-TASK-LOCATION
            Goal: MOVE-TO-TASK-LOCATION
                [USE POSITION-CURSOR-METHOD]
            Goal: LOOKUP-TASK-FUNCTION
        Goal: EXECUTE-UNIT-TASK
            SELECT: [INSERT-METHOD, DELETE-METHOD,
                      COPY-METHOD, MOVE-METHOD,
                      TRANSPOSE-METHOD]

(B) Method for Deleting any Text String

Goal: DELETE-TEXT
    Goal: PRESS-DELETE-KEY
    Goal: CHECK-DELETE-PROMPT
    Goal: SELECT-RANGE
        [USE SELECT-RANGE-METHOD]
    Goal: VERIFY-DELETE
    Goal: PRESS-ACCEPT-KEY
    Goal: FINISH-DELETE

Figure 2-1: Examples of GOMS analyses taken from the model of the manuscript editing task, Verb-Noun editor, used in the Polson, Bovair, and Kieras (1987) experiment

Simon, 1975; Karat, 1983; text comprehension: Kieras, 1982). Anderson (1976, 1982, 1983) extends Newell and Simon's (1972) architectural arguments and develops a general theory of cognition based on a production system formalism.

Polson and Kieras (1985), Polson, Muncher, and Engelbeck (1986) and other researchers have shown that production system models based on the original Kieras and Polson (1985) formalism make successful quantitative predictions for training time, transfer performance, and productivity. The models described in these papers represent the user's knowledge of how to perform tasks as collections of rules. Predictions for training time and transfer performance are derived from static analyses of a set of rules. Simulated executions of the task by the model generate performance predictions and validate the sufficiency of the representation: that is, the model can actually perform the task. The simulation program has two components: (1) a production system model of a user performing a task, and (2) a model of the system that simulates its input-output behavior. The input-output behavior of a system is for-malized as a generalized transition network. This formalism is described in Kieras and Polson (1983, 1985) and will not be discussed further here.

2.2.1 An Overview Of Production System Models

A production system is made up of three components: (a) a collection of **rules** describing the knowledge required to perform a task; (b) a **working memory** containing a representation of a user's immediate goals, intermediate results generated during the execution of a method, and a representation of the external behavior of the system; and (c) an **interpreter** that controls execution of the rules.

A rule is a condition-action pair of the form

IF (condition) THEN (action)

where the condition and action are both complex. The **condition** represents a pattern of information in working memory that specifies when a physical action or cognitive operation represented in the **action** should be executed. The condition includes a description of an explicit pattern of goals and subgoals, the state of the environment, (e.g., prompts and other information on the CRT display), and other needed information in working memory (e.g., a document name or some other parameter).

The interpreter operates in cycles by alternating back and forth between **recognize** and **act** modes. At the beginning of each cycle, the inter-preter, in the recognize mode, matches the conditions of all rules against the contents of working memory. The rule that matches is said to fire, and the system changes to the act mode. In the act mode, the action is executed. The action includes a physical or cognitive operation as well as the addition and deletion of goals and other information from working memory. Deleting and adding goals and changes in the environment caused by a user action modify the pattern of information in working memory. When the production system changes back to the recognize mode, a new production will fire, generating the next action or cognitive operation.

2.2.2 Production Rules And The GOMS Model

The production system models described in Sections 3 to 5 were derived by first performing a GOMS analysis and then writing a production system model to implement the methods and control structures described in the GOMS models. GOMS models are better structural and qualitative descriptions of the knowledge necessary to perform tasks. They directly represent the hierarchy of methods and goal structures that characterize the organization of a user's knowledge of the actions and cognitive operations necessary to accomplish a task.

A production system is a "flat", uniform representation of the same knowledge. A given rule describes the conditions under which a specific action or cognitive operation is to be executed. The organization of the knowledge, in a collection of rules that performs a complete task, has to be inferred from study of the interrelationships among the conditions of different rules or by tracing the execution time behavior of the system. Expressing this same knowledge in the production system formalism permits the derivation of well-motivated, quantitative predictions for training time, transfer, and execution time for various tasks.

Kieras and Bovair (1986), Polson and Kieras (1985), Polson, Muncher, and Engelbeck (1986), and others have successfully tested assumptions underlying these predictions. These authors have shown that (1) the amount of time required to learn a task is a linear function of the number of new rules that must be learned in order to successfully execute the task and (2) execution time for a task is the sum of the execution times for the rules that fire in order to complete the task. They have shown that transfer of training can be characterized in terms of shared rules.

2.3 Transfer

The dominant theoretical approach for explaining specific transfer effects is based on a framework proposed in experimental psychology by Thorndike and Woodward (1901) and Thorndike (1914). Transfer between two tasks is mediated by **common elements** assumed to be stimulus-response associations. Associations acquired in a first task that successfully generalize to a second do not have to be relearned during the acquisition of the second task. Only those associations unique to the second task have to be acquired. If a large number of the associations required to successfully perform the second task transfer from the first task, there can be a dramatic reduction in training time compared to the training time required for the second task without experience on the first.

Kieras and Bovair (1986) and Polson and Kieras (1985) proposed that a common elements theory of transfer could account for positive transfer effects during the acquisition of operating procedures. They assumed that the common elements are individual rules. In a consistent interface, common methods are used to achieve the same goals even when these goals occur in different task contexts. These shared methods are represented by rules common to models of the different tasks. It is assumed that these shared rules, once learned, are always incorporated into the representation of a new task at little or no cost in training time. After a user has had some experience with an application program with a consistent user interface, learning a new task requires the acquisition of a small number of unique rules. These new rules may be a small fraction of the total number of rules necessary to execute the new task. Rules representing the common methods transfer and do not have to be relearned. In a consistent interface, these common methods can be a large part of the knowledge required to perform the new task. Detailed illustrations of the transfer process are given in the next section; see Tables 3-3 and 3-4 and the associated explanations.

The transfer processes outlined above are the basis for derivations of models which are fit to data from experiments described in Sections 3 to 5. These transfer processes incorporate three strong assumptions. First, there is no characterization of nonspecific transfer effects, (e.g., generalized practice effects); it is assumed that improvements and performance are mediated by common rules. Second, these shared rules are recognized and utilized in novel contexts. Third, common rules can be incorporated into the representation of a new task at no cost in training time.

3. Transfer Within an Application

The experiment described in this section evaluated transfer predictions across tasks within an application. The theoretical analysis and confirming experimental results pinpoint the locus of these transfer effects and demonstrate the magnitude of reductions in training time across tasks for a consistent user interface. An earlier version of this study was reported in Polson, Muncher, and Engelbeck (1986).

3.1 Tasks And Production System Models

This experiment and the fourth experiment discussed in this chapter (Engelbeck, 1987) required subjects to learn utility tasks such as printing a document, changing the line spacing from single to double, and duplicating a diskette for a well-known, menu-driven, stand-alone word processor. Each utility task involved a series of menu selections leading to a menu associated with a specific task. The task menu was filled in with necessary parameters, and exiting that menu then caused the associated utility function to be completed. Some tasks involved manipulating diskettes containing documents; the diskette unit was simulated with a diagram and prompts presented on the CRT screen and operated by labeled function keys.

3.2 Theoretical Analysis

The GOMS model for each of the nine tasks used in this experiment has a very simple structure. Each task is represented as a linear sequence of steps. However, each step is complex and requires the execution of a method to perform the step. The methods common to all tasks were: load a diskette containing documents into the right slot of the diskette drive, go to the next menu, select an item from a menu, enter a parameter into a menu, enter a diskette name, and enter a document name. Figure 3-1 shows the GOMS model for the check spelling task.

Goal: INSERT-WORK-DISKETTE-IN-RIGHT-SLOT
    [USE INSERT-WORK-DISKETTE-IN-RIGHT-SLOT METHOD]

Goal: CHECK-SPELLING
    Goal: GOTO-CHECK-SPELLING-MENU
        [USE GOTO-NEXT-MENU-METHOD]
    Goal: VERIFY-GOTO-CHECK-SPELL-MENU
    Goal: SELECT-CHECK-SPELLING-FROM-MENU
        [USE SELECT-ITEM-FROM-MENU-METHOD]
    Goal: ENTER-DISKETTE-NAME
        [USE ENTER-DISKETTE-NAME-METHOD]
    Goal: ENTER-DOCUMENT-NAME
        [USE ENTER-DOCUMENT-NAME-METHOD]
    Goal: VERIFY-SPELLING-CHECK-COMPLETE
    Goal: GOTO-TASK-SELECTION-MENU
        [USE GOTO-NEXT-MENU-METHOD]

Goal: VERIFY-GOTO-TASK-SELECTION-MENU

Figure 3-1:   A GOMS analysis of check spelling task from the Polson, Muncher, and Engelbeck (1986) experiment

The production system model for a task has a structure identical to that of the GOMS model. Each rule in the production system model executes a single step, calling a method if necessary. The methods perform the operations necessary to complete each step. For example, the method to enter a document name reads the document name from the instructions, enters the name in response to the appropriate prompt, verifies the entry, and returns to the calling routine. The number of rules in the production system model for each method is shown in the bottom half of Table 3-3; it is the first non-zero entry in each row.

3.3 Testing Learning And Transfer Assumptions

The learning and transfer assumptions of CCT were evaluated by having subjects in different experimental conditions master sequences of utility tasks that varied in similarity and serial position of a given task. The nine tasks used in this experiment are listed in Table 3-1. The four experimental groups learned three pairs of highly similar tasks. These pairs were always presented in a fixed order, shared an identical initial sequence of steps, and could share a common final sequence of steps. The pairs appeared in different serial positions across the four groups.

CCT predicts that the total training time for all six tasks is constant and independent of training order; the same **unique** productions have to be mastered independently of training order. However, large differences in serial position curves across groups are predicted. The number of **new** productions that have to be learned to master a task is determined by its position in the training order and by the particular tasks that were learned previously. The assumption that there were no context effects was evaluated by showing that rules representing common methods and common initial and final sequences of steps transferred independent of the particular task context in which they were learned.

The nine tasks used in this experiment are listed in Table 3-1. Tasks 1 through 4 manipulated format parameters. The first two tasks changed default format parameters, and the second two manipulated the parameters for a specific document. Tasks 1 and 3 and Tasks 2 and 4 involved the same format change and required an identical terminal sequence of menu selections and parameter entries for each pair. The shared initial sequences for the task pairs 1-2 and 3-4 and the shared terminal sequences for the task pairs 1-3 and 2-4 were so constructed that if the subject learned any three out of four of these tasks, the theory predicted that the fourth task required the acquisition of a single new rule.

Tasks 5 and 6 were very similar duplicate diskette procedures that required users to remove a diskette from the left slot of the diskette unit and load another diskette into the slot in the middle of a sequence of menu selections and parameter entries. This novel sequence of actions is represented by a unique series of rules. Thus, it was predicted that this novel sequence of actions in Task 5 would make it relatively difficult independent of its serial position in a training order but that Task 6 would be learned more rapidly because the novel unique sequence had been mastered during the acquisition of Task 5 and would transfer to Task 6.

Table 3-1:   Task descriptions

Task Number	Task Description
Default Format Tasks	
1	Change the default first typing line from 5 to 7.
2	Change the default spacing from double to single.
Document Format Tasks	
3	Load diskette containing documents. Change the first typing line for a document from 5 to 7.
4	Load diskette containing documents. Change the spacing for a document from double to single.
Work Diskette Duplication Tasks	
5	Load diskette containing documents. Duplicate the diskette.
6	Load diskette containing documents. Condense diskette.
Miscellaneous Tasks	
7	Print a document.
8	Check a document for spelling errors.
9	Change the name of a document.

Adapted from Polson, Muncher, and Engelbeck (1986), Table 1.

The fifth group of subjects was a control for nonspecific transfer effects like generalized practice. This group first learned three unrelated tasks, 7, 8, and 9, followed by the four tasks involving the manipulation of format parameters. It was assumed that if nonspecific transfer is a significant component of the transfer process, then training on the three unrelated tasks should make the four format manipulation tasks less difficult to learn than predicted by the common elements model of transfer.

In summary, there were five groups. The four experimental groups learned the common set of six tasks arranged in three pairs with two members of every pair appearing in the order shown in Table 3-1. The training orders for the five groups are shown in Table 3-2.

Table 3-2: Training orders

Group	Task Number Serial Position						
	1	2	3	4	5	6	7
1	1	2	3	4	5	6	
2	3	4	1	2	5	6	
3	5	6	1	2	3	4	
4	5	6	3	4	1	2	
C	7	8	9	1	2	3	4

Adapted from Polson, Muncher, and Engelbeck (1986), Table 4

This experiment tests two types of transfer predictions. The first is that a common method once acquired transfers perfectly to any task later in the training sequence making use of the method. The second type of prediction involves shared steps in the pairs of tasks shown in Table 3-1. Recall that each step is represented by a rule that calls the appropriate method. The transfer theory assumes that transfer occurs at the level of individual shared rules. Thus, common initial and final sequences of steps are assumed to transfer perfectly. The magnitudes of transfer effects are calculated from the number of common rules in the representations of common methods and identical sequences of steps.

The mean time to the learning criterion for a task is determined by the number of **new rules** a user must learn in order to master the task. If a task appears in the first serial position of a training order, then all rules are new and the subject must acquire all of the rules representing the individual steps of the tasks as well as the common methods used in the task.

These calculations are shown in detail for the first experimental group and for the control group in Tables 3-3 and 3-4 respectively. The rows of each table are components of the tasks: common sequences of steps and shared methods. The columns represent each task in its corresponding serial position in the training sequence. An entry is either an asterisk, a zero, or a number greater than zero. An asterisk means that

Table 3-3: Calculation of number of new rules for each position in training sequence, Experimental Group 1

| | Number of Rules to be Learned | | | | | |
Subsequence or Common Method	1	2	3	4	5	6
Task						
Steps Unique to Task	1	1	1	1	5	5
Initial Steps for Default	3	0	*	*	*	*
Initial Steps for Document	*	*	8	0	*	*
Final Steps for Typing Line	7	*	0	*	*	*
Final Steps for Spacing	*	7	*	0	*	*
Steps for Insertion of Diskette	*	*	*	*	20	0
Common Methods						
Load Diskette	*	*	12	0	0	0
Go To Next Menu	5	0	0	0	0	0
Select Item From Menu	5	0	0	0	0	0
Enter Parameter	5	0	0	0	*	*
Enter Diskette Name	*	*	5	0	0	0
Enter Document Name	*	*	5	0	*	*
Number of New Rules	26	8	31	1	25	5
Total Number of Rules	26	26	53	53	52	52

Adapted from Polson, Muncher, and Engelbeck (1986), Table 2

this component does not occur in this task. A number greater than zero is the number of rules that must be acquired at this point in the training order for a component appearing for the first time. An entry of zero means that the rules representing this component were acquired earlier in the training sequence; the theory assumes that these rules transfer perfectly. The sum of numbers in each column is the number of new rules required to master the task learned in this serial position. This number predicts training time. The last line shows the total number of rules in the production system model for the task; this is the number of rules that would have to be learned if this task appeared first in the training order. Table 3-5 presents the number of new rules for all five groups and each serial position. CCT predicts that the corresponding cell means will be a linear function of these entries.

Table 3-4: Calculation of number of new rules for each
position in training sequence, Control

Number of Rules to be Learned

Subsequence or Common Method	Task Number						
	7	8	9	1	2	3	4
Task							
Steps Unique to Task	9	9	11	1	1	1	1
Initial Steps for Default	*	*	*	3	0	*	*
Initial Steps for Document	*	*	*	*	*	8	0
Final Steps for Typing Line	*	*	*	7	*	0	*
Final Steps for Spacing	*	*	*	*	7	*	0
Methods							
Load Diskette	*	*	*	*	*	12	0
Go To Next Menu	5	0	0	0	0	0	0
Select Item From Menu	*	5	0	0	0	0	0
Enter Parameter	*	*	5	0	0	0	0
Enter Diskette Name	5	0	0	*	*	5	0
Enter Document Name	5	0	0	*	*	5	0
Number of New Rules	24	13	16	11	8	21	1
Total Number of Rules	24	28	36	26	26	53	53

Adapted from Polson, Muncher, and Engelbeck (1986), Table 3

3.4 Method And Procedure

The results reported below are from two replications of the experiment described in the preceding section. All subjects were recruited from introductory psychology courses. Fifteen subjects were run in the first replication reported in Polson, Muncher, and Engelbeck (1986). Twenty subjects were run in the second replication, giving a total of 35 subjects in each of the five experimental conditions.

Subjects learned either six or seven of the utility tasks listed in Table 3-1 in the training order appropriate for their experimental condition shown in Table 3-2. The utility tasks were performed on a high-fidelity simulation of the word processor that also incorporated a computer assisted instruction (CAI) subsystem.

Table 3-5: Number of new rules

Group	Number of New Rules Serial Position*						
	1	2	3	4	5	6	7
1	26	8	31	1	25	5	
2	53	8	4	1	25	5	
3	52	5	16	8	9	1	
4	52	5	26	9	4	1	
C	24	13	16	11	8	21	1

Adapted from Polson, Muncher, and Engelbeck (1986), Table 4
*See Table 3-2 to determine which task occurred in a given serial position.

Each task was learned to a criterion of three consecutive perfect recitations by the anticipation method. The simulation presented subjects with the appropriate display for each step in a task. The subject had to anticipate the correct action for each step. The program responded in a manner identical to the actual word processor if the correct action was made. Minimal feedback was provided on a first error; the style of this feedback was consistent with the actual word processor. On the second error, control was transferred to the CAI subsystem, and subjects were given detailed feedback. The simulated display was replaced with a feedback screen which provided subjects with information about the current step, the goal for the next step, and the correct user action for the next step. Users could study feedback screens for as long as they wished. Then the simulated display for the current step was represented, and the subject had to anticipate the correct action.

3.5 Results

The training time and transfer predictions were evaluated by fitting both the cells' means and the individual training times for each task. The observed and predicted mean training times as a function of serial positions for the five groups are shown in Figures 3-3 (Panels A and B), 3-4

(Panels A and B), and 3-5. Figure 3-2 plots cell means as a function of the number of new rules.

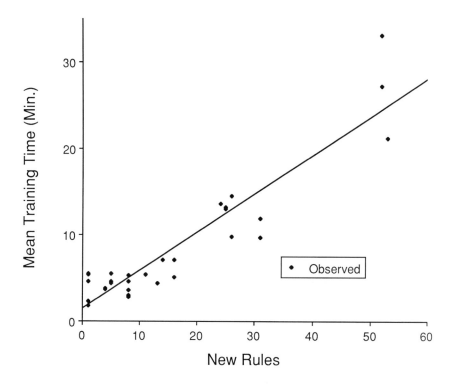

Figure 3-2: Observed mean training times plotted as function of number of new rules

The first set of predictions was calculated by fitting a simple model to the mean training times for each combination of serial position and group, a total of 31 cell means. The cell means are assumed to be a linear function of the number of new rules; the slope of the best fitting straight line is an estimate of the training time per new rule. The intercept is the time taken to perform the criterion run and other processes not involving acquisition of rules. The number of new rules for each cell is shown in Table 3-4. The observed training time per rule was 26.9 seconds, and the intercept was 84.1 seconds. The model accounted for 88% of the variance of the 31 means. There were only two significant differences between observed and predicted values for the 31 means. One occurred on Serial Position 1 for Experimental Group 4; the other was found in Serial Position 6 for the control group.

A more complex model was fit to the individual training times. This model included three sets of predictors: each subject's mean, the number of new rules, and the number of newly generalized rules. CCT does not include any explanation of individual differences. In order to account for individual differences, each subject's mean was included in the regression equation. Including the number of newly generalized rules in the equation permits a test of the hypothesis that there is no cost for generalizing a rule, enabling it to be used in a new task. A newly generalized rule is a rule that was acquired during some previous task and is now transferring for the first time on the current task. The number of newly generalized rules can be calculated from Tables 3-3 and 3-4 by tracing across each row, finding the first non-zero entry, and then continuing across the row to the first zero entry. This zero entry is the task on which the rules must be generalized in order to fire in the new context defined by a different task.

The model accounted for 70% of the variance of the individual data points. The estimated training time per rule was 28.7 seconds, very similar to the value found by fitting the simpler model to the cell means. The training time for newly generalized rules was 3.5 seconds, and this parameter was significantly different from zero. This result calls into some question the assumption that the transfer process is cost free. The standardized regression coefficients for the subject's own mean, the number of new rules, and the number of newly generalized rules were .30, .83, and .10 respectively.

Being able to generate a consistent account for both cell means and individual data points is an important test of the theory. The data from such learning experiments are highly variable; the ratios of the slowest subject to the fastest in a given cell can range from 5 to 1 to 10 to 1. Card, Moran, and Newell (1983) found similar individual differences in their data from experiments on skilled users of text editors. Accounting for 70% of the variance of the individual data points is thus an impressive

Panel A

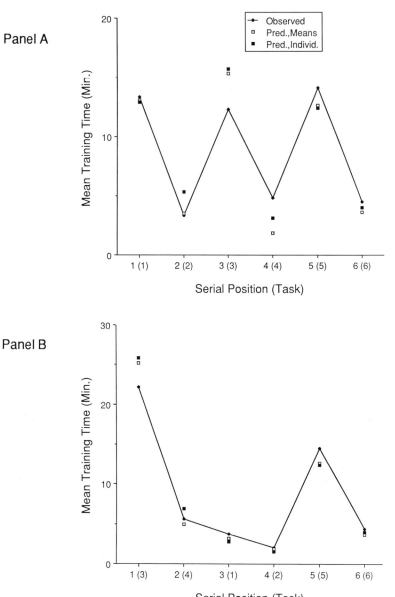

Figure 3-3: Observed and predicted mean training times plotted as a function of serial position (task) for Experimental Group 1 (Panel A) and Experimental Group 2 (Panel B)

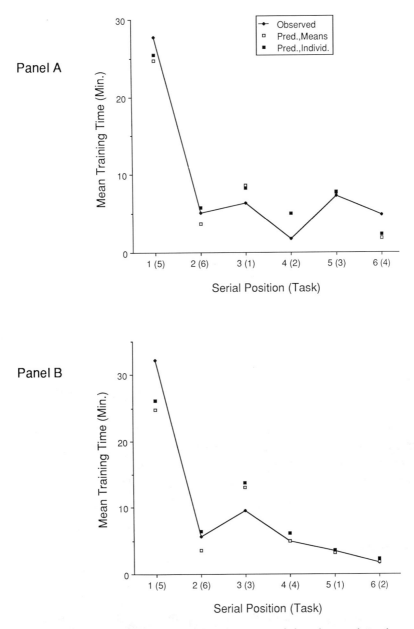

Figure 3-4: Observed and predicted mean training times plotted as a function of serial position (task) for Experimental Group 3 (Panel A) and Experimental Group 4 (Panel B)

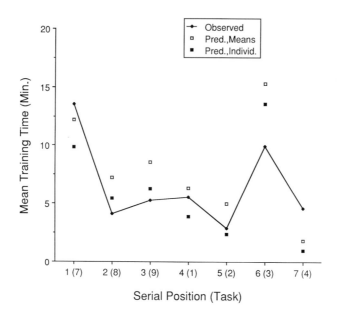

Figure 3-5: Observed and predicted mean training times plotted as a function of serial position (task) for the Control Group

accomplishment for such a model. Even more important is the finding that the number of new rules is a better predictor of a subject's performance than his or her's own mean. The standardized regression coefficient for the number of new rules was .83, and the coefficient for the subject's own mean was .30.

3.6 Conclusions

The excellent fits to the complex patterns of transfer results shown in Figures 3-3 (Panels A and B), 3-4 (Panels A and B), and 3-5 and the linear relationship between observed means and number of new rules shown in Figure 3-2 support the conclusions that transfer is mediated by very specific relationships between successive tasks and that CCT can provide a quantitative account of these transfer effects.

4. Transfer Between Different Editors

This section describes the use of the cognitive complexity framework to analyze transfer between different versions of the same application. Polson, Bovair, and Kieras (1987) modelled transfer between two similar, full-screen, text editors. Singley and Anderson (1985) found large positive transfer effects between very different line editors and from line editors to a screen editor. This analysis of the transfer process also accounts for the large transfer effects observed by Singley and Anderson (1985).

4.1 Theoretical Analysis

Polson, Bovair, and Kieras (1987) had subjects learn two very similar full-screen text editors. The first editor has a verb-noun command structure in which the editing operation is specified first, followed by range selection. The second editor has a noun-verb command structure; the select range operation occurs first, followed by specification of the editing function. Otherwise, the two editors are identical. They share a common method for inserting text, and the details of the range selection and cursor positioning operations are also identical.

Polson and Kieras (1985) developed a production system model for the first editor. The model for the second editor was determined by the model for the first editor and involves only small changes dictated by the different organization of commands, noun-verb vs. verb-noun. In the production system representation, only a few rules are required to describe the differences in the overall organization of the two editors, and the user is predicted to transfer large amounts of knowledge. On the other hand, knowledge representations that assume that transfer is at the level of complete methods would predict that differences in these methods, however subtle, would require users to relearn the new similar methods.

4.1.1 The Editors

The editors were two very similar full-screen text editors with five functions: insert, delete, copy, move, and transpose. The editing commands were selected by pressing labeled function keys: INSERT, DELETE, COPY, MOVE, and TRANSPOSE. All were block mode commands in which the text to be operated on by an editing function was specified by a generalized range selection function. All editing operations were terminated by an ACCEPT or REJECT key. Pressing the REJECT key undid the current edit and positioned the cursor at the end of the last edit. The insert function was identical for both editors and was a command of the form verb-noun.

In the verb-noun editor, performing an edit involved the following sequence of steps: (1) pressing the appropriate labeled function key, (2) specifying a range for the edit, (3) specifying a to-location for the copy, move, and transpose commands, (4) specifying a second range for the transpose command, and (5) finally pressing the ACCEPT or REJECT key. The delete command was executed immediately at the end of the first range selection step. The cursor keys were used to move the cursor to the to-location which was designated by pressing the ENTER key. The copy and move commands were executed immediately after designating the to-location. The transpose command was executed after completing the selection of the second range.

Performing an edit with the verb-noun editor involved the following sequence of steps: (1) pressing the SELECT key, (2) specifying a range for the edit, (3) pressing the appropriate labeled function key, (4) specifying a to-location for the copy, move, and transpose commands, (5) specifying a second range for the transpose command, and (6) finally pressing the ACCEPT or REJECT key. The delete command was executed immediately on pressing the DELETE key. The cursor keys were used to move the cursor to the to-location which was designated by pressing the ENTER key. The copy and move commands were executed immediately after designating the to-location. The transpose command was executed after completing the selection of the second range.

4.1.2 The Models

Production system models for both editors are based on Card, Moran and Newell's (1983, Chapter 6) GOMS analysis of manuscript editing in which the task is decomposed into a sequence of unit tasks, each defined by a single edit. The top-level control structure is a do-while loop that terminates when there are no more unit tasks. Performance of a unit-task involves: (1) acquiring the task (e.g., positioning the cursor at the beginning of the range and determining that the operation to be performed is delete), (2) execute the unit-task (e.g., perform the delete operation), and (3) verify correct execution of the unit-task (e.g., verify that the delete was performed correctly). The GOMS analyses for the top-level control structure and the delete method for the verb-noun editor are shown in Figure 2-1.

The model for each editor has seven methods: a cursor positioning method, a select range method, and one method for each of the five editing functions. The verification phase is the last step of each editing method. The goal structures for the five editing methods are linear sequences of the actions and verification steps including range selection, necessary to complete an edit. Table 4-1 shows the number of rules for the top-level control structure and for each method and the number of shared or common rules for each component of the model. Both models share identical methods for cursor positioning and the insert function and the top level control structure.

4.2 Method And Procedure

There were four groups of subjects: two transfer groups and two retention controls. The two training days occurred 24 or 48 hours apart. Group 1 learned the verb-noun editor followed by the noun-verb editor; Group 2 learned the noun-verb editor followed by the verb-noun editor. The two retention control groups were tested on the same editor on Day 2. Within each group, subjects learned 5 different editing methods in one of two training orders. Sixteen subjects were run in each of the four conditions defined by the two transfer groups and the two training orders. Eight subjects were run in each of the four conditions for the retention controls.

Table 4-1: Number of rules for Verb-Noun and Noun-Verb editors

Component Description	Number of Rules		
	Verb-Noun	Noun-Verb	Common
Top-level Task Control Structure (Core)	9	9	9
Cursor Positioning Method (uses arrow keys)	14	14	14
Select Range Method (use single-character find)	15	17	12
Insert Text Method	9	9	9
Delete Method	7	6	3
Copy Method	11	10	6
Move Method	11	10	6
Transpose Method	12	11	4

Adapted from Polson, Bovair, and Kieras (1987), Table 1.

The experimental procedure was controlled by two interacting programs, which implemented an editor and a computer-assisted instruction system. There were two CRTs, one displaying the material to be edited and the other presenting instructions and feedback. The same general procedure was used for both Day 1 and Day 2. Subjects were first given general instructions that included information about the general structure of the task, the layout of the keyboard, and use of the cursor positioning keys. Subjects then learned 5 text editing methods one at a time in an order specified by the particular training order that they received.

Subjects were given detailed instructions on how to perform each editing function. They then had to successfully complete a practice task that required them to make ten changes on a two page manuscript using the particular editing function. After each practice edit, subjects were given feedback if they made an error. Subjects then had to review the instructions for the particular editing method. The criterion for learning was one error-free repetition of all ten edits.

Subjects who could type and who had no computing or word processing experience were recruited through a newspaper ad and were paid $25 for participating in the experiment.

4.3 Theoretical Results

Models for the two transfer groups and the combined retention control groups were fit to the 60 training time cell means defined by the combination of three training groups, two training orders, two days, and five serial positions. The training time for a method was the reading time for the instructions plus the time required to complete the practice edits using the method. Figures 4-1 (Panels A and B) and 4-2 plot the observed and predicted mean training times as a function of serial position and day for each of the three groups.

The number of new rules are shown in Table 4-2 for the group learning the verb-noun editor on Day 1 followed by the noun-verb editor on Day 2 and in Table 4-3 for the group learning the two editors in the reverse order. Each table has 20 entries for the cells defined by two training orders, two days (original learning, Day 1, vs. transfer learning, Day 2) and five serial positions. Observe that the profiles of the number of new rules as a function of serial position in a given training order are very similar for the two editors on both Day 1 and Day 2. There are larger differences between the two training orders caused by the shift of transpose, the most difficult method, from Serial Position 5 in Training Order 1 to Serial Position 2 in Training Order 2.

The details of the calculations for the entries for Day 1 in Tables 4-2 and 4-3 are very similar to the calculations leading to Tables 3-3 and 3-4. The number of rules to be learned to perform the insert method presented in Serial Position 1 for both training orders and both editors is the sum of the number of rules for the top-level control structure (9), the cursor positioning method (14), and the insert text method (9) which is 32. The number of new rules that must be acquired to learn the delete

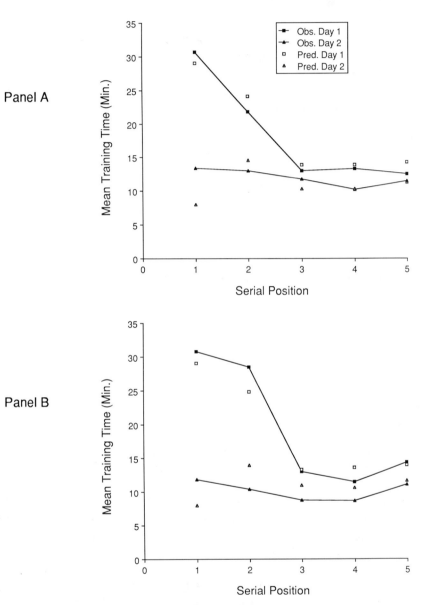

Figure 4-1: Observed and predicted mean times to criterion plotted as a function of serial position in training order averaged over training orders for the Noun-Verb to Verb-Noun (Panel A) and the Verb-Noun to Noun-Verb (Panel B) Training Groups

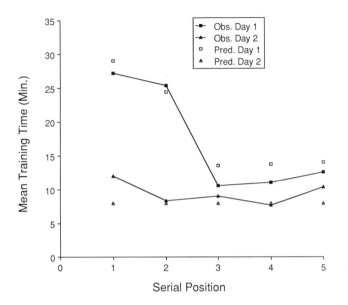

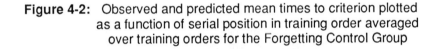

Figure 4-2: Observed and predicted mean times to criterion plotted
as a function of serial position in training order averaged
over training orders for the Forgetting Control Group

method for the verb-noun editor in Serial Position 2 is the sum of the new
rules associated with the following components: top-level control structure (0), cursor positioning method (0), range selection method (15), and
delete method (7). The only other piece of information needed to
calculate the other entries in Table 4-2 is that the copy and move
methods share four rules.

There are two sources of positive transfer on Day 2: (a) rules acquired
while learning the first editor and (b) transfer between editing methods on
the second editor. Examination of Table 4-1 shows that both editors
share an identical top level or core, insert method, and cursor positioning
methods. There are also common rules in the select range methods and
the five editing methods. On Day 2, the editing method presented in

Table 4-2: Number of new rules learned during original learning
(Verb-Noun Editor) and transfer (Noun-Verb Editor)

Training Order 1

	Insert	Delete	Copy	Move	Transpose	Total
Verb-Noun Editor	32	22	11	7	12	84
Noun-Verb Editor	0	8	4	3	7	22

Training Order 2

	Insert	Transpose	Delete	Copy	Move	Total
Verb-Noun Editor	32	27	7	11	7	84
Noun-Verb Editor	0	12	3	4	3	22

Adapted from Polson, Bovair, and Kieras (1987), Table 3

Serial Position 2 for both transfer group and the two training orders groups requires that subjects learn both the text editing and the select range methods for the new editor. The number of rules to be learned is reduced by the number of common rules for range selection and the editing method acquired on Day 1. The editing methods in the remaining serial positions require learning only the rules involved with each method.

Assuming no forgetting, the Day 2 predictions for the insert function in all conditions and for the two forgetting controls are straightforward. Performing the insert function requires knowing the top-level control structure, the cursor positioning method, and the insert method, which are all identical for both editors; and thus no new rules have to be learned. Similar arguments lead to the prediction that no new rules are learned on Day 2 in either of the two forgetting control conditions.

Table 4-3: Number of new rules learned during original learning
(Noun-Verb Editor) and transfer (Verb-Noun Editor)

		Training Order 1				
	Insert	Delete	Copy	Move	Transpose	Total
Noun-Verb Editor	32	23	10	7	11	83
Verb-Noun Editor	0	7	5	3	8	23

		Training Order 2				
	Insert	Transpose	Delete	Copy	Move	Total
Noun-Verb Editor	32	28	6	10	7	83
Verb-Noun Editor	0	11	4	5	3	23

Adapted from Polson, Bovair, and Kieras (1987), Table 4

Predictions were calculated by fitting a linear function to the points
defined by the 60 cell means. The predictor for each cell mean is the
number of new rules that have to be learned in order to master a new
editing method at a given serial position in a training order. The
parameters of the models were estimated using regression techniques.
The estimated value of training time per rule is .66 min (39.6 sec); the
intercept is 7.91 min. The number of new rules accounts for 77% of the
variance in the 60 cell means. The observed and predicted means are
shown in Figures 4-1 (Panels A and B) and 4-2 for each training group.
The observed and predicted total training times summed across serial
positions and averaged over training orders are shown in Table 4-4.

Table 4-4: Observed (predicted) and mean total training times
in minutes

Training Group	Day 1	Day 2
Verb-Noun	91.3(95.2)	59.9(54.4)
Noun-Verb	97.8(94.6)	50.6(55.0)
Control	86.8(94.9)	47.6(39.8)

Adapted from Polson, Bovair, and Kieras (1987), Table 6

4.4 Conclusions

These results provide strong support for the extension of the cognitive complexity framework to the characterization of transfer between different versions of the same application. Furthermore, they show that it is possible for the framework to account for the large positive transfer effects observed by Singley and Anderson (1985).

5. Transfer Between Different Applications

The study summarized in this section examines transfer between different applications, text, and graphic editors. Ziegler, Vossen, and Hoppe (1986) evaluated models of transfer between the text and graphics editors on the Xerox STAR workstation derived from the cognitive complexity framework. Will a method learned in the context of one application, (e.g., delete text string), generalize to another context defined by a different application, (e.g., delete graphic object)? Gick and Holyoak (1983) and Hayes and Simon (1976) have shown that subjects have great difficulty in transferring knowledge about a common underlying solution between problems with different cover stories.

The designers of the Xerox STAR workstation (Smith et al., 1982) claimed to have developed **universal commands** for operations like delete, copy, move, and manipulation of properties. Furthermore, basic commands in different applications involved first selecting an object and then specifying the operation by pressing a labeled function key. There are specialized methods for selecting different kinds of objects--a character, word, arbitrary string of text, or graphical object for example--but the methods are fairly similar, and a mouse is used to make all selections. Thus, there is a large amount of similarity between the methods for delete text object and delete graphic object. However, as Gick and Holyoak (1983) have shown, it is quite possible that surface differences between tasks may block transfer. The Ziegler et al. (1986) experiment is the first to attempt to evaluate the claims of the STAR's designers.

5.1 Tasks

Ziegler et al. (1986) had subjects with no computing experience learn four sets of editing methods which were defined by the dimensions text vs. graphics and content vs. form. All tasks required selection of the object to be manipulated and then specification of the operation. The four tasks involved editing of text content, text form, graphics content, and graphics form. Content editing operations were delete, copy, and move. Form editing operations involved changing the form of an existing object by using the properties command on the STAR. The properties command displays a property sheet, and the attributes that can be manipulated depend on the object. Using the mouse, the user selects the new values of various attributes from the property sheet. The text properties were font, size, and text features such as italics and bold face. The graphics properties were line width, shading of a figure, and texture.

5.2 Theoretical Analysis

The basic structure of the CCT models for both graphics and text tasks were identical. These models were very similar to the CCT models presented in the last section for the two text editors. There is a common top-level control structure and identical methods for delete, copy, move, and change attribute functions. There is a common method for basic cursor positioning operations with the mouse and specialized selection methods for text and graphics objects. The identical assumptions concerning learning and transfer underlying quantitative predictions for the two previous experiments were the basis for derivations of transfer predictions in the Ziegler et al. study. The same processes were used to calculate the number of new rules as a function of serial position and training order. The details of the calculations are contained in the explanations of the entries in Tables 3-3, 3-4, and 3-5 and Tables 4-2 and 4-3.

5.3 Method And Procedure

Subjects were trained on four different sets of methods: text content modifications (TC), text form modifications (TF), graphics content modifications (GC), and graphics form modifications (GF). Four groups of 20 subject each learn the sets of tasks in different training orders. The training orders are shown in Table 5-1. The content modification operations were delete, copy, and move. Form modification operations changed properties of an existing object. For texts, changes were made in fonts, sizes, and text features such as italics and bold face. For graphics objects, changes were made in line width, shading of a figure, and texture.

Table 5-1:   Training orders for Ziegler et al. (1986) experiment

Group	Serial Position			
	1	2	3	4
Text to Graphics	TC	TF	GC	GF
Graphics to Text	GC	GF	TC	TF
Function to Form	TF	GF	TC	GC
Mixed	GF	TC	TF	GC

Adapted from Ziegler, Vossen, and Hoppe (1986), Figure 14

Subjects were given a minimal introduction to each set of methods. They then went through a series of texts or figures on which they had to carry out three different form or structure modifications on each text or figure. Subjects were run individually by one of six experimenters. The experimenters provided instruction and corrective feedback if subjects made mistakes. The criterion for learning was three successive error-free sets of modifications on three different texts or figures. Timing data and errors were recorded by experiments on a separate terminal running on another system.

5.4 Results

The observed and predicted mean times to reach the first of the three criterion trials are shown in Figures 5-1 (Panels A and B) and 5-2 (Panels A and B) for the four groups. An analysis of variance showed that no significant effects were caused by the differences in the six experimenters. Improvement performance as a function of serial positions shown in the four figures are highly significant. As predicted by CCT there were no differences in the total training time for the four groups.

These results show that subjects are capable of perceiving similarities across applications and of transferring the appropriate skills. Ziegler et al. did not give their subjects any explicit instruction about the relationship between various tasks. Subjects were simply encouraged to make use of the knowledge they acquired previously. Thus, subjects can successfully transfer the relevant underlying structural features of methods across tasks with different surface features.

A linear function was fit to the 16 cell means defined by the combinations of four training orders and four serial positions with the number of new rules as the predictor. The number of new rules for each of the 16 cells is given in Table 5-2. The slope, the observed training time per rule, was 18.8 sec and the intercept was 195.6 sec. The number of new rules accounted for 90% of the variance between the 16 cell means.

Table 5-2: Number of new rules in each serial position

Group	Serial Position			
	1	2	3	4
Text to Graphics	44	24	9	3
Graphics to Text	40	24	13	3
Function to Form	50	12	18	0
Mixed	46	31	3	0

Adapted from Ziegler, Vossen, and Hoppe (1986), Figure 15

5.5 Conclusions

The results shown in Figures 5-1 (Panels A and B) and 5-2 (Panels A and B) exhibit the same large transfer effects across the four classes of tasks that have been observed across tasks within the same application and between two highly similar text editors. The results of the Ziegler et al. (1986) study strongly support the generality of the cognitive complexity framework and show that methods can transfer across different applications.

6. Consistent Interfaces and Transfer of User Skills

The cognitive complexity framework provides a common explanation for the large positive transfer effects observed (1) between tasks with the same application (Polson et al., 1986), (2) between different versions of the same application (Polson et al., 1987; Singley & Anderson, 1985; Anderson, 1987), and (3) between different applications on a system with a consistent user interface (Ziegler et al., 1986).

The large transfer effects observed during the acquisition of utility tasks

Panel A

Panel B

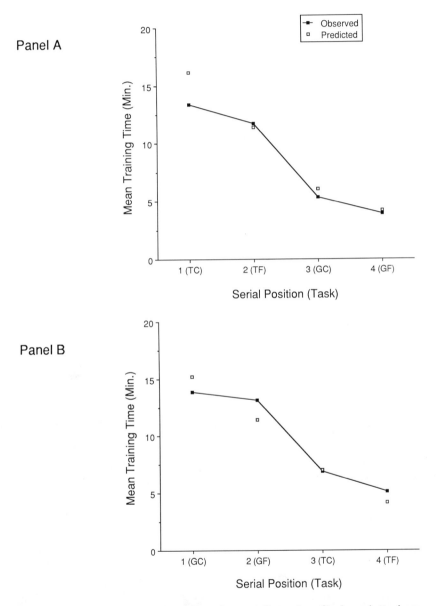

Figure 5-1: Observed and predicted mean times to criterion plotted as a function of serial position for the Text to Graphics Group (Panel A) and the Graphics to Text Group (Panel B)

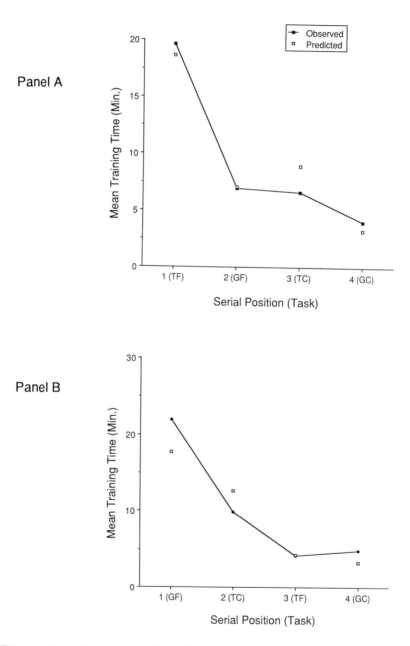

Figure 5-2: Observed and predicted mean times to criterion plotted as a function of serial position for the Function to Content Group (Panel A) and the Mixed Group (Panel B)

executed on a menu-based, stand alone, word processor with a consistent interface were mediated by methods common to tasks (Polson et al., 1986). These methods generate the user actions necessary to navigate through the menu hierarchy, enter diskette and document names, and enter parameters into menus. Individual steps in a task involved a single rule which calls a method. The typical task has from five to nine steps; thus a completely unrelated task would require that the user learn five to nine new productions. The complete model for the task and the common methods could have 50 rules. Consistency dramatically reduces the cognitive complexity of new tasks once the common methods have been mastered.

Most of the tasks in the initial serial position of a training order were difficult because the subject had to acquire the knowledge necessary to perform each of them as well as a significant percentage of the methods that were common to all tasks. Subjects are capable of recognizing common methods that appear in different task contexts and transferring this knowledge to new contexts. Such common methods are characteristic of a consistent interface. These results show that users will exploit such consistencies and that acquisition of the common methods dramatically reduces training time for tasks that appear in later serial positions of a training order.

The other component of the transfer was transfer of the knowledge necessary to make common sequences of menu transitions that were shared by the various task pairs. Here transfer is at the level of individual rules, and the results show that the predicted transfer effects in fact do occur. The rather dramatic sawtooth, serial-position curve shown in Figure 3-3, Panel A, is in large part due to transfer of common sequences of menu transitions.

The cognitive complexity framework and Anderson (1987) have similar explanations for the large positive transfer effects observed between different text editors. The top-level control structure is a description of the structure of the manuscript editing task that is independent of the details of a particular editor. An important component of the knowledge that subjects have about text editing is how the task is to be organized into a collection of unit-tasks in which each unit task is an individual edit.

Cursor positioning and other low-level editing methods are very similar for given classes of editors. These shared methods are the other component that mediates the large observed transfer effects. The cognitive complexity framework enables us to predict the magnitudes of these effects.

The results of Ziegler et al. (1986) demonstrate that the cognitive complexity framework can be extended to make predictions both across very different applications, text versus graphic editors, as well as different kinds of tasks within those applications, content versus form modifications. These results also suggest that the positive transfer mechanisms are quite robust in that subjects can recognize common methods acquired in a very different task context and successfully transfer them to a new task context.

These results seem to contradict the findings of Gick and Holyoak (1983) showing that differences in surface structure block the transfer of common problem solving methods that apply to superficially different problems. It is possible to generate versions of the same underlying puzzle-like problem and that they would have no superficial similarities at all. However, in all of the transfer experiments discussed in this chapter, there are a large number of external cues that enable users to relate old and new context: (1) different tasks are performed on the same computer system; (2) tasks performed on different systems are identical (e.g., text editing); (3) consistent methods across tasks within the same application display identical prompts and other surface information. In the Xerox Star, the universal commands are associated with identical dedicated function keys. In summary, identical tasks, prompts, function keys, and other information appearing on the display provide surface cues which may play an important component in mediating the successful transfer of user skills from one task context to another. These similarities trigger retrieval of the common methods in new contexts. Users then attempt to apply these methods in new contexts. On a system with a consistent user interface, such attempts are successful.

7. The Impact of Inconsistencies

This section explores the impact of inconsistent methods on competent users of computer systems. Inconsistent interfaces for systems or different application programs require that users employ different methods in various contexts to achieve the common goals. Such inconsistencies can impact users in three different ways. First, inconsistencies prevent transfer of existing user skills across different applications and systems. Second, inconsistencies may accelerate forgetting of associations between a goal and the several inconsistent methods used to achieve the goal in different contexts. An experiment by Engelbeck (1987) provides support for this conjecture. Third, inconsistencies between old and new methods associated with a goal may cause interference in the process of learning new methods.

Competent users have difficulties in learning to use a new application even when they understand it's functions and general principles of operation; the problem is that they lack the knowledge of the novel methods for achieving common goals (Karat, Boyes, Weisgerber, & Schafer, 1986). For example, in two versions of a popular word processing package, the command to center text is control-shift c in the first version and control-shift x in a second version hosted on another computing system.

Inability to remember methods limits and frustrates competent users. They do not forget general principles of operation for applications, (e.g., a spreadsheet, text editor, or document compiler). However, they cannot make effective use of infrequently used applications or functions because they cannot remember the associated methods. In a popular graphics package for a well-known personal computer, axis labels and other text material are edited by highlighting characters and words, deleting the highlighted material, and entering new text. Function keys F7 to F10 control the highlighting function.

Retention of methods is made more difficult by the fact that they are often both arbitrary, having no logical relation to the associated goal, and meaningless, being single control or function keys. Thus, users have to memorize meaningless associations between goals and sequences of meaningless actions that accomplish the goal. Inconsistencies further compound a user's difficulties. Methods associated with the same goal in different versions of an application are different sequences of meaningless actions. The new methods have to be looked up in a reference manual and then memorized.

7.1 Classical Research On Memory

Failures of transfer and retention are problems in human-computer interaction where 100 years of research on the psychology of human memory can contribute. Verbal learning tasks involving the memorization of arbitrary associations between meaningless items were used in the first scientific studies of memory (Ebbinghaus, 1885/1964). Similar tasks were employed for the next 80 years in the study of the processes of learning, transfer and forgetting (Postman, 1971). Today, many researchers argue that these results have little or no relevance to the dynamics of memory processes outside the laboratory since humans typically memorize events and materials that are meaningful and highly organized (Neisser, 1982; Jenkins, 1974; Anderson, 1985).

However, most computing systems and applications programs recreate the tasks used in the verbal learning literature to study learning, transfer, and forgetting. Nonsense associations are difficult to learn and remember. The structure of inconsistencies in the relationships between goals and their associated methods both across and within applications are analogous to the experimental tasks that were used to study processes that interfere with learning and retention (Postman, 1971). Thus, the classical verbal learning literature is directly relevant to understanding the difficulties faced by competent users of modern applications programs (Nielsen et al., 1986).

7.2 Retention Of Rules

Engelbeck (1987) performed an experiment that suggests that classical results from verbal learning literature on forgetting apply to the retention of individual rules. He tested memory for rules in an experiment that used the utility tasks from the menu-based, stand-alone word processor used in the Polson et al. (1986) study. Engelbeck assumed that reten-tion errors are caused by forgetting of rules that perform individual steps of a task. These rules call methods that generate sequences of actions to perform steps. They are associations between the goal of performing a given step and the method that accomplishes the goal.

7.2.1 Interference

Engelbeck (1987) then applied the basic assumptions of interference theory (Postman & Underwood, 1973) as a model of the forgetting process. The identical goal may be associated with different methods if tasks require inconsistent methods to accomplish the goal. Let A represent the common goal and B and C represent the inconsistent methods. Thus, the two rules are of the form A-B and A-C. This relationship is a classical interference paradigm. Interference theory predicts that such rules should interfere with each other and lead to for-getting. Engelbeck varied the relative frequencies of use of A-B and A-C rules. The rule that appears more frequently was predicted to interfere with the retention of the less frequent version of the rule.

7.3 Method And Procedure

Engelbeck (1987) used the menu-based word processor simulation and computer-aided instruction system and employed the basic training pro-cedure described in Section 3. Subjects were trained to perform seven utility tasks on the simulated word processor and then were brought back a day later for a retention test. The retention tests involve retraining subjects on the same set of utility tasks.

Engelbeck's subjects first learned the method for loading the diskette in the right slot and then learned six other utility tasks: check spelling, print a document, go to the typing area, delete a document, change the printer setup, and change the line format parameter for a document. Three of the six tasks contained A-C rules, the low-frequency exceptions to the A-B rules. These tasks also contain many rules that were consistent across all six tasks. The other three tasks contained no inconsistent rules and were the primary source of the high-frequency A-B rules.

Engelbeck's experiment manipulated the training orders of tasks with consistent and inconsistent rules in order to examine the effects on acquisition as well as the retention of these inconsistencies. This discussion focuses on retention. The tasks containing only consistent rules were delete a document, change a printer setup, and change the line format on a document. The tasks containing one or more inconsistent rules were check spelling, print a document, and go to the typing area. Each rule in production system models of each task represents a step in one of the six utility tasks or in the method for loading a diskette. The rules were then classified as C-D (unique) rules and A-B or A-C rules.

The retention testing session in Engelbeck's experiment lasted one hour. Retention was measured by having subjects relearn the seven utility tasks they had acquired on the previous day to a criterion of a single errorless repetition of the task.

7.4 Results

A retention error was defined as an error made by a subject on the first attempt at a given step of a given task. Because each step can be associated with a rule, it was possible to tabulate the number of errors associated with each rule type. There was a total of 61 steps across all seven tasks, and 60 subjects were tested for retention on all tasks. The overall probability of an error was .076. The observed probability of an error was .56 for the four low-frequency A-C rules. Over half the errors observed in this study were made on these four steps. The probability of an error on a low-frequency C-D rule was .046.

7.5 Conclusions

The results from the Engelbeck's (1987) experiment strongly suggest that the extensive body of literature on interference and forgetting in list learning tasks (Postman, 1971) is applicable to the domain of human-computer interaction. Engelbeck's results suggest that interference results can be very powerful. Nearly half of the total number of errors made on the retention tests were due to the loss of 4 out of 61 rules. All four of these rules were the low-frequency member of an A-B, A-C pair.

Engelbeck's results must be interpreted with some caution because two variables (a) whether a given rule was unique or a member of an interfering pair, and (b) the frequency of application of the different kinds of rules, were not orthogonal in the experimental design. Nevertheless, Engelbeck's experiment was run on a very high-fidelity simulation of an actual product.

8. Summary and Design Implications

8.1 Consistency

The results from the three transfer experiments demonstrate that consistent user interfaces mediate positive transfer within an application across tasks, between two versions of the same application, and across different applications. These results should surprise no one; the important fact is their magnitude. In the Polson et al. (1986) and Ziegler et al. (1986) studies, the same task appeared in different serial positions of different training orders across groups. Three- or four-to-one reductions in training times were observed when a task was presented in the first serial position vs. later serial position in a training order.

There are pervasive communalities across different tasks and applications in systems with consistent interfaces. High level methods characterizing general task structure are independent of the details of a given interface such as a particular text editor. A consistent system, by definition, has identical low-level methods and these transfer, too. Finally, the accurate predictions of performance for all three of these experiments were derived from a theory that assumes that improvements in performance are due solely to the transfer of individual rules.

8.2 Inconsistency

Inconsistent methods block positive transfer; the user must acquire new rules representing the inconsistent methods. Engelbeck's (1987) results suggest not only that inconsistent rules are more likely to be forgotten but also that to remember inconsistent rules, users have to spend additional time acquiring representations that can be successfully retained.

Results from experiments on transfer between inconsistent text editors show that inconsistent methods do not interfere with the acquisition of new methods (Polson, Muncher, & Kieras, 1987; Polson et al., 1987). User just have to acquire the new rules representing the inconsistent methods. However, the impact of inconsistencies on learning and the user should not be underestimated. Karat et al. (1986) examined transfer between three versions of the same word processing systems hosted in different system environments. The first system was a stand-alone word processor. The follow-on systems were intended to facilitate transfer of user skills from the stand-alone version to new versions hosted on a general purpose personal computer and on a departmental computing system.

Karat et al. found that although there was some transfer, users experienced serious difficulties in transferring their skills to the new versions. The inconsistencies were caused by differences in the assignments of functions keys leading to inconsistent methods for common functions. The stand-alone version of the system has specialized, labeled function keys. Users had to learn and retain the locations of corresponding function keys on unlabeled, generic keyboards for versions on both the general purpose personal computer and the departmental computer system. Users had trouble learning the new function key assignments because they attempted to discover the new key assignment by trial and error and almost always failed, requiring experimenter intervention. The reference documentation was available, but users rarely made use of it.

8.3 Relationships Between Transfer and Interference

The large transfer effects observed in the experiments reported in this chapter are mediated by methods common to different tasks within an application, shared by the same application running on different systems, and shared across different applications. Variations of the same goals occur again and in different contexts across different tasks and applications, (e.g., enter or edit text, move or copy object, and the like). What these results show is that these common methods make up a very significant part of the total knowledge required to use an application to perform a task. Inconsistent methods for these functions block positive transfer and cause interference. Thus, the user is penalized twice by such inconsistencies. First, useful skills fail to transfer. Second, the newly acquired novel methods are easily forgotten.

The commercial success of the most popular personal computing systems is in large part due to the very rich collection of highly functional software written by various independent organizations. However, there is no consensus on standards for low-level methods or even the assignment of functions to the keypad. Application programs have embedded unique user interfaces. The cost of this anarchy is a decrease in usability: failure to transfer user skills and difficulty in remembering the unique methods used by different software packages.

Acknowledgements

This chapter summarizes several of the experiments conducted as part of a collaborative research program with David Kieras and Susan Bovair of the University of Michigan. My co-workers at Colorado include George Engelbeck, Elizabeth Muncher, Mary Gravelle, and Peter Foltz. I am grateful to Raymonde Guindon for her detailed, critical review of an earlier version of this chapter. Thanks to her efforts, this version is a much more effective presentation of the results of the Cognitive Complexity Project. This research was supported by International Business Machines Corporation. The opinions and conclusions contained within this paper are those of the author and not necessarily those of IBM.

References

Anderson, J. R. (1976). *Language, memory, and thought.* Hillsdale, N.J.: Lawrence Erlbaum Associates.
Anderson, J. R. (1982). Acquisition of cognitive skill. *Psychological Review, 89*, 369-406.

Anderson, J. R. (1983). *The architecture of cognition.* Cambridge, MS: Harvard University Press.

Anderson, J. R. (1985). Ebbinghaus's century. *Journal of Experimental Psychology: Learning, Memory, and Cognition, 11,* 436-439.

Anderson, J. R. (1987). Skill acquisition: Compilation of weak-method solutions. *Psychological Review, 94,* 192-211.

Card, S. K., Moran, T. P., & Newell, A. (1983). *The psychology of human-computer interaction.* Hillsdale, N.J.: Erlbaum.

Carroll, J. M., & Rosson, M. B. (1987). The paradox of the active user. In J. M. Carroll (Ed.), *Interfacing thought: Cognitive aspects of human-computer interaction* (pp. 80-111). Cambridge, MS: Bradford Books/MIT Press.

Ebbinghaus, H. (1964). *Memory: A contribution to experimental psychology.* New York: Dover. (Original work published 1885; translated 1913.)

Engelbeck, G. E. (1986). *Exceptions to generalizations: Implications for formal models of human-computer interaction.* Unpublished master's thesis, Department of Psychology, University of Colorado, Boulder.

Engelbeck, G. E., & Polson, P. G. (1987). *An interference theory explanation of retention errors.* Poster presented at CHI'87 Human Factors in Computer Systems. Toronto, Canada.

Gick, M. L., & Holyoak, K. J. (1983). Schema induction and analogical transfer. *Cognitive Psychology, 12,* 306-355.

Jenkins, J. J. (1974). Remember that old theory of memory? Well, forget it! *American Psychologist, 29,* 785-795.

Hayes, J. R., & Simon, H. A. (1977). Psychological differences among problem solving isomorphs. In N. J. Castellan, Jr., D. B. Pisoni, & G. R. Potts (Eds.), *Cognitive theory, Vol. II* (pp. 21-41). Potomac, MD: Lawrence Erlbaum Associates.

Karat, J. (1983). A model of problem solving with incomplete constraint knowledge. *Cognitive Psychology, 14,* 538-559.

Karat, J., Boyes, L., Weisgerber, S., & Schafer, C. (1986). Transfer between word processing systems. In M. Mantei & P. Orbeton (Eds.), *Proceedings CHI'86 Human Factors in Computer Systems* (pp. 67-71). New York: Association for Computing Machinery.

Kieras, D. E. (1982). A model of reader strategy for abstracting main ideas from simple technical prose. *Text, 2,* 47-82.

Kieras, D. E., & Bovair, S. (1986). The acquisition of procedures from text: A production-system analysis of transfer of training. *Journal of Memory and Language, 25,* 507-524.

Kieras, D. E., & Polson, P. G. (1983). A generalized transition network representation of interactive systems. *Proceedings of the CHI 1983 Conference on Human Factors in Computing.* Boston, MS: ACM.

Kieras, D. E., & Polson, P. G. (1985). An approach to the formal analysis of user complexity. *International Journal of Man-Machine Studies, 22*, 365-394.

Neisser, U. (1982). *Memory observed: Remembering in natural contexts.* San Francisco, CA: W. H. Freeman.

Newell, A., & Simon, H. A. (1972). *Human problem solving.* Englewood Cliffs, New Jersey: Prentice-Hall.

Nielsen, J., Mack, R. L., Bergendorff, K. H., & Grischkowsky, N. L. (1986). Integrated software usage in the professional work environments: Evidence from questionnaires and interview. In M. Mantei & P. Orbeton (Eds.), *Proceedings CHI'86 Human Factors in Computing* (pp. 162-167). New York: Association for Computing Machinery.

Norman, D. A. (1981). The trouble with UNIX: The user interface is horrid. *DataMation*, 139-150.

Polson, P. G. (1972). A quantitative analysis of the conceptual processes in the Hull paradigm. *Journal of Mathematical Psychology, 9*, 141-167.

Polson, P. G. (1987). A quantitative theory of human-computer interaction. In J. M. Carroll (Ed.), *Interfacing thought: Cognitive aspects of human-computer interaction* (pp. 184-235). Cambridge, MS: Bradford Books/MIT Press.

Polson, P. G., Bovair, S., & Kieras, D. E. (1987). Transfer between text editors. In P. Tanner & J. M. Carroll (Eds.), *Proceedings CHI'87 Human Factors in Computer Systems* (pp. 27-32). New York: Association for Computing Machinery.

Polson, P. G., & Kieras, D. E. (1985). A quantitative model of the learning and performance of text editing knowledge. *Proceedings of the CHI 1985 Conference on Human Factors in Computing* (pp. 207-212). San Francisco: ACM.

Polson, P. G., Muncher, E., & Engelbeck, G. (1986). A test of a common elements theory of transfer. In M. Mantei & P. Orbeton (Eds.), *Proceedings CHI'86 Human Factors in Computer Systems* (pp. 78-83). New York: Association for Computing Machinery.

Polson, P. G., Muncher, E., & Kieras, D. E. (1987). *Transfer of skills between inconsistent editors* (Tech. Rep. No. 87-10). Boulder: University of Colorado, Institute of Cognitive Science.

Postman, L. (1971). Transfer, interference, and forgetting. In J. W. King & L. A. Riggs (Eds.), *Woodworth and Schlosberg's experimental psychology* (pp. 1019-1132). New York: Holt, Rienhart, and Winston.

Postman, L., & Underwood, B. J. (1973). Critical issues in interference theory. *Memory and Cognition, 1*, 19-40.

Rubenstein, R., & Hersh, H. M. (1984). *The human factor: Designing computer systems for people.* Burlinton, MS: Digital Press.

Simon, H. A. (1975). Functional equivalence of problem solving skills. *Cognitive Psychology, 7*, 268-286.

Singley, K., & Anderson, J. (1985). Transfer of text-editing skills. *International Journal of Man-Machine Studies, 22*, 403-423.

Smith, D. C., Irby, C., Kimball, R., Verplank, B., & Harslem, E. (1982). Designing the STAR user interface. *Byte, 7*(4), 242-282.

Smith, S. L., & Mosier, J. M. (1986). *Guidelines for designing user interface software* (EDS-TR-86-278, MTR 10090). Bedford, MS: MITRE Corp.

Thorndike, E. L. (1914). *The psychology of learning.* New York: Teachers College.

Thorndike, E. L., & Woodward, R. S. (1901). The influence of improvement in one mental function upon the efficiency of other functions. *Psychological Review, 8*, 247-261.

Ziegler, J. E., Vossen, P. H., & Hoppe, H. U. (1986). *Assessment of learning behavior in direct manipulation dialogues: Cognitive complexity analysis* (ESPRIT Project 385 HUFIT, Working Paper B.3.3). Fraunhofer-Institut fur Arbeitswirtschaft und Organisation, Stuttgart, West Germany.

3
Computer-Aided Reasoned Discourse or, How to Argue with a Computer

PAUL SMOLENSKY
BARBARA FOX
ROGER KING
CLAYTON LEWIS

Reasoning is a demanding intellectual task that is greatly facilitated by appropriate notational systems. This chapter reports a new notational system we are developing for supporting *reasoned discourse*: the construction, communication, and assessment of reasoned arguments about non-formal domains. The new notation is an active system: a computer environment called EUCLID. In EUCLID, arguments are displayed in tabular and graphical forms; a library of argument types provides users with tools for constructing arguments, and EUCLID's knowledge of argument structure offers users tools for argument comprehension and assessment. EUCLID rests on a language called ARL for formally representing argument structure; argument content is expressed in natural language. Our development of EUCLID involves research on: the structure of actual examples of reasoned discourse, the representation of argument structure using a formal language, the management and modeling of large data structures representing arguments; and the nature and effectiveness of human reasoning when the new notational system is used.

1. Introduction

Spoken language, writing, and mathematical notation and proof are symbolic systems that have profoundly affected human reasoning capacity. Modern computers are powerful, active symbolic systems with the potential, we believe, to provide significant further advances in human reasoning ability.

In this chapter, we describe a tool we are developing for helping people create and assess reasoned arguments and communicate these arguments to others. The tool provides reasoners with a *language*, ARL, for expressing their arguments in a clear, precise, and relatively standardized fashion. The medium in which this language is realized is a computer environment we call EUCLID.

In EUCLID, the computer plays a role analogous to acoustic or print media in verbal or written argumentation: it provides a medium - an extremely powerful one - for supporting logical discourse among human users. We are *not* proposing to use computer reasoning to replace human reasoning. Our goal is to give users the expressive and analytic power necessary to elevate the effectiveness of their own reasoned argumentation.

In this chapter we offer an argument for the potential value of the EUCLID project. The top-level structure of our argument is summarized in Figure 1-1, which also serves as a table of contents. We begin in Section 2 by elaborating the goal for the EUCLID project, and describing the capabilities ARL and EUCLID are ultimately intended to offer. Next, in Section 3, we argue that a system with the capabilities we strive for can significantly enhance the effectiveness of human reasoning. This includes an analysis of the means by which notational systems amplify cognitive abilities. Then, in Section 4, we discuss other research that we can build upon; this also allows us to clarify our objectives by relating them to those of other projects. We focus on this issue because we have found when discussing this research with colleagues that our goals are frequently misunderstood.

Numbers coincide with sections of the chapter.

2. *Definition*: The goal: enhancing reasoned discourse
   Definition: ARL and EUCLID (functional specifications)
   Example: Using EUCLID to read the Chinese room
   argument of John Searle.

3. *Claim*: EUCLID can contribute significantly to achieving the goal.
   Argument summary: Analysis of sources of the power of
   notation to overcome cognitive limitations suggest that
   EUCLID should be effective.

4. *Claim*: A system meeting EUCLID's specifications does not
   yet exist, but previous research provides much to build upon.
   Argument summary: Consideration of several existing projects
   show they provide valuable foundations, but that considerable
   further research is necessary.

5. *Claim*:   Development of EUCLID is feasible.
   Argument summary: Methodologies exist for developing the
   necessary theoretical constructs and for effectively implementing
   them. These methodologies fall into several subareas,
   corresponding to the following particular claims.

   5.1. *Claim*: It is feasible to perform a task
        analysis of argumentation
        that reveals the aspects of the task on which people need
        support. This analysis fills in the details of the
        specifications that ARL and EUCLID are to meet.
        Argument summary: Discourse analysis provides a number of
        techniques for analyzing examples of reasoned discourse,
        and the literature on informal logic offers normative analysis
        of argumentation.

   5.2. *Claim*: It is feasible to develop a language meeting
        the specifications of ARL.
        i[Argument summary]: Predicate calculus techniques
        can be used to develop ARL through testing on
        actual large-scale academic arguments. (See appendix.)

   5.3. *Claim*: It is feasible to develop a computer
        environment meeting the specifications of EUCLID.
        Argument summary: Object-oriented data
        representation, semantic data modeling, and
        graphical interface techniques can be used.

   5.4. *Claim*: The effectiveness of EUCLID can be assessed.
        Argument summary: Empirical techniques like those
        employed in human computer interface evaluation
        can be used.

Figure 1-1 : Top level of the argument offered in this chapter

In the major portion of the chapter, Section 5, we describe the techniques that we are employing in developing EUCLID. The proposed research can be usefully divided into four parts. The first part, considered in Section 5.1, is a task analysis in which argumentation is analyzed to elucidate those aspects of argumentation for which people need most support. The second part, described in Section 5.2, is the development of ARL, a language which has sufficient expressive power to represent realistically sophisticated arguments, and which explicitly offers the support that the task analysis shows people need. The third part, considered in Section 5.3, is the development of EUCLID, a computer environment that provides the necessary support for effectively using ARL. The final part, considered in Section 5.4, is the evaluation of the effectiveness of the evolving EUCLID system.

These four research components draw primarily upon techniques from the research disciplines of the four principal investigators. The task analysis is an application of discourse analysis from linguistics to the special discourse type we call *reasoned discourse*. ARL is an application of artificial intelligence knowledge representation techniques to knowledge of informal logic. EUCLID can be viewed as an application of semantic database modeling to a special database with the semantics of argumentation. Evaluation of EUCLID exploits techniques from the field of user interface design for the assessment of human computer systems. The four components respectively call upon the specialties of Fox, Smolensky, King, and Lewis.

2. Reasoned Discourse and EUCLID

2.1 The Goal: Enhancing Reasoned Discourse

A central activity in theoretical research is the construction of reasoned arguments supporting theoretical conclusions. The problem we address is a practical one: how can this activity be effectively supported? While our focus is on argumentation of the type found in research papers (for we intend to develop our tool while using it ourselves in our work), we also consider, to a lesser extent, related forms of argumentation. Other examples of *reasoned discourse*, in addition to research papers, include policy advocacy for decision making (e.g., reasoned letters to the editor), pedagogy in theoretical disciplines such as linguistics and physics, and to a certain extent, reasoned argumentation in everyday conversation.

The domains of analysis we have in mind are ones that are not strictly formal, so that mathematically rigorous proofs are not possible. Our goal is to enhance reasoned discourse that now occurs in natural not formal language.

We take the goal of enhancing reasoned discourse to integrally incorporate both support of explicit discourse processes (like reading and writing) and also support of reasoning itself. A clear distinction between cognition and communication is particularly problematic in the area of reasoning. Argumentation is the construction of a symbolic structure intended to persuade through conformity to certain social conventions: reasoning is intrinsically a discourse phenomenon. The point is underlined by a substantial body of research on writing which suggests that what writers most need support for is the *planning* of documents: the main problem is deciding exactly what to say, and devising an overall presentation plan (Flower & Hayes, 1980; Gregg & Steinberg, 1980; Kellogg, 1985a, 1985b). Even in the writing of business letters of a few paragraphs, people spend two-thirds of their time planning (Gould, 1980). In the domain of reasoned discourse, it is clear that planning the laying out of a line of argumentation is a crucial and almost completely unsupported activity. The process of planning a research paper - the working out of the claims to be made and the arguments to support them - is essentially the process of carrying out the theoretical component of the research itself.

Our goal, then, is to provide a tool to facilitate reasoning and enhance reasoned discourse, particularly writing.

2.2 The Proposed Tool

In this section we specify the functionality that ARL and EUCLID are intended to provide. Methods for realizing these systems will be discussed in Sections 5.2 and 5.3, respectively, after we have argued for the value of the proposed functionality and have considered related research.

2.2.1 ARL: An Argumentation Representation Language

Our fundamental hypothesis is that in constructing an argument, two kinds of knowledge are brought to bear: knowledge of the subject domain, and knowledge of argumentation per se. These respectively manifest themselves as argument content and argument structure. A *general purpose* argumentation tool helps the user by virtue of its knowledge of argument structure, not argument content.

Drawing a clear line between structure and content is so crucial to this research that we find it useful to give that line a concise name: *the Divide*. Content information is *below* the Divide; structure information is *above* the Divide. Examples of assertions *below* the Divide are:

- Lower interest rates lead to bull markets.

- Linguistic principle X is universal.

- Approach Y to knowledge representation is seriously flawed.

Above the Divide we find statements such as:

- Claim C_1 supports claim C_2.

- Claim C is the main point of argument A.

- Claim C is made by author S.

- Claim C_1 made by author S_1 contradicts claim C_2 made by author S_2.

- Term T is used by author S_1 to mean phrase D_1 but by author S_2 to mean phrase D_2.

This latter sort of information is often not explicitly stated in text, but in it lies the structure that characterizes reasoned discourse. (The crucial importance of information above the Divide has also been emphasized by Zukerman and Pearl (1985). In the tutoring context, they have studied how such information is introduced through natural language expressions they call *meta-technical utterances*.)

Information below the Divide involves terms and predicates that vary completely from one domain of argumentation to another. But information above the Divide involves a reasonably constant vocabulary: the examples above use the terms *claim C, argument A, author S* and the predicates *supports, main-point, asserts, contradicts.* This vocabulary is characteristic of reasoned discourse in any domain. (In Section 5.2 we address the issue of variations in *styles* of argumentation across fields.)

ARL is intended to offer a set of primitive term-types and primitive predicates for formally describing argument structure, such as those mentioned in the previous paragraph. In addition, it should incorporate high-order structures formally defined by combining simpler ones. Examples that will be explicitly discussed in Section 5.2 include high-level standard schematic structures for arguments, arguments by analogy, allegations of misrepresentations, and argument refutations.

To give users the expressive power needed in real argumentation, ARL must let users extend the language's set of primitives and must provide the machinery for them to formally create their own high-order constructs.

The ARL statement corresponding to "Claim C_1 supports claim C_2" uses the formal predicate **supports** to relate two entities that have formal type **claim**. The content of each claim is not expressed formally, but *informally*, in natural language. For example, the content of C_1 might be "Lower interest rates lead to bull markets." Thus ARL is a *semi-formal* language: argument *structure* information (above the Divide) is represented *formally*, while argument *content* (below the Divide) is represented *informally*. The computer has access to the semantics of the formal information, but only the user has access to the semantics of the informal information.

2.2.2 EUCLID: An Environment for User Construction of Logical Informal Discourse

A formal representation of the structure of the argument in a theoretical research paper is too large for anyone to explicitly represent without the help of a data manager. The computer environment EUCLID[1] must keep track of ARL representations, allowing users to select portions of the argument to be displayed on a high-resolution graphics terminal. In addition to displaying ARL structures, EUCLID must allow users to add new structures and to modify old structures. Users should be able to state that they want to create a new instance of a higher-level construct (say an analogy), whereupon EUCLID would prompt the user for the necessary inputs and manage the details of creating the necessary data structures. Information must be displayed by procedures specially designed to show the various argument components. For example, there must be special procedures for displaying analogies, refutations, or retrieval requests like "show all claims whose validity depend on this one." Along with the capability to create new types of argument structures, users need the capability to specify new procedures for displaying them. Of course users should have considerable opportunity for choice among alternative display methods.

An argument created in EUCLID would contain full pieces of text: EUCLID is intended to provide a unified environment for working out an argument *and* expressing it in text. A specific example will be illustrated in the next section; to give the general idea, reading a "journal article" in EUCLID might proceed like this. After reading the abstract, the user would decide what further information is of most interest: an experimental procedure, a source for a "fact," a theoretical argument, the theoretical assumptions, etc. The requested information would be retrieved and displayed according to the type of information. The retrieved information might be a piece of text, like a section of a paper, or perhaps a table or graph. In one unified ARL data structure is contained both the underlying logical structure and the pieces of text that present the argument. In this sense, EUCLID is a *hypertext system* specially tailored for logical material reasoned discourse.

_____

[1]The environment EUCLID is unrelated to the programming language Euclid (Lampson, Horning, London, Mitchell, & Popek, 1977; Holt, 1983).

2.2.3 An Example: The Chinese Room Debate

As an example of how EUCLID might look to a user reading an argument, we will consider an argument that has been our testbed: the "Chinese room" argument of John Searle (1980). This argument claims to show that instantiating an AI program, even one that could answer questions indistinguishably from a human and thereby pass the Turing test, cannot be sufficient grounds for saying that a machine "understands" in the full sense of the word. The core of the argument is the following analogy. A Chinese story is slipped under the door of a closed room, and then Chinese questions about the story are slipped in. Back under the door come Chinese answers to the questions, indistinguishable from those of a native speaker. As it happens, inside the room is Searle himself, working away at copying Chinese symbols he doesn't understand from big books under the guidance of a complex set of English instructions. According to Searle's analogy, the Chinese characters are to the Searle in the room as English is to a question answering computer: completely meaningless forms being manipulated without any understanding.

The commentary from numerous cognitive scientists that was published with the article revealed a tremendous diversity of outlooks, and appeared to evidence a considerable amount of confusion about just what Searle's argument was. The argument is still highly active today, meriting an entire session of the 1986 meeting of the Society of Philosophy and Psychology. Our goal is to use EUCLID to delineate, as clearly as possible, the positions taken by the numerous participants in the published debate; in the process, the expressive adequacy of ARL and the usability of EUCLID will be challenged by a truly worthy argument.

Figures 2-1 through 2-6 illustrate how EUCLID might be used to study an ARL representation of the Chinese Room debate. We imagine the user has read the text, and is ready for an analysis. Figure 2-1 gives a tabular display of the top level of Searle's argument. This is a relatively clean display, in which a lot of relational information is implicit in the arrangement of items on the screen.

Strong AI	Searle
An AI program (running on a von Neumann machine) that can pass the Turing test; lacks no important element of understanding	An AI program that can pass the Turing test; lacks an important element of understanding that would be present if the program were implemented on a machine with the causal powers of the brain.
The argument from information processing	The argument from formality
The argument from behavior	Just behaviorism
The argument from implementation independence	Just modern-day dualism
	The argument from formality: The Chinese room
The systems reply	The internal Chinese room
The robot reply	The internal Chinese room + peripherals
The brain simulator reply	The argument from water pipes
	The argument from lactation

Figure 2-1: Tabular display of the top level of Searle's argument

Figure 2-2 shows the relationships explicitly. The left side of the diagram are claims and arguments that Searle attributes to his opponents, those accepting the position of "strong AI." On the right side of the diagram are the claims and arguments that Searle accepts. At the very top of the left side is the main claim of the strong AI view. Immediately beneath the strong AI position are three arguments supporting it, which Searle attributes to his opponents; to the right of each one is Searle's counter-argument. Below these counter-arguments are Searle's arguments in favor of his position, the main claim of which is stated at the top of the right column. To the left of Searle's arguments are refutations of them which them he attributes to his opponents and to the right of these are his counter-arguments.

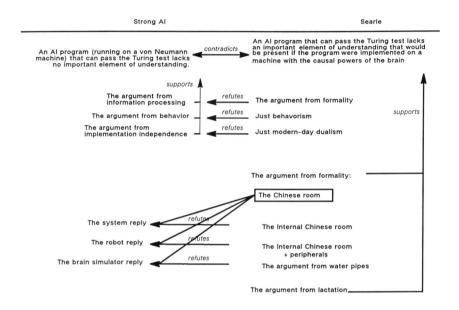

Strong AI   Searle

An AI program (running on a von Neumann   *contradicts*   An AI program that can pass the Turing test lacks
machine) that can pass the Turing test lacks   an important element of understanding that would
no important element of understanding.   be present if the program were implemented on a
                                                           machine with the causal powers of the brain

supports

The argument from   *refutes*
information processing   ◄───────── The argument from formality   *supports*

The argument from behavior   *refutes*
                               ◄───────── Just behaviorism

The argument from   *refutes*
implementation independence   ◄───────── Just modern-day dualism

The argument from formality:

The Chinese room

The system reply   *refutes*

The robot reply   *refutes*   The internal Chinese room

                                                 The internal Chinese room
The brain simulator reply   *refutes*   + peripherals

                                                 The argument from water pipes

The argument from lactation

Figure 2-2: Tabular display of the top level of Searle's argument with
explicit relationships between elements

A user facing the austere display of Figure 2-1 might request that all
implicit relationships be made explicit, giving rise to Figure 2-2. Next we
suppose the user to have selected "The Chinese Room" for further information about Searle's key argument. As in all hypertext systems, this
selection leads to a new display, Figure 2-3, which expands upon the
selected item. (Note that the new display is coherently displayed without
intervention by the user.) Figure 2-3 shows the form of the Chinese
Room argument: it is an analogy, and is displayed in an appropriate
form. On the left side of the Chinese Room display are the elements of
the Chinese Room domain; on the right side are the corresponding elements of the AI system. Searle's analogy is a mapping that carries elements and claims from the Chinese Room domain into elements and
claims of the AI domain.
Having been shown the explicit form of the Chinese Room analogy, we
next suppose that the user wishes to consult the text to check the ac-

curacy of the analysis given for the analogy. Figure 2-4 shows the text separated into pieces that are explicitly connected to components of the analogy analysis. Deciding this representation of the relationships is too messy, the user requests a simpler representation. Figure 2-5 shows the text, unbroken, next to the analogy analysis. After selecting a particular item in the analysis, the corresponding parts of the text become under-lined.

After studying the analysis side-by-side with the text, the user decides to accept the analysis for the time being and to proceed. A request to remove the text and the explicit relationships gives the relatively clean screen of Figure 2-6, from which it is now reasonable to proceed by selecting another part of the overall argument for analysis.

2.2.4 Creating Arguments

Having described the kinds of capabilities EUCLID is intended to provide for reading arguments, we now consider argument generation. It is use-ful to distinguish a number of processes which must all be supported by EUCLID. These processes are closely related to processes that have been studied in the creation of ordinary text (Flower, Hayes, Carey, Schriver, Stratman, to appear; Hayes & Flower, 1980). The processes are intermingled, and should not be viewed as serial phases.

- *Dump*: Generate terms and assertions the author feels to be central to the argument. EUCLID serves as electronic paper.

- *Reader-preprocess*: Indicate for various terms and asser-tions what they assume about the reader: background, inter-ests, what other items have been previously read (**prerequisite** relations), etc. EUCLID stores this infor-mation for use in the linearization process (below).

- *Organize*: Insert definitions of terms, relations between assertions (e.g., **supports**, **contradicts**). EUCLID serves as ARL structure editor and browser.

- *Fill in*: Generate missing terms, claims, and arguments. EUCLID provides templates for common arguments types, checks for missing components of these argument templates, and satisfies useful database queries (e.g., "find

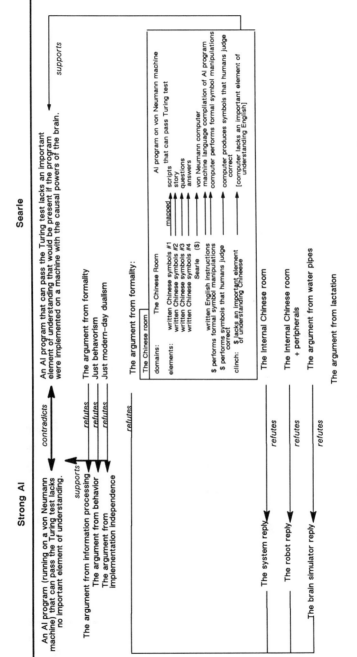

Figure 2–3:   Display of the Chinese Room argument as an analogy

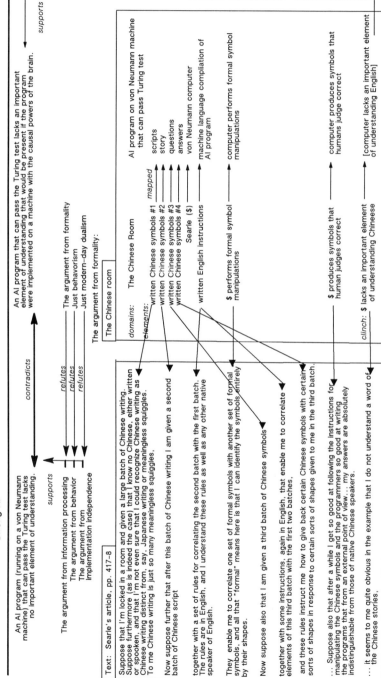

Figure 2-4: Text of the Chinese Room argument separated into pieces explicitly connected to the analogy

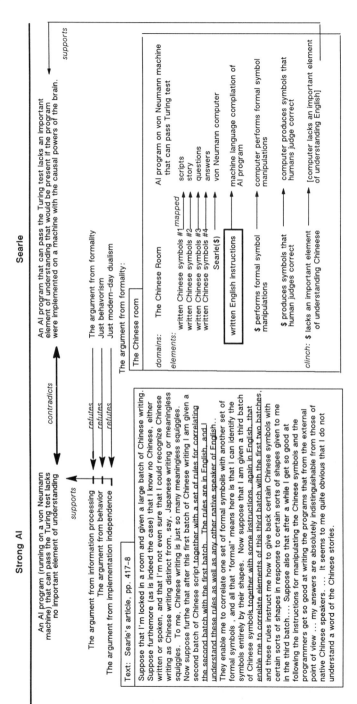

Figure 2–5: Text of the Chinese Room argument next to the analogy analysis

Strong AI	Searle
An AI program (running on a von Neumann machine) that can pass the Turing test lacks no important element of understanding.	An AI program that can pass the Turing test lacks an important element of understanding that would be present if teh program were implemented on a machine with the causal powers of the brain

The argument from information processing	The argument from formality
The argument from behavior	Just behaviorism
The argument from implementation independence	Just modern-day dualism

The argument from formality:

The Chinese room

domains:	The Chinese Room	AI program on von Neumann machine that can pass the Turing test
elements:	written Chinese symbols #1	scripts
	written Chinese symbols #2	story
	written Chinese symbols #3	questions
	written Chinese symbols #4	answers
	Searle ($)	von Neumann computer
	written English instructions	machine language compliation of AI program
	$ performs formal symbol manipulations	computer performs formal symbol manipulation
	$ performs symbols that humans judge correct	computer produces symbols that humans judge correct
clinch:	$ lacks an important element of understanding Chineese	[computer lacks an important element of understanding English]

The system reply	The Internal Chinese room
The robot reply	The Internal Chinese room + peripherals
The brain simulator reply	The argument from water pipes

The argument from lactation

Figure 2-6:   Chinese Room argument with text and explicit relationships removed

claims lacking **supports** links"). EUCLID's library of examples of different argument types lets the user browse for possible approaches.

- *Linearize*: Impose on parts of the argument graph a linear order, thereby generating a document. EUCLID partly automates this process, making use of **prerequisite** relations, and filtering the database on intended readers' background and interests. Schemas for document types help guide this process.

- *Edit prose*: Generate readable text. EUCLID functions as text editor integrated into ARL structure editor.

The support provided by EUCLID in these processes is substantial. While the activity of expressing an argument in ARL form is itself helpful in developing the argument, the support that EUCLID can supply on the basis of the formal ARL relations that it can process is a major part of the benefit of using EUCLID instead of pencil and paper for developing arguments. On the other hand, we feel that the process of expressing an argument in ARL form requires extensive human processing and that the prospects for automating the process are dim.

3. Effectiveness of EUCLID

In this section we argue that a system with the capabilities that EUCLID is intended to offer can significantly enhance human reasoning capability. By offering abstraction tools, EUCLID can assist users in comprehending and constructing arguments. By considering the example of algebraic notation, we enumerate three powerful techniques by which a language can extend cognitive abilities. We then show how EUCLID incorporates those techniques.

3.1 Techniques for Overcoming Cognitive Limitations

Arithmetic word problems that we cannot solve intuitively "in our heads" can often be readily solved by the use of algebraic notation. How does this notation overcome our cognitive limitations?

To address this issue we adopt a simplified picture of human information processing which is crude but sufficiently accurate for our purposes. The value of such simple cognitive models in the analysis of human computer interaction has been advocated (and demonstrated) by a number of researchers; see, for example, Card, Moran, and Newell (1983); and Norman and Draper (1986). A critical cognitive limitation is the small capacity of working memory. Since cognitive operations can be performed only on the contents of working memory, it is crucial that relevant operands be in working memory at the time of each operation. Problems that introduce enough information to exceed the very limited capacity of human working memory thus pose serious difficulties.

One technique afforded by algebraic notation is simply the *elimination of irrelevant information* from attention, thereby freeing up working memory capacity. The algebraic representation of a word problem has discarded much information in the problem that is irrelevant to its solution: whether *x* represents "the age of Peter's father" or "the number of nickels" is not expressed by the notation, and when solving the equations we can free our minds of these distractions.

A second technique algebraic notation uses is *explicit chunking*. New variables can be introduced for combinations of others, and parentheses can also be used to isolate subexpressions. Then the entire chunk can be manipulated as a single entity, taking up much less working memory capacity than if the constituents were individually represented. For example, we can see that the next operation to perform is to take the square root of an entire subexpression in parentheses, while being temporarily oblivious to the contents of that subexpression.

A third technique algebra affords is *explicit decomposition*. Parentheses can be used to group together elements into subexpressions. Individual equations also form explicitly delimited subparts of the entire problem representation. Attention can be focussed on individual limited components and the rest of the problem representation can be temporarily ignored. If the subexpressions or equations that are created are sufficiently small, they can individually be contained in working memory and operated upon. Once the component has been processed, attention can return to the context in which it is embedded. The notation keeps in *external memory* the relation between the component and the context, so we know how to incorporate the new result into the temporarily forgotten context.

The techniques of explicit chunking and explicit decomposition are in fact two sides of the same coin. Explicit chunking allows us to ignore what goes on *inside* a substructure, while explicit decomposition permits us to ignore what goes on *outside* a substructure. Each of these aspects is so powerful that they merit separate consideration.

In the next section we will argue that EUCLID can apply these three techniques to the domain of argumentation. While individual practitioners of reasoned discourse no doubt have various personal devices, explicit and implicit, for achieving the ends of these three techniques, we believe there is considerable advantage in developing a *standard, explicit notational system* for representing arguments.   Before the widespread dissemination of algebraic notation, it was no doubt true that experts with "word problems" had personal methods for solving them: but consider the fact that today nearly any child can solve such problems.   This is because of the powerful social advantages of using a standardized explicit representation:

- Since the same standard approach to problem representation and solution is used over and over, procedures for representation and solution can be *automatized*. Thus after explicitly using parentheses for chunking for a long time, we learn to *see* chunks without explicitly marking them with parentheses. This represents a truly significant expansion of cognitive ability.

- A standard explicit notation enhances information retrieval.

- A standard explicit notation permits explicit, systematic *instruction*.

- An explicit representational system can be *studied*. It can be perfected for power, consistency, and naturalness.

- A standard representational system can be *publically shared*. This means it can evolve under the benefit of multiple users, and, most of all, that a common language is provided as a basis for communication.

It may be too much to hope that a system like EUCLID, after the benefit of decades of development and cultural evolution, would make it possible for school children to assess the soundness of an argument with an effectiveness that is limited today to expert reasoners.   Nonetheless, we believe there is ample reason to believe that resources expended in this project will be well repaid.

3.2 EUCLID: Sources of Power

The three techniques of the previous section are all exploited by EUCLID, as we now argue. Our arguments are rather similar to those given for the domain-independent decision support systems GODDESS and CONVINCE developed by Judea Pearl and collaborators: Kim (1984) and Pearl, Leal, and Saleh (1982). In EUCLID, however, the user performs a greater portion of the analysis, so our arguments are more crucial. We begin by considering EUCLID's support of argument comprehension.

3.2.1 Applications to Argument Comprehension

The formal relations of ARL represent the structure of an argument and ignore its content. For many aspects of argumentation, of course, content is essential, but for many other aspects, details of content are irrelevant. EUCLID exploits the *elimination of irrelevant information* technique by letting users focus attention on structural issues and ignore content, when this is appropriate. When an argument is recognized as an *ad hominem* attack, for example, the content of the attack is usually irrelevant: what is important is just the structural fact that what is being attacked is the *source* of a claim and not the claim itself. *Once an argument has been expressed in ARL*, there are many important tasks that can proceed without reference to content:

- determination of whether a certain claim is supported or assumed;

- determination of whether a group of claims are alleged to be consistent;

- finding all claims which become unsupported if a given claim is denied;

- finding pivotal claims on which a large fraction of the conclusions depend.

In fact all of these could be defined as formal operations which the computer could carry out automatically. These operations correspond to those that can be performed on algebraic expressions without attention to what the variables denote.

Perhaps the single most difficult aspect of assessing an argument is finding components of the argument to focus on that are small enough to be understood and evaluated yet large enough to be self-contained. The argument structuring operations of ARL allow argument creators to help the reader with this task. The author can clearly mark the main claims as such, mark which claims are used to support each of these, and which claims are used to support each of these, and so on down to the unsupported assumptions at the base of the argument. This permits readers to assess the argument in small pieces. A reader adopting a top-down strategy would pick one of the main claims and ask EUCLID to present the first layer of claims on which it is based. The author should have structured the argument so that, after a reasonable period of attention, this first layer of claims can all be held simultaneously in working memory. The reader can then assess whether the alleged conclusion does indeed follow from the premises offered. If so, the reader can proceed to assess each of the premises in exactly the same manner. A reader preferring a bottom-up strategy would start with the unsupported claims (the assumptions), and examine each for acceptability. This reader would then ask EUCLID to supply the layer of claims that the author has supported solely by the assumptions, and would examine each to see if it is indeed a justified conclusion. In either case, whenever an inference or claim is deemed unacceptable by the reader, EUCLID can automatically display which parts of the argument then become invalidated. If the reader is uncertain about a claim, EUCLID can automatically display the parts of the argument to which this uncertainty propagates. (Ultimately EUCLID will be extended to support *numerical* assignment and propagation of uncertainty.) Thus the technique of *explicit decomposition* is at the center of EUCLID's power.

One of the central mechanisms of ARL is the encapsulation of parts of the overall argument into discrete subarguments, and the encapsulation of the conclusions of each subargument into discrete claims. Thus the technique of *explicit chunking* is heavily used.

There is an important reason to believe that with practice EUCLID can provide readers of reasoned discourse with substantially improved comprehension compared to ordinary text. Research in text comprehension has shown how important it is for understanding and retention for readers to construct mental *macrostructures* in which the contents of the text are abstracted and integrated (e.g., van Dijk & Kintsch, 1983; Guindon & Kintsch, 1984). What EUCLID provides is a way for authors to make macrostructures *explicitly available* to readers rather than relying, as in ordinary text, on many subtle and often ambiguous cues for implicitly communicating macrostructural information. Of course, we do not mean that EUCLID will remove all possibilities for multiple interpretations of a text; it will merely narrow the range of interpretations, to the extent pursued by the author. The advantages cited in the previous section for having standard, publically shared, explicit notations rather than implicit, idiosyncratic representations apply with considerable force to macrostructures.

In a related vein, it can be noted that by supporting those processes of document creation described in Section 2.2.4, EUCLID provides some of the help that research into the cognitive aspects of writing has shown that writers need: support for the intricate planning needed to satisfy the many constraints implicit in the difficult task of writing (Collins & Gentner, 1980; Flower & Hayes, 1980).

3.2.2 Applications to Argument Construction

The three techniques discussed in Section 3.1 offer considerable power during the construction of arguments as well as during their comprehension. As in ordinary writing, the author of a EUCLID argument spends considerable time wording sentences. However, with EUCLID, the author's real work has just *begun* when all the claims are framed. Now the author must explicitly represent the relationships between the claims using the formal relations of ARL. Here is where the power of EUCLID comes into play.

Explicitly representing the structure of arguments (e.g., by diagramming) appears to be quite helpful to students of informal logic (Govier, 1985). Explicitly indicating that a certain claim allegedly follows from a definite set of other claims defines a separate component of the entire argument which can be examined in isolation. Focusing one's attention completely on this component often reveals an inadequacy in the inference, and forces reformulation of the claims or abandonment of the argument component. This is an example of the usefulness of explicit decomposition in argument construction.

In the process of explicitly indicating the structural relations in an argument, the following will occur rather often. In looking to attach a claim to the conclusion that it supports, no explicit claim will be found. This is because it is common in ordinary text for a "point" (or conclusion) of a passage to be implicit in the entire passage, never being explicitly stated in a single sentence. The attempt to attach a link to the sentences of such a passage to the conclusion they support will fail, because the conclusion is not written down anywhere. The result will be the creation of a new claim that explicitly states a conclusion of the argument in the passage. This is one way EUCLID encourages explicit chunking: the new claim encapsulates many others.

Of course, during the construction of an argument an author must continually assess the current state of the argument, so that the advantages EUCLID offers argument comprehension are also advantages for argument construction. For example, the fact that EUCLID can display those claims currently not explicitly supported by other claims can be used by an author to check whether the set of unsupported claims is the intended set of assumptions or whether there remain claims that were intended to be supported but are not. Here the author benefits from the ARL formalization of argument *structure* that results from the elimination of irrelevant (*content*) information.

4. Relation of EUCLID to Existing Systems

There is a large amount of research related to the EUCLID project. In this section we discuss the considerable previous work that EUCLID can benefit from. We also consider a number of existing projects with goals that have been frequently confused with those of EUCLID. Certain serious (but illusory) obstacles tend to appear as a result of these confusions.

4.1 Projects Requiring Formalization of Domain Knowledge

There are a number of research projects related to EUCLID that involve formalization of domain knowledge. It is useful to contrast these with EUCLID, in which domain information is represented *informally*: it is below the Divide.

Unlike AI projects in text comprehension and generation, the EUCLID project does not involve a computer program that "understands" natural language statements about a domain. Such understanding requires formalizing domain knowledge. In EUCLID, the user, not the computer, deals with natural language statements about the domain. Thus, the necessity to specify massive quantities of background knowledge about the domain of argumentation is avoided, which would be lethal to EUCLID.

Several existing AI projects in text comprehension deal specifically with argumentation. The *argument molecules* of Birnbaum, Flowers and McGuire (Birnbaum, 1982; Birnbaum, Flowers, & McGuire, 1980; Flowers, McGuire, & Birnbaum, 1982) and the *argument units* of Alvarado, Dyer, and Flowers (1985) are important examples of higher-level constructs that are definable in ARL. In EUCLID, however, these structures are used to help people build and comprehend arguments, not to get AI programs to understand them.

Some of the most impressive research in philosophy, formal semantics, and AI addresses the formalization of human reasoning. Formalization of reasoning about uncertainty and counterfactuals has led these researchers to various forms of nonmonotonic logic, such as circumscription and default logic (e.g., *Artificial Intelligence*, 1980) to fuzzy logic (e.g., Zadeh, 1979, 1984), to logics with modal operators (e.g., Hintikka, 1969) and to other sophisticated forms of logic. The semantic problems lead to complex issues of model theory (e.g., Asher, Bonevac, Kamp, & Smith, 1983). The point here is that these subtleties have arisen from attempts to *formally* characterize the *validity* of realistic arguments. In EUCLID, validity is not assessed by the computer but by the human. Again, assertions about the domain, upon which validity rests, are below the Divide, and their content is not formalized in EUCLID. Since no attempt is made to formally assess the validity of arguments, EUCLID avoids the subtleties and complexities that would entail.

As an example of the alternative strategy, Bennett (1984a, 1984b, 1985; Isard & Lewis, 1984) is applying sophisticated formalizations of reasoning to computer assessment of the validity of arguments in political policy. Such a project is considerably more ambitious than EUCLID, although, for reasons argued in the previous section, we feel that EUCLID could significantly contribute to argument assessment in areas such as policy analysis.

Like Bennett's project, the OWL (McGee, 1986) is an attempt to formalize the *content* of arguments. It differs from Bennett in that the logic used is propositional calculus: arguments must be coded in terms that avoid the complexities often found in real arguments. These simplifications make formal assessment of the validity of arguments infeasible in the OWL, which, like EUCLID, leaves assessment up to the user. The formal internal structure of claims "if p then q " is used only for information retrieval: a search for p produces a list of those claims containing p , separated according to whether p is in the antecedent or consequent role. We are encouraged by the successful application of the OWL to policy issues of realistic scale.

While the methods of the OWL seem appropriate for the applications to which it has been applied, we feel a more elaborate structure is needed to represent general arguments. The OWL analysis of arguments distinguishes "claims" from "evidence": each claim can have a piece of evidence supporting it (such as a reference or a "fact"). By contrast, in EUCLID, argument structure is recursive: an argument is a network of claims which are supported not by atomic entities called "evidence" but rather by potentially highly complex entities which are themselves arguments. Thus the OWL does not address itself to the issue of argument structure in the sense of EUCLID. The OWL approach seems appropriate to a special class of arguments that involve shallow reasoning from a broad base of data.

4.2 Projects Not Formalizing Domain Knowledge

There are a number of research areas that do not involve formalization of domain information and on which EUCLID can build.

Normative theory of informal logic is readily available in the philosophical literature on argumentation (e.g., Acock, 1985; Engel, 1980; Fogelin, 1982; Govier, 1985). The argument strategies and fallacies identified in this literature provide higher-order argument structures, some of them quite complex, that should be formalizable in ARL; they have played a large role in the development of ARL to date, and will continue to do so. (Specific examples are discussed in the Appendix.)

Formal proof techniques (Solow, 1982) are also suggestive in this regard, for standard procedures like proof by contradiction, proof by induction, and the like have their counterparts in informal reasoning. It will be interesting to see how well EUCLID can support the proof technique of adapting an existing proof to a similar problem. We are also interested to determine the extent to which another highly stylized form of argumentation, legal reasoning, can provide us with useful insights. There are a number of techniques common to legal argumentation and, say, that of Searle (such as analogy and emotional coloration); at the same time, the strong dependence of American legal reasoning on particular cases gives it a rather distinctive style.

A pair of projects at Xerox Palo Alto Research Center have goals that are quite close to those of EUCLID. The first is NoteCards^{TM} (Brown & Newman, 1985; Halasz, Moran, & Trigg, 1987), which gives the user computerized files of notecards. The user can create types of links between cards and use them for cross-referencing. When a new notecard is selected, it appears on the bit-mapped screen, to be given a convenient location by the user.

Like EUCLID, NoteCards allows the user to interrelate pieces of text. It was, at least in part, conceived as a system to support argumentation. However, it is not specialized to the argumentation domain, and it is up to the user to work out a personal argument representation system. Also, the user must continually manage the screen to keep it usable. At least for a user who is an AI researcher, the system has proved to be most valuable in strengthening arguments (VanLehn, 1985).

EUCLID can be thought of as a kind of specialization of NoteCards to the argumentation domain. A standard set of argument-structuring relations are provided, which the user can extend if necessary. The standard argument structures are recognized by EUCLID as having certain natural display forms, so that the management of the screen is handled automatically in a way driven by the semantics of the specialized domain. For the user who wishes to extend the argument-structuring relations, tools are provided for specifying appropriate displays for the new relations.

Another Xerox project, IdeaSketch (Brown & Newman, 1985), provides tools for structuring pieces of text. Here there is a conceptually infinite two-dimensional electronic blackboard allowing pieces of text to be written and related items to be connected by lines. EUCLID is intended to offer views of arguments as such graphs (see Figure 2-3); EUCLID graphs, however, are constrained by the structure of the argumentation domain, and contain links with labels whose semantics are known to the computer. The graphical representation is only one of those available in EUCLID, and one good only for displaying certain kinds of information formally represented in ARL (binary relations such as **supports**).

Another related project is Notepad© , developed at the University of California, San Diego by Allen Cypher. This system offers tools like those of NoteCards for managing interrelated pieces of data, but also provides support for managing interrelated *activities*. Like NoteCards, Notepad is a very general tool, and EUCLID can be viewed as specializing the functionality of Notepad to the domain of reasoned discourse. The EUCLID user is offered support for activities such as information retrieval and editing that is driven by the semantics of the argumentation domain.

A popularly used piece of software that is relevant is the ThinkTank™ system for constructing outlines. Like EUCLID, it aims to help users sort out their ideas and to prepare for writing a well-organized piece of text. However, for argumentation, ThinkTank is simultaneously too general and too constrained a tool. Outlines are basically trees with a single type of link. This single link, if taken to cover all the relations in an argument, is much too general to offer crucial distinctions between relations in argumentation. If the single link is taken to represent a specific argument relationship, then the system allows consideration of only one relation at a time, and the imposition of tree structure is an inappropriate constraint.

Finally, the Hypertext idea championed by Ted Nelson (1974) also shares an inspiration with EUCLID. Hypertext is an active, computerized extension of text in which users continually make selections of further material to be added to the screen. A hypertext is a collection of textual (or graphical) elements linked with explicit structural relations. The chapter by Fairchild, Poltrock and Furnas discusses techniques to display and browse large numbers of information units, such as found in hypertext systems. Structural issues in a hypertext-inspired approach to on-line documentation are analyzed in O'Malley et al. (1983) and in Smolensky, Monty, and Conway (1984). The hypertext idea is appealing, but constraining the course of events towards relatively fruitful interactions turns out to be a serious problem. In passing from the completely static form of standard text to a completely unconstrained form of hypertext, the possibility of guidance from a capable author gets lost and so do readers. EUCLID has the dynamic aspects of hypertext, but in a context that is well constrained by ARL and the structure of argumentation. EUCLID can be looked upon as a form of hypertext specialized to reasoned discourse. For a comprehensive review of hypertext systems and issues with their use, see Conklin (1986).

5. Feasibility of EUCLID

5.1 Task Analysis

5.1.1 Informal Logical Argumentation: A Learned Skill

It is clear from looking at argumentation in natural conversations that the sort of reasoned discourse required in academic discussions, which EUCLID is intended to promote, is a learned, non-natural skill. Argumentation in conversations does not involve step-by-step reasoning from premise to conclusion, with each step supported and justified by mutually agreed upon sources of evidence. Although participants involved in a conversation are sensitive to pressures to produce evidence to support their claims, at least in this society most often disagreements center on claims based on personal experience or personal belief, and these claims tend to be supported by repeated reference to personal statements ("I think x") or by reference to "common" knowledge ("nobody does x" or "everyone knows y"). Often if one type of support does not clinch the disagreement, another, logically contradictory, type is offered. Parties in a disagreement are sometimes dismissed by argument ad hominem, where their character, rather than their arguments, is impuned. The most common types of support for claims we have found in spontaneous conversations are the following:

1. citing personal experience;

2. citing someone else's experience;

3. citing a higher authority;

4. appeal to "common" knowledge;

5. simple restatement of claim; and

6. impuning character of interlocutor.

A close examination of academic argumentation reveals a rather different set of common strategies for supporting a claim:

1. citing other people in the field (higher authority);

2. citing self;

3. presentation and analysis of data;

4. appeal to widely accepted premises which lead deductively to claim;

5. appeal to something said earlier in the article;

6. providing an analogy;

7. giving an example; and

8. support by reputation (i.e., no support for a claim need be given overtly if the writer is considered an expert on the point being made).

The strategies common in conversation tend to involve personal experience and personal involvement (cf. Pomerantz, 1984), while the strategies common in academic argumentation tend to involve abstract knowledge external to the writer's everyday experience. This finding is echoed in the cross-cultural psychology literature, particularly in the work of Scribner (1977). In her research in Liberia, Scribner found that people without formal western education solved syllogisms by invoking their knowledge about their immediate environment rather than by using abstract deductive reasoning, whereas people with even a limited amount of formal western schooling used some version of deductive reasoning to solve the problems. And even American students thoroughly grounded in western education make consistent mistakes in working through the implications of syllogistic premises (Johnson-Laird, 1983). Thus, for the most part people wishing to write academic articles must learn a new way of thinking about reasoning and evidence (although academic argumentation certainly involves some use of everyday strategies, even impuning the character of the "opposition").

Furthermore, the overall structure of academic argumentation is quite different from that of conversational disagreements and must be learned, much as any style of writing must be learned (Akinasso, 1982; Fox, 1984; McHouh, 1982; Nystrand, 1982; Rubin, 1980; and van Dijk & Kintsch, 1983, discuss differences between writing and speaking in general). We know from previous studies (e.g., Fox, to appear; Ochs, 1979) that sequences in conversation tend to have relatively little hierarchical structure compared to pieces of writing, and therefore, that following the structure of a conversation requires less cognitive effort than does understanding and remembering the structure of a piece of writing (van Dijk & Kintsch, 1983; see also the chapter by Guindon in this volume on the structure of user-adviser dialogues in spoken or written communication). When the constraints of informal logical argumentation are added, the difficulty of both production and comprehension of a tightly organized, highly complex and logically coherent argument becomes enormous, far beyond the demands of natural conversation. Since this task is so profoundly difficult, even writers who utilize strategies to facilitate ease of composition and comprehension (see Kieras, 1982, and Meyer & Rice, 1982, for discussion of these strategies), and readers who are skilled at learning from complex texts (Kintsch & van Dijk, 1978), often experience lack of success when dealing with informal logical argumentation.

It should be clear from this discussion that the skills needed for successful communication in the domain of informal logical argumentation are extremely difficult to develop, especially given that they are learned relatively late in life (see Fromkin & Rodman, 1978, on the advantages of learning language-related skills early in life) and are foreign to our everyday experience. If the situation were otherwise, there would be little need for a system like EUCLID.

5.1.2 Proposed Research

If EUCLID is to be successful as a writing aid, it must provide clear links between principles of everyday argumentation and principles of logical argumentation, so that users find EUCLID useful and easy to learn. If EUCLID promotes strategies of writing that are unnaturally methodical, i.e., that violate basic principles of coherent English discourse, or if it encourages a mode of argumentation that is too radically removed from what users find desirable, or if it offers a mode of text representation that users find ineffective, then it will fail as a writing aid. It is therefore critical that the semantics of ARL be oriented to the principles of everyday argumentation, of natural written expository prose, and of logical argumentation, and that the mode of representation be psychologically and linguistically insightful. Since these principles have received little study (some exceptions include Fox, 1984; Mann & Thompson, 1985; and Reichman, 1981a, 1981b), one component of the research we are proposing entails discovering principles of these key areas. We therefore propose the following research:

1. Analyzing argumentation in conversation to understand the processes involved in everyday conversation. As we have seen, the processes of everyday argumentation differ from those of informal logic, but it is unclear exactly what happens in the former, since natural conversation has received so little attention in this regard. Reichman (1981a, 1981b) looks at debates in spontaneous conversations, but her data must be taken as non-representative of what we mean here by everyday argumentation, since most of the participants in her conversations are academics, and academics are unusual in having been strongly shaped by informal logic. We propose to analyze instances of conversational disagreement and persuasion, which will be culled from a large variety of conversations already taped and transcribed for other purposes.

Since this research involves in part examining how people say how they know something (i.e., giving evidence), it will be relevant to look at the work in linguistics in the area of evidentiality (Chafe & Nichols, 1986), which describes grammatical systems found in some languages (predominantly AmerIndian languages) for indicating how the speaker knows what is being claimed (because it is generically true, because the speaker witnessed it, because the speaker saw evidence of it, etc.). We expect that languages with such evidential systems have institutionalized patterns that are extremely common in other languages where they are handled at the discourse level rather than the grammatical level (Givon, 1979).

The techniques that will be used for analyzing these disagreements come from the tradition of Conversational Analysis (Schegloff & Sacks, 1973; Schegloff, 1976; Schenkein, 1979), which is a subarea within the framework of ethnomethodology.

2. Analyzing well-written, well-argued academic articles to understand what kinds of structures are typical of this genre. The texts that EUCLID will support should be as coherent and natural as any well-written academic article. We therefore propose to understand better the structural organization of such academic articles by analyzing a large number of academic articles, initially drawn from the disciplines of cognitive science. We will explore several methods of analysis, including an analytic technique known as Rhetorical Structure Analysis (Fox, 1984; Mann & Thompson, 1985), context space theory (Reichman, 1981a, 1981b), macrostructure-based analysis (van Dijk & Kintsch, 1983) and the method developed by Meyer and Rice (1982). The overall approach will be to view higher-level discourse structures as dynamically created from local structures (Fox, to appear; McClelland, Rumelhart, & the PDP Research Group, 1986; Rumelhart, McClelland, & the PDP Research Group, 1986; Rumelhart, Smolensky, McClelland, & Hinton, 1986; Smolensky, 1986, in preparation a).

By relating the analyses of everyday argumentation to those of well-argued academic discourse, we can clarify those aspects of reasoned discourse on which people can most use support, and thereby focus and direct the goals of the EUCLID system. We will use the preceding techniques to analyze texts constructed with EUCLID, compare these analyses to those of well-written articles, and use these comparisons to direct the EUCLID design.

5.2 ARL

In Section 2.2.3 and Figure 2-1 to 2-6 we considered what a real argument might look like to a EUCLID user. Behind the various displays lies an ARL data structure that can be presented to the user in graphical and tabular forms but which is fundamentally represented internally in a symbolic form. In the Appendix, we discuss the underlying ARL form of argument representation: the form stored in the EUCLID database and manipulated by retrieval, editing, and display procedures. What we describe is the current conception of the language, which is still in an early stage of development.

5.2.1 Argumentation Domains to be Studied

To ensure the expressive adequacy of ARL, it is important to test it during development on sophisticated and complex arguments. We have been using the Searle Chinese Room debate as our testing ground, and will continue to analyze it until we have a thorough ARL representation of the entire debate. (Of course, there is no claim about the uniqueness of the analysis.) After the Chinese Room debate, we will consider actual examples of argumentation from other areas of theoretical research, such as linguistics, physics, and computer science. It is important to ensure that ARL offers the power necessary to cope with the types of argumentation found in a variety of fields. We will also use ARL in our other research to see how well it supports argument creation in realistic situations. To test the applicability of ARL to other types of reasoned discourse, we will consider arguments from everyday conversation, as discussed in Section 5.1, and a sample of written arguments from a variety of areas; for example, those collected in texts such as Fogelin (1982).

ARL offers the exciting prospect of characterizing, with considerable precision, the *styles* of argumentation found in various academic disciplines and, more broadly, in various subtypes of reasoned discourse. For example, an ARL analysis of American legal reasoning would give a formal characterization of a very stylized form of case-based argumentation. We hope to make interesting contributions in this respect as a by-product of testing the generality of ARL.

5.3 EUCLID

Development of a EUCLID prototype is well underway. This prototype assumes for the most part that the database of the argument is in (virtual) memory. The next implementation will include a database management system to handle extensive databases. Figure 5-1 gives a block level description of one configuration of the expanded EUCLID system. The heart of the system, the object manager and the user interface, will be written in Common Lisp and is here shown running on a Symbolics Lisp machine; a Sun workstation running an object-oriented database management system is shown managing data archival.

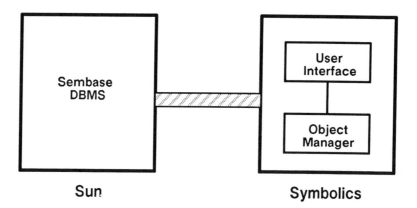

Figure 5-1: EUCLID system configuration

Certain retrieval tasks in EUCLID amount to the instantiation of predicate calculus expressions containing variables. For these tasks, a Prolog-like interpreter is convenient. By implementing such an interpreter in Lisp, we can readily exploit the advantages of logic programming while retaining the powerful advantages of the unified Lisp environment.

5.3.1 Object Management

The object manager will maintain the various ARL structures as objects, along with the various methods for performing analysis and constructing displays. The ARL database used by EUCLID is a heavily interconnected network of objects of many types, including terms, claims, arguments, documents, **support** relationships, and so on. An object-oriented approach is natural for providing an extensible set of data types and for defining special types of arguments. Message-passing and procedural inheritance make it easy to define display procedures for different structures that can be specially tailored where desired and inherited from more general structures otherwise. The data contained in objects will be cross-referenced, so that, for example, the object for a DOA, a domain of assertion, will possess pointers to the claims it contains, and the objects for various arguments will contain pointers to those same claims. A detailed definition of DOA is given in the Appendix.

In order for EUCLID to be a useful research tool it is important that argument structures that are carefully worked out be accessible for multiple uses. Over the past four years, an object-oriented database management system called Sembase (for Semantic database system; King, 1984; Farmer, Myers, & King, 1985) has been developed. It it written in C, runs under Unix, and supports recursively-defined objects and type/subtype (or ISA) hierarchies. Another tool, called Cactis (for Colorado ACTIve Semantics data; Hudson & King, 1986) has been developed. This system uses attributed grammars and specialized implementation techniques to support complex object structures in a fashion which allows very fast retrieval. (For an overview of object-oriented and semantic database systems, see Hull & King, 1986.)

As these tools already exist, the implementation efforts required to build a version of EUCLID which may handle large problem domains will be greatly eased. When an ARL database grows beyond that which may be stored in memory in the Symbolics system, EUCLID will use Sembase and Cactis as an external store. In order to support a multi-user environment and to allow a user to work in parallel on various pieces of a large argument structure, we will employ a demand-driven architecture in which the database component of EUCLID can process multiple requests in parallel.

An important basic operation in EUCLID is search of the database for information that pertains to a given subject. This is done both through searches of natural language strings for relevant words, and by following explicit pointers from data objects denoting topics that have been explicitly created by the user as retrieval keys. In either case, requiring exact matching between strings or keys and retrieval cues is a very restrictive constraint. A potentially powerful alternative exploits *spreading activation* to find items indirectly related to, but not exactly matching, a given search cue. This "connectionist" approach to search is directly inspired by models of human memory and offers considerable power and flexibility (Hinton & Anderson, 1981; McClelland et al., 1986; Rumelhart, McClelland, & the PDP Research Group, 1986; Smolensky, in preparation a, in preparation b; see also the chapter by Jones in this volume). We will test the value of connectionist retrieval techniques in the EUCLID context. Preliminary investigations of connectionist retrieval in a keyword bibliographic database (Mozer, 1984) are very encouraging.

5.3.2 The User Interface

To be useful EUCLID must present a large quantity of information to the user in readable formats. The figures in Section 2.2.3 illustrate two information-rich display techniques to be heavily used by EUCLID: graphs and tables. Graphical representation of the **supports** relation provides a vivid display of the overall logical structure of an argument. Tabular display of particular argument types, like analogies, allows complex interrelations to be implicitly displayed by relative locations of items in the table. Other dynamic display techniques, such as highlighting elements on the screen with intensity or color, allow the display of elements possessing a property (e.g., **unsupported**) that the user wants to concentrate attention upon.

The demanding display requirements of the EUCLID system are handled by a general tool we are developing for manipulating database *perspectives* and *views*. A database perspective is a set of items currently of interest to the user. A view is a perspective together with information about how the items in that perspective are to be displayed on the screen. Changing perspective has the effect of adding or deleting items from the screen; changing views of a given perspective amounts to changing how the same information is displayed on the screen. Perspectives are being implemented as trees which specify the flow of control for producing displays. Views are implemented as particular inheritance hierarchies of display procedures for the various data types. Thus in different views, different procedures may be used for displaying the same type of object. See the chapter by Fairchild, Poltrock, and Furnas in this volume for a related discussion about the selective display of large networks of symbolic information.

On input, as is customary in object-oriented systems, we use pop-up menus heavily, along with forms. If the user wishes to create an argument by analogy, for example, the definition of that subclass of the argument class allows EUCLID to prompt the user for the necessary elements, by providing a form to fill in or a menu of options to select. The system uses the ARL definition of an analogy to manage the details of creating all the constituent ARL structures for the user.

All EUCLID input/output is handled through a set of high-level graphics procedures; a *mouse-sensitive graphics package* has been specially designed for EUCLID by Brigham Bell, but is of extremely general applicability. The use of these high-level input/output graphics routines makes EUCLID highly portable: to port EUCLID to any machine running Common Lisp requires only the porting of the mouse sensitive graphics package, and, if necessary, porting the flavors system of object-oriented programming. Neither of these tasks require extensive effort, and both provide extremely general functionality that extend well beyond the EUCLID application.

5.4 Evaluation

We feel it is extremely important to monitor the effectiveness of the evolving EUCLID system by testing it with real users. We have three related but distinct objectives in this evaluation; they must be clearly separated because different methods are applicable to each. Our general framework is based on Gould and Lewis (1985).

Objective 1: Determine revisions to the EUCLID design needed to make it more useful for realistic tasks. Gould and Lewis stress the need for early attention to user tasks and requirements. While preliminary design work has been based on contact with a subpopulation of users, namely ourselves, it is clearly essential to obtain continuing feedback from a broader class of users who are not involved in the design of the system. We will follow the methodology successfully used by the NoteCards project (Brown & Newman, 1985; VanLehn, 1985): the system is used for meaningful tasks, in argument creation and analysis, by volunteer users outside the project team. Trial users will select some tasks from their own work domain, as well as performing tasks we provide. Logs will be kept of user activities, comments, and suggestions.

Objective 2: Collect detailed information about features of the EUCLID interface that users find difficult. While this objective is related to the broader one just discussed, getting specific feedback on interface features requires a different methodology. This specific feedback is needed to support the design iteration that good user interface design demands. We will use the "thinking aloud" technique (Ericsson & Simon, 1984), as adapted to user interface evaluation by Lewis (1982). In this approach, users are asked to make verbal comments in real time as they work with the system. These comments often pinpoint problems in the interface that are difficult to discover from performance data or post-hoc comments. We will collect thinking-aloud data on a sampled basis from the trial users discussed above.

Objective 3: Measure the effectiveness of EUCLID. Measurement of performance in complex tasks such as those supported by EUCLID is complicated by the likelihood of wide individual differences in skill and approach. Nevertheless, we will attempt to gather data bearing directly on some of the goals of EUCLID.

To assess the effectiveness of EUCLID as an argument creation and presentation tool, we will adapt a methodology developed by Gould (1978a, 1978b, 1980, 1981, 1982) to study differences in communication media. Participants will be asked to prepare arguments supporting a stated conclusion; they will use EUCLID to prepare some arguments and will generate others without aid. Users will provide text representations of the arguments prepared using EUCLID, so that we will have three products to compare: arguments in text prepared without EUCLID, arguments in text prepared with EUCLID, and arguments prepared with EUCLID presented in EUCLID form. Judges will rate the effectiveness of all arguments. With appropriate balancing of treatments we can then assess how method of preparation and presentation influence rated effectiveness.

To assess the effectiveness of EUCLID as an analytical tool we will ask readers to indicate flaws in arguments presented in text form. Readers will have the use of EUCLID in examining some arguments and not others. Some of these arguments will be selected from texts on informal logic (e.g., Acock, 1985; Engel, 1980) which provide normative grounds for evaluating readers' performance. On other arguments, readers will then be asked to compare their findings with flaws listed by other readers or suggested by us, and indicate whether they accept these putative flaws as such. This will allow us to determine whether flaws accepted by most readers are more likely to be found by readers using EUCLID, providing an effectiveness measure requiring no a priori norms.

How users feel about using the EUCLID system is to some extent independent of the quality of what they produce. We will therefore directly assess the attitude of users towards the system, to see how EUCLID affects their confidence in constructing arguments.

We have so far considered the assessment of EUCLID's benefits. An adequate evaluation must also assess costs, in performance time and learning. While tradeoffs relating quantitative measures of benefits to costs are difficult to assess, we will measure time used, and training time required, in the studies just described.

Acknowledgements

This research has been supported by a grant from Symbolics, Inc., and by the Department of Computer Science and Institute of Cognitive Science at the University of Colorado at Boulder.

References

Acock, M. (1985). *Informal logic examples and exercises*. Belmont, CA: Wadsworth.

Akinasso, N. (1982). On the difference between spoken and written language. *Language & Speech, 25*, 97-125.

Alvarado, S. J., Dyer, M. G., & Flowers, M. (1985). Memory representation and retrieval for editorial comprehension. *Proceedings of the International Joint Conference on Artificial Intelligence.*

Artificial Intelligence. (1980). Special issue on non-monotonic logic. Volume 13, Numbers 1-2.

Asher, N., Bonevac, D., Kamp, H., & Smith, C. (1983). Discourse representation. Proposal to the National Science Foundation.

Bennett, J. P. (1984a). Data stories: Learning about learning from the U.S. experience in Vietnam. In S. Sylvan & S. Chan (Eds.), *Foreign policy decision making: Perception, cognition, and artificial intelligence*. Praeger.

Bennett, J. P. (1984b). No second thoughts about 'no first use' How can the policy analyst undertake subjunctive reasoning in political argument? Manuscript.

Bennett, J. P. (1985). Pre-theory for comparing national security policies. Paper prepared for New Directions in the Comparative Study of Foreign Policy, Columbus, OH.

Birnbaum, L. (1982). Argument molecules. *Proceedings of the American Association for Artificial Intelligence.*

Birnbaum, L., Flowers, M., & McGuire, R. (1980). Towards an AI model of argumentation. *Proceedings of the American Association for Artificial Intelligence.*

Brown, J. S., & Newman, S. E. (1985). Issues in cognitive and social ergonomics: From our house to Bauhaus. *Human Computer Interaction, 1*, 359-391.

Card, S. K., Moran, T. P., & Newell, A. (1983). *The psychology of human-computer interaction*. Hillsdale, NJ: Erlbaum.

Chafe, W., & Nichols, J. (Eds.). (1986). *Evidentiality*. Norwood, NJ: Ablex.

Collins, A., & Gentner, D. A. (1980). A framework for a cognitive theory of writing. In L. W. Gregg & E. R. Steinberg (Eds.), *Cognitive processes in writing*. Hillsdale, NJ: Erlbaum.

Conklin, J. (1986). *A survey of Hypertext* (Tech. Rep. STP-356-86). Austin, TX: Microelectronics and Computer Technology Corporation.

Cypher, A. (1986). The structure of users' activities. In D. A. Norman & S. W. Draper (Eds.), *User centered system design*. Hillsdale, NJ: Erlbaum.

Engel, S. M. (1980). *Analyzing informal fallacies.* Englewood Cliffs, NJ: Prentiss-Hall.

Ericsson, K. A., & Simon, H. A. (1984). *Protocol analysis.* Cambridge, MA: MIT Press/Bradford.

Farmer, D., Myers, D., & King, R. (1985). The semantic database constructor. *IEEE Transactions on Software Engineering, SE-11,* 583-590.

Flower, L. S., & Hayes, J. R. (1980). The dynamics of composing: Making plans and juggling constraints. In L. W. Gregg & E. R. Steinberg (Eds.), *Cognitive processes in writing.* Hillsdale, NJ: Erlbaum.

Flower, L. S., Hayes, J. R., Carey, L., Schriver, K., & Stratman, J. (to appear). Detection, diagnosis and the strategies of revision. *College composition and communication.*

Flowers, M., McGuire, R., & Birnbaum, L. (1982). Adversary arguments and the logic of personal attacks. In W. G. Lehnert & M. G. Ringle (Eds.), *Strategies for natural language understanding.* Hillsdale, NJ: Erlbaum.

Fogelin, R. J. (1982). *Understanding arguments: An introduction to informal logic.* New York: Harcourt, Brace, Javanovich.

Fox, B. (1984). *Anaphora and discourse structure in written and conversational English.* Ph.D. dissertation, UCLA.

Fox, B. (to appear). *Discourse structure and anaphora in written and conversational English.* Cambridge, England: Cambridge University Press.

Fromkin, V., & Rodman, R. (1978). *Introduction to language.* New York: Holt, Rinehart, & Winston.

Gentner, D. A. (1983). Structure-mapping: A theoretical framework for analogy. *Cognitive Science, 7,* 155-170.

Givon, T. (1979). *On understanding grammar.* New York: Academic.

Gould, J. D. (1978a). An experimental study of writing, dictating, and speaking. In J. Requin (Ed.), *Attention and performance, VII.* Hillsdale, NJ: Erlbaum.

Gould, J. D. (1978b). How experts dictate. *Journal of Experimental Psychology: Human Perception and Performance, 4,* 648-661.

Gould, J. D. (1980). Experiments on composing letters: Some facts, some myths, and some observations. In L. W. Gregg & E. R. Steinberg (Eds.), *Cognitive processes in writing.* Hillsdale, NJ: Erlbaum.

Gould, J. D. (1981). Composing letters with computer-based text editors. *Human Factors, 23,* 593-606.

Gould, J. D. (1982). Writing and speaking letters and messages. *International Journal of Man-Machine Studies, 16,* 147-171.

Gould, J. D. & Lewis, C. H. (1985). Designing for usability: Key principles and what designers think. *Communications of the ACM, 28*, 300-311.

Govier, T. (1985). *A practical study of argument.* Belmont, CA: Wadsworth.

Gregg, L. W. & Steinberg, E. R. (Eds.). (1980). *Cognitive processes in writing.* Hillsdale, NJ: Erlbaum.

Guindon, R., & Kintsch, W. (1984). Priming macropropositions: Evidence for the primacy of macropropositions in the memory for text. *Journal of Verbal Learning and Verbal Behavior, 23*(4), 508-518.

Halasz, F., Moran, T. P., & Trigg, R. (1987). NoteCards in a nutshell. *Proceedings of CHI + GI 87.* Toronto, Canada.

Hayes, J. R. & Flower, L. S. (1980). Identifying the organization of writing processes. In L. W. Gregg & E. R. Steinberg (Eds.), *Cognitive processes in writing.* Hillsdale, NJ: Erlbaum.

Hintikka, K. J. J. (1969). *Models for modalities.* Dordrecht: Reidel.

Hinton, G. E. & Anderson, J. A. (1981). *Parallel models of associative memory.* Hillsdale, NJ: Erlbaum.

Holt, R. C. (1983). *Concurrent Euclid, the UNIX system, and Turis.* Reading, MA: Addison-Wesley.

Hudson, S., & King, R. (1986). Cactis: A database system for specifying functionally-defined data. *Proceedings of the International Workshop on Object-Oriented Database Systems.*

Hull, R., & King, R. (1986). Semantic database modeling: Survey, applications, and research issues (Tech. Rep. TR-86-201). Computer Science Department, USC.

Isard, W., & Lewis, B. (1984). James P. Bennett on subjunctive reasoning, policy analysis, and political argument. *Conflict Management and Peace Science, 8*, 71-112.

Johnson-Laird, P. N. (1983). *Mental models.* Cambridge, MA: Harvard University Press.

Kellogg, R. T. (1985a). Computer aids that writers need. *Behavior Research Methods, Instruments, & Computers, 17*, 253-258.

Kellogg, R. T. (1985b). *Why outlines benefit writers.* Paper presented to the Psychonomic Society, Boston, MA.

Kellogg, R. T. (in press). Designing idea processors for document composition. *Behavior Research Methods, Instruments, & Computers.*

Kieras, D. E. (1982). A model of reader strategy for abstracting main ideas from simple technical prose. *Text, 2*, 47-82.

Kim, J. H. (1984). *CONVINCE: A CONVersational INference Consolidation Engine* (Tech. Rep. UCLA CSD 84). Computer Science Department, UCLA.

King, R. (1984). Sembase: A semantic database management system. *Proceedings of the First International Workshop on Expert Database Systems.*

Kintsch, W., & van Dijk, T. A. (1978). Toward a model of text comprehension and production. *Psychological Review 85*, 363-394.

Lampson, B. W., Horning, J. J., London, R. L., Mitchell, J. G., & Popek, G. J. (1977). Report on the programming language Euclid. *SIGPLAN Notices, 12*(2).

Lewis, C. H. (1982). Using the "thinking-aloud" method in cognitive interface design (Report RC-9265). Yorktown Heights, NY: IBM Research.

Mann, W., & Thompson, S. (1985). Relational propositions. *Proceedings of the Berkeley Linguistics Society.*

McClelland, J. L., Rumelhart, D. E., & the PDP Research Group. (1986). *Parallel distributed processing: Explorations in the microstructure of cognition* (Volume II: Psychological and biological models). Cambridge, MA: MIT Press/Bradford.

McGee, V. E. (1986). The OWL: Software support for a model of argumentation. *Behavior Research Methods, Instruments, & Computers, 18*, 108-117.

McHouh, A. (1982). *Telling how texts talk: Essays on reading and ethnomethodology.* New York: Routledge and Kegan Paul.

Meyer, B., & Rice, G. (1982). The interaction of reader strategies and the organization of text. *Text, 2*, 141-154.

Mozer, M. C. (1984). Inductive information retrieval using parallel distributed computation (Tech. Rep. 8406). La Jolla, CA: UCSD, Institute of Cognitive Science.

Nelson, T. H. (1974). *Dream machines.* South Bend, IN: The distributors.

Norman, D. A. & Draper, S. W. (1986). *User centered system design.* Hillsdale, NJ: Erlbaum.

Nystrand, M. (Ed.). (1982). *What writers know.* New York: Academic.

Ochs, E. (1979). Planned and unplanned discourse. In Givon (Ed.), *Syntax and Semantics, 12.* New York: Academic.

O'Malley, C., Smolensky, P., Bannon, L., Conway, E., Graham, J., Sokolov, J., & Monty, M. L. (1983). A proposal for user centered system documentation. *Proceedings of the CHI 1983 Conference on Human Factors in Computing Systems.*

Pearl, J., Leal, A., & Saleh, J. (1982). GODDESS: A goal-directed decision structuring system. *IEEE Transactions on Pattern Analysis and Machine Intelligence, PAMI 4*, 250-262.

Pomerantz, A. (1984). Giving a source or basis: The practice in conversation of telling [How I know'. *Journal of Pragmatics.*

Reichman, R. (1981a). Modeling informal debates. *Proceedings of the International Joint Conference on Artificial Intelligence.*

Reichman, R. (1981b). Plain speaking: A theory and grammar of spon-
    taneous conversation (Tech. Rep. 4681). Cambridge, MA: Bolt,
    Beranek & Newman.
Rubin, A. (1980). A theoretical taxonomy of the differences between oral
    and written language. In R. Spiro, B. Bruce, & W. Brewer (Eds.),
    Issues in reading comprehension. Hillsdale, NJ: Erlbaum.
Rumelhart, D. E., McClelland, J. L., & the PDP Research Group. (1986).
    Parallel distributed processing: Explorations in the microstructure
    of cognition (Volume I: Foundations). Cambridge, MA: MIT
    Press/Bradford.
Rumelhart, D. E., Smolensky, P., McClelland, J. L., & Hinton,
    G. E. (1986). Schemata and sequential thought processes in
    parallel distributed processing. In J. L. McClelland,
    D. E. Rumelhart, & the PDP Research Group, Parallel distributed
    processing: Explorations in the microstructure of cognition
    (Volume II: Psychological and biological models). Cambridge,
    MA: MIT Press/Bradford Books.
Schegloff, E. (1976). Some questions and ambiguities in conversation
    [Pragmatics Microfiche 2.2:D8]. England: University of
    Cambridge, Dept. of Linguistics.
Schegloff, E., & Sacks, H. (1973). Opening up closings. Semiotica, 8,
    289-327.
Schenkein, J. (Ed.). (1979). Studies in the organization of conversation
    interaction. New York: Academic.
Scribner, S. (1977). Modes of thinking and ways of speaking: culture
    and logic reconsidered. In P. N. Johnson-Laird & P. C. Wason
    (Eds.), Thinking: Readings in cognitive science. Cambridge,
    England: Cambridge University Press.
Searle, J. R. (1980). Minds, brains, and programs. The Behavioral and
    Brain Sciences, 3, 417-457.
Smolensky, P. (1986). Information processing in dynamical systems:
    Foundations of harmony theory. In D. E. Rumelhart,
    J. L. McClelland, & the PDP Research Group, Parallel distributed
    processing: Explorations in the microstructure of cognition
    (Volume I: Foundations). Cambridge, MA: MIT Press/Bradford.
Smolensky, P. (in preparation a). Connectionist models of cognition.
    Hillsdale, NJ: Erlbaum.
Smolensky, P. (in preparation b). Principles of connectionist artificial
    intelligence.
Smolensky, P., Monty, M. L., & Conway, E. (1984). Formalizing task
    descriptions for command specification and documentation.
    Proceedings of the International Federation of Information
    Processing Conference on Human Computer Interaction.
Solow, D. (1982). How to read and do proofs, an introduction to math-
    ematical thought process. New York: Wiley.

van Dijk, T. A., & Kintsch, W. (1983). *Strategies of discourse comprehension.* New York: Academic.

VanLehn, K. (1985). *Theory reformulation caused by an argumentation tool* (Report). Palo Alto, CA: Xerox Palo Alto Research Center.

Zadeh, L. A. (1979). A theory of approximate reasoning. In J. E. Hayes, D. Michie, & L. I. Mikulich (Eds.), *Machine Intelligence, 9.* New York: Wiley.

Zadeh, L. A. (1984). Syllogistic reasoning in fuzzy logic and its application to reasoning with dispositions (Tech. Rep. 16). Berkeley, CA: UCS, Cognitive Science Program.

Zukerman, I., & Pearl, J. (1985). *Tutorial dialogs and meta-technical utterances.* Manuscript. UCLA, Computer Science Department.

Appendix: ARL

In this appendix we address some of the more technical aspects of the argument representation language ARL, as it stands in its present early stage of development.

ARL uses a predicate calculus representation which is rarely (if ever) seen by casual users; it is most important to developers and extenders of the language. We shall use more or less standard predicate calculus notation in this appendix; we are still exploring various alternative notations.

1. Primitives

1.1 Data Types

The basic data types of ARL include:

    terms
    definitions
    claims
    arguments
    documents
    strengths
    domains of assertion

Terms, definitions, and atomic claims are primitive entities with associated strings giving their natural language expressions. Complex claims can be built up from simpler ones using functions introduced below. For example, **asserts(SEARLE, AI programming is basically trivial)** is a composite claim that Abelson makes in the Chinese Room debate.

Arguments are either simple, a single claim, or complex, built up out of claims using the logical operators of predicate calculus. Thus a conjunctive argument **a** may be constructed from several claims as **a = (c1 & c2 & c3)**. Below we give examples of argument types that are defined by fairly complex constructions.

In addition to pure argument structures, the EUCLID database also contains pieces of text, potentially quite extensive. When using EUCLID to write an academic paper, for example, not only is an argument structure constructed, but a document is also created. Thus ARL contains the data type **document**. Most documents are complex structures comprised of ordered sequences of sub-documents: a paper is a sequence of sections, a section is a sequence of subsections, and so on. Thus documents are generally hierarchical structures built of other documents. At the bottom of this hierarchy are primitive documents which are simply pieces of text. A primitive document may be the natural language expression of the content of a term, definition, claim, or argument.

Strengths exist so users may optionally mark assertions with a strength or confidence level; they can be numbers or strings as the user prefers.

A *domain of assertion* (DOA) is a set of claims that are embraced by one participant in an argument. Often a DOA can be labelled by a person, but DOAs at other scales are also important. Thus a DOA can be associated with a whole school of thought ("strong AI"), an individual ("Skinner"), a period in an individual's career ("late Wittgenstein"), a document ("Schank's commentary on Searle's paper"), or even a portion of an argument where some hypothetical state of affairs is entertained. Because DOAs are sets of claims, they are subject to the usual set-theoretic operations and relations (intersection, inclusion, etc.).

1.2 The Model of Argumentation

Domains of assertion form the basis for our model of argumentation. Participants in an argument are each entitled to a private set of claims. The semantic constraint (not syntactically enforced in ARL) is that the claims in a domain of assertion, when semantically interpreted, should be mutually consistent. The goal of persuasion is to make another participant realize that, because of claims that are already accepted, others should be accepted too to avoid inconsistency. Unlike in formal proofs, there is no prior agreement on a finitely-specified set of axioms. At any point, a participant can arbitrarily assert "if p then q" (as though this were axiomatic) and use it to derive q from p. To be persuasive, however, the claim "if p then q" must be one that someone else will accept as it stands, otherwise it should be justified by further argumentation.

1.3 Predicates and Functions

ARL contains functions that construct composite claims from simpler constituents. A very basic function is **asserts**; in the example above,

asserts(SEARLE, AI programming is basically trivial)

we construct the claim meaning "Searle asserts that AI programming is basically trivial" by inserting the DOA **SEARLE** and the atomic claim meaning "AI programming is basically trivial" into the function **asserts**. This is in fact a claim that Abelson makes in the Chinese Room debate.

We will display the syntax of the **asserts** function as

asserts(DOA, claim; strength)

where the data type of the arguments are indicated, and the arguments following ";" are optional. (In the preceding example, there is no indication of the strength with which Searle is claimed to make his assertion.) Examples of other basic functions for constructing composite claims include:

supports(argument, claim; strength)
contradicts(claim1, claim2)
relevant-to(claim1, claim2)
requires(argument, claim)
definition-of(term, definition, DOA)

There are also functions that construct claims about documents, including:

expresses(document, argument)
topic(document, term)
summary(long-document, short-document)
paraphrase(document1, document2)

Then there are some basic ARL predicates that relate terms, claims, arguments, and documents. Examples include:

contains(super-document, sub-document)
precedes(sub-document, sub-document, super-document)
contains-term(claim, term)
conjunct-of(argument, claim)
constituent-of(argument, claim)

2. Extensions

Users can extend the primitive data types, functions, and predicates of ARL. As a simple example, to define the argument type **confusion**, a user might create a primitive function

confuses(DOA, claim1, claim2)

meaning that the point of view of DOA has confused **claim1** with **claim2**. Or to define the argument type **argument_by_analogy**, a user might choose to create the predicates

domain-of(claim, term)
maps(analogy_map, term1, term2)

The idea here is that an analogy consists of two domains: the antecedent domain about which information is presumed known (e.g., "the Vietnam war"), and the consequent domain about which a conclusion is being argued for (e.g., "Central American involvement"). The argument consists of a set of claims about each domain, and the assertion that there is a mapping between the terms occurring in those claims that takes true statements in the antecedent domain into true statements about the consequent domain. This idea will be formalized into an ARL definition below.

3. Constructs

ARL lets users define higher-order, composite data types. This is a crucial feature of ARL, one that illustrates the true sense in which ARL provides users with a *language* with real generative power. For this reason we provide a number of examples in this section of the construction of higher-order argument types. These examples are intended to convey the flavor of ARL.

We shall consider constructions of increasing complexity. For the more complex cases, we find the expressions to be considerably more transparent when infix notations are used for the central functions **asserts** and **supports**. Thus for **asserts(SEARLE, claim)** we write **SEARLE: claim** and for **supports(argument, claim)** we write **argument → claim**. To familiarize the reader with the infix notations, we shall initially write all expressions in both the more verbose and the more compact notations. In all cases we will paraphrase the formal definitions in English. Throughout this appendix we use upper-case variables (e.g., **X**) to denote DOAs (e.g., **SEARLE**) and lower-case variables (e.g., **arg,cl**) for everything else: arguments, claims, etc.

The first two constructions we illustrate would be used to argue that someone is misrepresenting another's claim. We define a **strong_misrepresentation** to exist when **X** says that **Y** asserts **cl** , but in fact **Y** asserts **-cl** (**not(cl)**). We write the definition, in the compact and verbose forms, as:

```
strong_misrepresentation( X, Y, cl) :=      strong_misrepresentation( X, Y, cl) :=
  X: Y: cl  &                                 asserts( X, asserts ( Y, cl))  &
  Y: -cl                                      asserts( Y, not( cl))
```

For example, in analyzing the Chinese Room debate, the following claim might be generated:

**SMOLENSKY: strong_misrepresentation(ABELSON, SEARLE,
writing a program to pass the Turing test
is basically trivial)**

Here Smolensky asserts that Abelson has strongly misrepresented Searle. The function **strong_misrepresentation** constructs from its inputs an argument that consists of the conjunction of the claim that

"Abelson says that Searle says **c**" and the claim that "Searle says **not-c**," where the meaning of **c** is "writing a program to pass the Turing test is basically trivial."

A related type of argument is:

```
weak_misrepresentation( X, Y, cl) :=     weak_misrepresentation( X, Y, cl) :=
    X: Y: cl  &                              asserts( X, asserts ( Y, cl))  &
    -Y: cl                                   not( asserts( Y, cl))
```

This argument claims that "**X** says that **Y** asserts **cl** but in fact **Y** does not assert **cl**."

Another rather simple construction is:

```
omission( X, arg, claim1, cl2) :=     omission( X, arg, cl1, cl2) :=
    X: arg → cl1  &                       asserts( X, supports( arg, cl1)  &
    requires( arg, cl2)  &                requires( arg, cl2)  &
    -justified( X, cl2)                   not( justified( X, cl2))
```

Here, the argument is: **X** has appealed to the argument **arg** to support the claim **cl1** , but **arg** actually requires for its validity that claim **cl2** hold, and **X** has not justified **cl2**. In other words, there is an omission in **X**'s argument. (**justified(X, claim)**) can be defined basically as "there exists an argument in the DOA **X** that supports **claim**." That an argument rests on an unstated claim cannot be derived from other ARL relationships, so **requires** is a primitive function.

An example of a rather more involved construction is:

```
confusion( X, arg, cl1, cl2) :=     confusion( X, arg, cl1, cl2) :=
    X: arg  &                           asserts( X, arg)  &
    X: arg → cl1  &                     asserts( X, supports ( arg, cl1))  &
    arg  &                              arg  &
    arg → cl2  &                        supports( arg, cl2)  &
    confused( X, cl1, cl2)              confused( X, cl1, cl2)
```

Here the argument is that **X** has mistakenly concluded **cl1** from **arg** instead of **cl2** , because **X** has confused **cl1** with **cl2**. Searle employs this argument, claiming that Strong AI has confused "observer-relative ascriptions" of understanding with "intrinsic" understanding.

The following more elaborate structure defines when one argument, **ref**, **refutes** another argument, **arg**:

```
refutes( ref, arg) :=
arg = claim cl1 &
        (E cl2) (contradicts( cl1, cl2) & ref → cl2)
or
arg = conjunction( a[ ] ) &
        (E i) refutes( ref, a[i])
or
arg = disjunction( a[ ] ) &
        (i) refutes( ref, a[i])
```

Here we use an informal notation in which **arg = claim cl1** means "the argument **arg** is simply a claim, **cl1** "; **arg = conjunction(a[ ])** means "the argument **arg** is the conjunction of the sub-arguments a[i], i = 1, ..., N"; **(E i)** means "there exists an **i** in 1, ..., N"; and **(i)** means "for all **i** in 1, ..., N".

Two important observations should be made about this definition. First, it shows the value of recursion in ARL. Second, using this definition, a user can ask to instantiate an argument **ref** to refute **arg**, and get significant support: EUCLID can inspect the ARL definition of **arg** to see if it is a simple claim, a conjunctive argument, or a disjunctive argument, and then use the definition to guide the user in constructing the refutation. In this sense, the definition of **refutes** offers a procedural semantics for the ARL primitives **conjunction**, **disjunction**, and **contradicts** .

Searle's Chinese Room analogy is displayed in tabular form in Figure 2-6, and some of the relationships are graphically displayed in Figure 2-3. In the following definition, there are an antecedent domain (**dom[1]**) and a consequent domain (**dom[2]**), a set of objects in the antecedent domain (**obj[1][j]**), a corresponding set of objects in the consequent domain (**obj[2][j]**), sets of corresponding properties or predicates (**pred[1][k]**, **pred[2][k]**) and claims (**cl[i][n]**) about the two domains that use the specified objects and predicates (see also Gentner, 1983). The conclusion of the argument by analogy is a claim about the consequent domain that corresponds to a certain claim - which we call the **clinch** - about the antecedent domain. The correspondences are set up by a mapping **m**, and the argument assumes that all the claim made about the domains, except the conclusion, are true. Here is a function that constructs an analogy **a**, a mapping **m**, and uses them to create an **argument_by_analogy** :

argument_by_analogy(a, conclusion, dom[ ], obj[ ][ ], pred[ ][ ], cl[ ][ ], clinch) :=

```
a := (i,j) domain-of( obj[i][j], dom[i])  &
     (i,k) domain-of( pred[i][k], dom[i])  &
     (i,n) domain-of( cl[i][n], dom[i])  &
     (j) maps( m, obj[1][j], obj[2][j])  &
     (k) maps( m, pred[1][k], pred[2][k])  &
     (n) maps( m, cl[1][n], cl[2][n])  &
     maps( m, clinch, conclusion)  &
     (i,n) cl[i][n]  &
     clinch
  &
a  →  conclusion
```

The **maps** statements are to be interpreted as follows. The mapping of objects and predicates from **dom[1]** to **dom[2]** are unconstrained stipulations that define **m**. Since the various **cl[i][n]** involve these objects and predicates, the assertion that **m** maps **cl[1][n]** onto **cl[2][n]** is semantically constrained to be consistent with the stipulations defining how **m** maps objects and predicates between the domains. Assessing this consistency involves the content of the claims, i.e., information below the Divide, and must be done by the user. This is part of the evaluation of the validity of any argument by analogy. As always, the ARL definition formally characterizes the *structure* of an argument by analogy, but the assessment of the *validity* of such an argument goes beyond the formal component of ARL.

The complex relations defined by **argument_by_analogy** can be conveniently displayed in tabular form, as illustrated in Figure 2-6. The tabular display is defined with reference to the preceding definition by:

a

domains:	**domain[1]**	**domain[2]**
elements:	**object[1][j]**	**object[2][j]**
	predicate[1][k]	**predicate[2][k]**
	claim[1][n]	**claim[2][n]**
clinch:	**clinch**	**[conclusion]**

Here it is implied that the entries for various values of **j,k,n** are to be stacked vertically.

As our final example, we consider a higher-order construct that can serve as a template for the top level of an argument. In fact, it is the top level of Searle's argument, and was shown in Figures 2-1 and 2-2. This type of argument might be called **refute_and_support** . The idea is that an opposing point of view is credited with a claim, and a series of arguments supporting this claim are presented and refuted. Then a contradictory claim is put forth and arguments supporting it are offered. Possible counterarguments may then be formulated and refuted.

An ARL definition for this argument schema, written in a chatty, second-person style, is:

```
refute_and_support( YOU, your_claim, my_claim, your_argument[ ],
    my_refutation[ ], my_argument[ ]; your_refutation[ ], my_counter[ ]) :=

YOU: your_claim  &
(i) YOU: your_argument[i]  → your_claim  &
(i) refutes( my_refutation[i], your_argument[i])  &
contradicts( my_claim, your_claim)  &
(j) my_argument[j]  → my_claim  &
(j) YOU: refutes( your_refutation[j], my_argument[j])  &
(j) refutes( my_counter[j], your_refutation[j])
```

As with the argument by analogy, the complex interrelations of the components of the **refute_and_support** argument lend themselves to tabular display, as shown in Figure 2-1. The tabular form is related to the preceding definition by:

YOU	ME
your_claim	my_claim
your_argument[i]	my_refutation[i]
	my_argument[j]
your_refutation[j]	my_counter[j]

Here **ME** represents the DOA in which the **refute_and_support** argument is made. (In Figure 2-1, **your_refutation[1]**, the Strong AI refutation for Searle's "argument from formality: the Chinese room," happens to be a disjunction of three sub-arguments. Thus **my_counter[1]** is a conjunction of three sub-arguments. **my_argument[2]** in Figure 2-1 is Searle's "argument from lactation," for which no refutations are shown.)

We now have a glimpse of what is going on behind the scenes of Figures 2-1 and 2-2. Internally, the top level of Searle's argument is represented in ARL as a **refute_and_support** structure. Associated with this type of argument is a data structure expressing the preceding tabular format. There is a display procedure that can use this data structure to display instances of **refute_and_support** arguments in tabular form. This is what generates the display in Figure 2-1. The relations between elements in the table are all encoded in the underlying ARL definition of **refute_and_support**; these relations can be retrieved and then explicitly displayed using a procedure that draws labelled arcs. This is how Figure 2-2 is generated. Similar procedures using the **argument_by_analogy** definition and tabular dispay format generate Figures 2-3 and 2-6. Figures 2-4 and 2-6 involve an ARL function that was mentioned in passing in Section 1.3: **expresses** . It links a claim in an ARL analysis of the Chinese Room debate to the piece of text in the original document that allegedly expresses the claim. Two alternative procedures for displaying the **expresses** function are respectively illustrated in Figures 2-4 and 2-5.

4
A Multidisciplinary Perspective on Dialogue Structure in User-Advisor Dialogues

RAYMONDE GUINDON

Tutoring or advising is often performed in spoken face-to-face dialogues. What happens to the structure of user-advisor dialogues when the dialogue is typed and the advisor is a computer system? Typed dialogues in a Wizard-of-Oz setting and spoken face-to-face dialogues are collected and analyzed in three steps: 1) a task structure is derived from an analysis of the users' task; 2) the task structure is then used to segment the dialogues into hierarchically-related subdialogues producing the dialogue structures; 3) the distributions of the antecedents of pronominal and of non-pronominal noun phrases in the dialogue structures and the distance between subdialogues in the task structure are compared between the spoken face-to-face and the typed dialogues. The task structure has more influence on the structure of the spoken face-to-face dialogues than on the structure of the typed dialogues: the typed dialogues in the Wizard-of-Oz setting are more similar to a sequence of independent queries than cohesive discourse. This is due to the low interaction level of typed communication and to users' beliefs in poor shared context between users and advisor. Implications for natural language front-ends to advisory systems are generated.

1. Introduction

Tutoring or advising is often performed in spoken face-to-face dialogues. What happens to the structure of user-advisor dialogues when the dialogue is typed and the advisor is a computer system? In this study, novices engage in help-seeking dialogues with an advisor to learn how to use an unfamiliar statistical package. The dialogues are collected in two communicative contexts: typed in a Wizard-of-Oz setting[1] and spoken in a face-to-face context. The main goal of this study is to investigate the effect of communicative context on the structure of user-advisor dialogues. Communicative context is the set of dimensions characterizing the context of the dialogues, such as spoken or typed modality, high or low level of interaction, shared or unshared physical context. The structure of user-advisor dialogues has great implications for the design of natural language interfaces to advisory systems, especially for the design of the modules to handle dialogue phenomena such as anaphora resolution.

Section 1 of the introduction details the notion of discourse and dialogue structure. The following two sections describe an application of the dialogue structure in natural language interfaces - anaphora resolution using a focusing mechanism.[2] The last two sections of the introduction highlight how focusing models of anaphora resolution are consistent with psychological findings about how conversants actually perform anaphora resolution and are consistent with linguistic studies of discourse.

Section 2 describes the method which is used to analyze the user-advisor dialogues in this study - the derivation of a dialogue structure based on a task structure.

Section 3 describes the results of the comparison between the antecedent distributions of spoken face-to-face and typed user-advisor dialogues. It also presents an analysis of the distance in the task structure between consecutive subdialogues in the two types of dialogues.

Finally, Section 4 summarizes the implications of these results for the design of natural languages interfaces to advisory systems.

---

[1]In a Wizard-of-Oz setting, users are being told that they are conversing with a "computerized" advisor. In fact, their utterances are sent to the monitor of an experimenter located in another room. The experimenter sends back replies to the user's monitor. It is a popular experimental technique in human-computer interaction to design and evaluate computer systems that are not yet fully developed.

[2]Another example of an application of the notion of discourse structure in the area of human-computer interaction is the work by Smolensky, Fox, King, and Lewis in this volume.

1.1 A Multidisciplinary View of the Non-Linearity of Discourse Structure

Psychological research has well established that many observed phenomena in discourse understanding and memory cannot be accounted for solely by the linear concatenation of discourse sentences, but must also be explained by the non-linear, often hierarchical, structure of discourse (see Kintsch & van Dijk, 1978; Sanford & Garrod, 1981; and van Dijk & Kintsch, 1983). The earliest studies on discourse structure, both in psychology and linguistics, share the assumption that certain discourse types, especially stories, have a pre-defined structure. Linguists, sociolinguists, and anthropologists have studied conventions in story writing across cultures and have noticed that certain genres, like folktales, do indeed have pre-defined structures (Colby, 1972; Lakoff, 1972; Propp, 1968). In fact, many discourse types have well-defined conventions about their structure, such as, argumentative discourse,[3] technical reports, and journal articles. Such structures are often observed or believed to be hierarchical (Rumelhart, 1975; Thorndyke, 1977; Mandler & Johnson, 1980). Figure 1-1 shows the typical hierarchical structure found in an article in experimental psychology. One reason to study dialogue structure is that anaphora resolution, a computationally complex phenomenon described in the next section, is believed to be affected by dialogue structure. It is hoped that determining dialogue structure will help anaphora resolution in natural language understanding systems, and more generally, help such systems interpret users' ambiguous and ungrammatical utterances.

1.2 The Complexity of Anaphora Resolution

Anaphors are expressions such as pronouns (e.g., *it, they*) or definite noun phrases (e.g., *the vector, the mean*) whose interpretation depends on previous expressions in the dialogue. The previous expressions are called antecedents. Anaphors are also called referring expressions.

---

[3]See the chapter by Smolensky, Fox, King, and Lewis in this book.

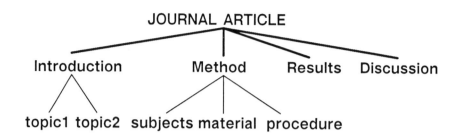

Figure 1-1: Hierarchical structure in psychology articles

Consider the following dialogue between speakers A and B:

    (1) A: There is a simple function that will calculate the mean.
    (2) B: O.K. And it is probably called "mean"?
    (3) A: That's correct.

People understand the pronouns *it* and *that* quite easily. The antecedent of *it* in (2) is *function* mentioned in (1), and the antecedent of *that* in (3) is the entire proposition in (2).

Anaphors do not refer to previous discourse entities, they refer to objects, properties, and events in the world, or more precisely, to objects, properties, and events in the mental models of the conversants about the situation described in the discourse. However, while anaphors do not refer to discourse entities, finding the antecedents in the discourse for these anaphors provide additional information to identify the referents of the anaphors. In (1) and (2), finding the antecedent of *it* provides one with the information that it is a function and that it is simple, in addition to how it is called. During a dialogue between a user and an advisor, each builds a model of the situation described in the dialogue. This situation model contains interrelated units corresponding to the characters, objects, properties, and events described in the dialogue. Anaphora resolution is the process of finding the antecedent of an anaphor in a discourse for the purpose of helping specify the referent of the anaphor in the situation model built by the conversants (Sidner, 1983).

1.2.1 Indeterminacy of Many Anaphors

Certain anaphors, such as pronouns, carry little information to help select the correct antecedent from the set of all antecedent expressions in the discourse. The pronoun *it* in (2) does not contain any information besides gender and number to help find its antecedent. In long dialogues, pronouns allow for a large number of previous noun phrases or verb phrases to be potential antecedents and the selection of a single antecedent can be very difficult with only gender and number restrictions.

1.2.2 Anaphora Resolution as a Search Problem

A dialogue makes available a broad range of semantic entities as possible antecedents for an anaphor, such as, individuals, sets, predicates, events, actions, states, etc. Since each utterance introduces a new set of potential antecedents, the set of available antecedents becomes prohibitively large and the search for an antecedent quickly becomes unmanageable. For example, one page of text with 25 sentences, each of which with two noun phrases, one verb, and one prepositional phrase, would introduce a total of at least 125 possible antecedents.

1.2.3 Anaphora Resolution as Reasoning

In some cases, an anaphor and its antecedent co-specify the same entity as in (4-5). It is not always the case that the semantic relation between an anaphor and its antecedent is the identity relation as in (4-5). Many other types of relations exist between an anaphor and its antecedent, such as the class-member relation in (6-7; 8-9) and the part-of relation in (10-11). For example, anaphors may co-specify different entities as in (8-9) where *they* refers to the class of recursive functions and not specifically to the recursive function mentioned in the previous sentence.

> (4) A: Where do I put the vector name?
> (5) B: Put *it* inside the parentheses.
>   (*it = vector name*)
>
> (6) Create a vector to contain the data.
> (7) The *data structure* should be of length 20.
>   (*data structure* has as a member *vector*)

(8) I wrote my first recursive function today.
(9) *They* are difficult to understand at the beginning.
      (*they* = *class of recursive functions* has as a member
      my first recursive function)

(10) Create a vector to contain the data.
(11) *The index* should run from 1 to 20.
      (*the index* is a part of *a vector*)

This section demonstrates the high complexity of anaphora resolution for a natural language understanding system. It also explains the interest by computational linguists in using the structure of the discourse to partition the discourse into segments which can be in focus. Focusing helps determine antecedents of anaphors by restricting the number of antecedents to search and test. The next section details how dialogue structure, focusing, and anaphora resolution are tied together.

1.3 Dialogue Structure and Focusing: A Key to Resolve Anaphors in Task-Oriented Dialogues?

Task-oriented dialogues are dialogues whose purpose is to accomplish another task. An example of a task-oriented dialogue is a dialogue between a novice and an expert where the novice seeks help from the expert to accomplish a task. Such dialogues are believed to exhibit a structure corresponding to the structure of the task being performed. Grosz (1977) hypothesizes that the task structure hierarchy imposes a hierarchy on the subdialogues. The whole dialogue is segmented into subdialogues in a way parallel to the segmentation of the whole task into subordinated subtasks. Figure 1-2 gives a part of the task structure, in this study, to compute the mean of a vector of values. It also gives its associated segmented subdialogues. A more complete version of this part of the task structure is given in Appendix II with associated subdialogues from the dialogue in Appendix I.

The segmentation of a dialogue into interrelated subdialogues is associated with shifts in focus occurring during the dialogue. As a subtask is performed (and its corresponding subdialogue expressed), the different objects, properties, and actions associated with this subtask come into focus. As this subtask is completed (and the corresponding

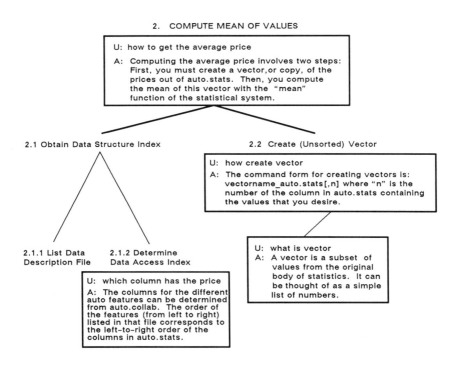

Figure 1-2: Partial task structure to compute the mean with associated subdialogues

subdialogue is closed), its associated objects, properties, and actions are likely to leave focus.

Grosz defines a focus space as that subset of the participant's total knowledge (which includes part of the dialogue itself) which is in the focus of attention and which is relevant to process a discourse segment. The partitioning of the participant's knowledge into a focus space allows more efficient reasoning because only a subset of the knowledge is used for computation. This is desirable for anaphora resolution because of the potentially great number of possible antecedents and the variety of possible semantic relations between antecedents and anaphors. Such partitioning establishes preferential restrictions on the set of potential antecedents and referents for an anaphor. This preferential restriction on the set of potential antecedents and referents has been called focusing (Grosz, 1977; Reichman, 1981; Sidner, 1983). Psychologically, this restriction is accomplished by maintaining the focused entities in working memory (Kintsch & van Dijk, 1978; Guindon, 1985).

The main point to emphasize is that in focusing theories of anaphora resolution, the discourse structure is assumed to play a crucial role in restricting the set of possible antecedents for an anaphor. The discourse structure is assumed to be partly determined by task structure. The task structure is used to determine the boundaries of subdialogues through recognition of changes in the goal of the conversants. The task structure is also used in determining the hierarchical relationships between sub-dialogues through recognition of goal and subgoal relationships. Moreover, the discourse entities in the current subdialogue, that is, the subdialogue fulfilling the current goal, are assumed to be in focus. Other discourse entities are also likely to be in focus, those introduced at the beginning of the dialogue and that stay relevant throughout the dialogue (Grosz, 1977). As a consequence, at any point in the discourse there is a dynamic preferential restriction of the set of possible antecedents. This is a possible solution to the computational complexity of anaphora resolution (i.e., the need for extensive search and reasoning). If a focusing mechanism of anaphora resolution is adopted, natural language interfaces need to keep a model of the dialogue structure and need to determine which subdialogues are in focus on the basis of task structure.

As a caveat, Grosz and Sidner (1985) point out that it is not necessary for the conversants to have pre-built mental models of the task structure for the task structure to influence the dialogue structure. For example, in a user-advisor dialogue about the use of a statistical package, the advisor can generate appropriate advice about how to compute a mean (i.e., advice about the task structure for computing a mean) using known elementary rules regarding the selection of numbers from a matrix, the summation of numbers, the division of two numbers, and the assignment of the result to a variable. From these elementary rules, the advisor may diagnose the user's problem and build a plan to solve the user's problem that is then conveyed to the user. Likewise, the user may plan and produce help-seeking utterances to the advisor on the basis of her developing mental model of the task structure.

To summarize, focusing theories of anaphora resolution have been proposed as a potential solution to the perceived great complexity of anaphora resolution in natural language understanding systems. Focusing theories of anaphora resolution are interesting because they are consistent with psychological findings on the use of working memory in text comprehension and they capture observations from linguistic studies of discourse, as will be seen in the next two sections.

1.4 Psychological Model of Discourse Comprehension and Anaphora Resolution

By far the most comprehensive and empirically validated model of discourse comprehension and production is by Kintsch and van Dijk (1978) and van Dijk and Kintsch (1983). The part most relevant to anaphora resolution is described in this section. It is well agreed that one can simultaneously apprehend in working memory only a small number of entities or chunks: the pure capacity of working memory is about 3 chunks (see Crowder, 1976, for a review) and the effective capacity is about 7 chunks (Miller, 1956; Simon, 1974). Moreover, relating ideas to each other, reasoning, and problem solving occur through working memory. Then, how does one understand, remember, and summarize a text when the amount of information provided by the text far exceeds the capacity of working memory? Kintsch and van Dijk (1978) propose that part of working memory is set aside as a buffer containing a subset of propositions from earlier parts of the text. During each cycle, basically defined as the processing of one sentence or clause, a subset of the current input propositions and a subset of the propositions already held in the buffer are selected to be held in the buffer for the next cycle. The criteria used to select propositions to be held in the buffer are assumed to maximize the probability that anaphors in the next set of propositions will have their antecedents in the buffer. This helps establish coherence of the text for the reader. The criteria used to select propositions to be held in the buffer for the next cycle are topicality (or importance) and recency. This selection procedure is called the leading-edge strategy.[4]When an anaphor is encountered whose antecedent is not in the buffer, it is necessary to perform a reinstatement search in episodic memory. Its antecedent is then reinstated in the buffer, effecting a context shift. This leads to increased reading time and comprehension difficulty.

According to the leading-edge strategy, the probability of an antecedent to be in the buffer, that is, to be in focus, depends on the topicality and recency of this antecedent. Recency is defined in terms of the number of clauses or sentences intervening between the antecedent and the anaphor. Antecedents for anaphors in the current sentence should become less frequent as recency decreases. Topicality is harder to define. In the context of user-advisor dialogues, topicality is defined in terms of the task structure. Given that the current subdialogue is about a certain subtask in the task hierarchy, the most topical elements are in the current subdialogue, in the parent subdialogue, and in the top-level subdialogue which introduces the overall task. The relationship between a dialogue and a subdialogue is one in which the subdialogue fulfills a subgoal of a goal introduced in the parent dialogue. The current subdialogue expresses entities that are recent and topical, the parent subdialogue expresses entities that are likely to be topical, and the top-level subdialogue introduces entities that are likely to be relevant throughout the dialogue. Since the elements in the current subdialogue are also recent, the distinguishing topical elements are in the parent subdialogue and in the top-level subdialogue. This definition of topicality in terms of the task structure is consistent with a psychological model of the process of abstracting and summarizing text (see van Dijk & Kintsch, 1983; Guindon & Kintsch, 1984).

However, this psychological model of anaphora resolution must be augmented by taking into account the different roles of anaphoric noun phrases in discourse. These different roles are described in the next section.

---

[4]The leading-edge strategy, the selection of items from a set based on topicality and recency, has been applied to graphical displays of information in the so-called Fish-Eye views. See the chapter by Fairchild, Poltrock, and Furnas in this book.

1.5 Some Determinants of Anaphor and Antecedent Distribution in Discourse

Pronominal anaphors, such as *it* and *they*, have been found to indicate topic continuity in discourse (Givon, 1983; Grosz, Joshi, & Weinstein, 1983). As a consequence, their antecedents should be mainly in focus. If entities in focus are selected on the basis of recency and topicality, the antecedents of pronominal anaphors are likely to be in the subdialogue containing the anaphor, in the parent subdialogue, and in the top-level subdialogue. Non-pronominal noun phrases, such as *the vector* and *the value*, are partly used to indicate change of topics or to introduce new topics (Givon, 1983; Grosz, Joshi, & Weinstein, 1983). Moreover, non-pronominal anaphors contain more semantic information than pronominal anaphors to describe their antecedents (e.g., *the vector* vs. *it*). As a consequence, the distribution of the antecedents of non-pronominal anaphors should be more widespread in the dialogue than the distribution of the antecedents of pronominal anaphors.

However, Fox (1984) found that general claims about the distribution of anaphors and their antecedents can be quite misleading when the data supporting these claims come from only one genre of discourse. She extensively studied the structure of three types of discourse: written ex-pository texts, spoken conversations, and written narratives. She observed rather different patterns of distribution of anaphors and their antecedents in these different genres due to their structural differences.

Let's now summarize the introduction and present the main hypotheses underlying this study. The distributions of antecedents of anaphors are influenced by the hierarchical structure of texts which vary across genres. In the context of user-advisor dialogues, the hierarchical structure of the dialogues is determined, at least partially, by the hierarchical structure of the task (Guindon, Brunner, & Conner, 1987; Guindon, Sladky, Brunner, & Conner, 1986). The structure of the task and the structure of the dialogue it determines are used in focusing theories of anaphora resolution to assign discourse elements to be in focus. Such focusing theories of anaphora resolution are consistent with psychologi-cal findings on discourse comprehension. However, none of the pre-vious linguistic or psychological studies have thoroughly looked at the distribution of antecedents of pronominal and non-pronominal noun phrases in user-advisor dialogues. Likewise, they have not compared the structure of user-advisor dialogues across communicative contexts. Altogether, these findings lead to the main hypothesis tested in this study: the structure of user-advisor dialogues may differ in different communicative contexts, such as spoken face-to-face and typed in a Wizard-of-Oz setting. As a consequence, the distributions of the antecedents of pronominal and non-pronominal anaphors may differ across communicative contexts. Such a finding would have implications on the proper design of natural language interfaces to handle typed user dialogues with an advisory system.

2. Task Structure and Dialogue Structure

Before presenting the results of the analyses regarding the influence of communicative context on the distribution of antecedents in user-advisor dialogues, the method used in deriving a task structure is described. For it is the task structure which is then used in deriving the dialogue structures.

2.1 Derivation of a Task Structure

The task structure is derived by performing a task analysis. A task analysis identifies the intrinsic constraints and possibilities in performing a certain task that are determined by the environment. In this study, the selected statistical package allows only a certain number of ways to perform a task, such as computing a mean. In the task analysis, all the possible ways that the statistical package allows for computing a mean are identified. A first step in performing a task analysis is to identify the *objects* involved in the task. In this case, these objects are vectors, matrices, columns, functions, values, etc. A second step is to identify all the *operators* in the task which when applied to one or more objects change the state of the completion of the task. In this case, these operators are the call of the function *mean*, the call of the function *variance*, the call of the function *sort*, etc. Of course, not all operators apply to all objects. A third step is to identify the *sequence of operators* which produces a desired state (the goal) from an initial state. Such a task analysis can be performed at many levels of abstraction, from high-level goal-oriented operators to low-level perceptual or motor operators. For a task that is goal-oriented and cognitive in nature, such as solving statistical problems with an unfamiliar statistical package, an appropriate level of analysis seems to be such as found in the GOMS model - Goals, Operators, Methods, Selection rules - (Card, Moran, & Newell, 1983). It is important to point out that, contrary to the GOMS model, this study is not describing a cognitive skill since the participants are learning how to use a statistical package and are requesting advice from an advisor. For this reason, the concept of a meta-plan is introduced below to explain how users recover from situations when their known plans do not allow them to reach their goals. Meta-plans are a superset of *selection rules*, such as defined in the GOMS model. In the notation used in our examples, we have used a slightly different terminology than in the GOMS model and have used the term *action* instead of *operator* and have used the term *plan* instead of *method*.

Let's now define the main concepts for the task analysis.

1. TASK STRUCTURE: An actual or possible composition of plans which describes how a task can be performed.

2. PLAN: A plan specifies a goal to achieve, prerequisites to execute the plan, a plan decomposition, and the intended effects of executing the plan.

3. GOAL: A desired state of the world (or INTENDED EFFECT).

4. PREREQUISITES: States which must be true to accomplish a plan, and which lead to subgoals if false. However, these do not correspond to a subtask in the task structure per se. For example, "FOLLOW some-stat-package SYNTAX" does not correspond to a particular subtask (as opposed to "CALL FUNCTION MEAN ON VECTOR"), but failure to follow the statistical package syntax will lead to a subgoal of correcting the syntax error.

5. PLAN DECOMPOSITION: The allowable ordering of necessary or optional plans and actions composing a plan.

6. EFFECTS: Changes in the state of the world brought upon by the execution of the plan. One of the effects is the goal of the plan.

7. ACTION: A plan that is not decomposed any further.

8. META-PLAN: A plan to reason about goals and plans. Possible examples of such reasoning are: If there are alternative plans to accomplish a goal, select the least expensive one. If the known plans to accomplish a task fail, learn new plans by requesting help from an advisor or by reading a manual.

The main determinant of the task structure is the actual procedures allowed by the statistical package used in the study. It is a command-oriented, interactive, commercially available, and general package for data analysis. Two raters, experienced with the statistical package, derived a task structure for each of the problems given to the participants. The instructions to the raters were to derive a task structure for a given problem which would include all alternative procedures and optional steps. There was very high initial agreement in the task structures derived by the two raters and almost all the initial differences were either missing alternative procedures or missing optional steps. The differences were all resolved through discussion. This is in itself an expected, but necessary, result: the concept of a task structure has validity, at least under the conditions set in this study.

An excerpt from a partial task structure to compute the mean in our study is presented in Figure 1-2 and in Appendix II with inserted dialogue segments. The prerequisites, effects, and constraints have been omitted from the excerpts to reduce the length of the examples. The procedure followed in segmenting user-advisor dialogues and in associating these segments to the task structure is described in the next section.

2.2 Steps in Deriving Dialogue Structure from Task Structure

A subdialogue is defined as a sequence, possibly interrupted, of user's and advisor's utterances which accomplishes one of the goals in the task structure or one of the communicative goals to be described below. Subdialogues are usually initiated by the user, followed by an utterance from the advisor. The coding decisions used to derive a dialogue structure from the task structure for each user-advisor dialogue are now described.

- If the user or advisor initiated a subdialogue which is the **statement of a plan or of a goal**, the subdialogue is "inserted" in the task structure at the location of the plan described.

- If the user or advisor initiated a subdialogue which is the **statement of a subplan** within the decomposition of its parent plan, the subdialogue is "inserted" in the appropriate daughter plan of the parent plan.

- If the user or advisor initiated a subdialogue which is the **statement of a subplan arising from the violation of a prerequisite** of the parent plan, then the subdialogue is "inserted" in a daughter plan of the parent plan.

Clarification subdialogues arise when the participants cannot achieve one of their plans regarding the use of the statistical package. For example, in this study, when the user is unable to compute the mean of selected values, she must ask help from the advisor aloud or by typing, and she is not allowed to consult manuals. This meta-plan, ASK-ADVISOR-HELP, itself has prerequisites, one of them being that the linguistic communication be successful. This leads to the linguistic clarification subdialogues when there are ambiguities in the message and they need to be resolved by requesting disambiguating information from the advisor. Another consequence of the meta-plan ASK-ADVISOR-HELP is the acknowledgement subdialogues whereby participants express that the communication is successful.

The other elements of the coding scheme are:

- The clarification subdialogues are subordinated to the dialogue mentioning the clarified concept (e.g., goal, plan, term).

- The acknowledgement subdialogues are subordinated to the subdialogue mentioning the acknowledged concept.

- The linguistic clarification subdialogues are subordinated to the subdialogue containing the utterance that is clarified.

Greater detail about the task structure notation, the derivation of the task structure, the segmentation of the user-advisor dialogues, and the derivation of the dialogue structures can be found in Guindon, Brunner, and Conner (1987).

3. A Study of User-Advisor Dialogues in Two Communicative Contexts: Spoken Face-To-Face and Typed in a Wizard-Of-Oz Setting

Participants had to use an unfamiliar statistical package to solve simple descriptive statistics problems. All participants had basic knowledge of statistics. There were two main restrictions imposed on the strategies employed to solve the problems: 1) the participants had to ask help from the advisor (no documentation available); and 2) all requests for help had to be said aloud in the spoken face-to-face condition or had to be typed in a help window on the screen in the typed Wizard-of-Oz condition.

3.1 Method

3.1.1 Subjects

Three and five college-educated subjects participated in, respectively, the spoken face-to-face condition and the typed Wizard-of-Oz condition. The five subjects in the typed condition were selected randomly from 35 subjects who previously had participated in a larger study of grammatical and ungrammatical structures of users' utterances (see Guindon, Shuldberg, & Conner, 1987a, 1987b).

All subjects had basic statistical knowledge and each solved up to eleven problems. None of the subjects had previously used the statistical package in the study but each of them had some previous experience with a statistical package. These are small numbers of subjects. However, the extensive time needed to derive a dialogue structure for each user-advisor dialogue and the need to have two judges each derive a dialogue structure for each user-advisor dialogue force such research to be on a small scale. This is not unlike verbal report studies where the number of subjects typically runs from three to five.

3.1.2 Material

Eleven simple descriptive statistics problems were constructed. The data were various measurements (e.g., price, repair record, mileage per gallon) performed on a large set of cars. The first problem was to list the names of the variables. Problems 2 to 8 were to compute the average, the variance, and the standard-deviation on selected variables and values of these variables. Problem 9 was to compute the interquartile range on one of the measurements. Problems 10 and 11 were to identify cars with a certain attribute (e.g., the car with the best repair record).

3.1.3 Procedure

The subjects were told that the goal of the study was to investigate how a novice user of a statistical package would make use of an advisor in trying to learn to use the statistical package to solve statistical problems. The subjects proceeded at their own pace and tried to solve as many problems as they could within one hour. The subjects were aware that they and their monitor's screen were videotaped. The subjects in the spoken face-to-face condition solved more problems than the subjects in the typed condition, replicating similar findings by Chapanis, Ochsman, Parrish, and Weeks (1972) and Chapanis, Parrish, Ochsman, and Weeks (1977). This performance difference is intrinsic to comparisons between typed and spoken modalities but is not believed to be directly relevant to the results of this study. This study is concerned about the structure of the user-advisor dialogues to perform a task and not about the users' performance on the task as measured by number of problems solved.

In the spoken face-to-face condition, the advisor was in the same room as the subject and sitting to her right. All utterances were recorded and transcripts were generated.

In the Wizard-of-Oz condition, the upper window on the subject's monitor was used to perform operations with the statistical package. The lower window was used to type utterances to the advisor and receive help from the advisor. The subjects were instructed to ask help in English from what they believed was a computerized advisor by typing utterances in the help window. The subjects were told that the advisor was capable of understanding English and that they should ask help in English, in the manner they felt most comfortable with. The subjects' and advisor's utterances were sent to each other's monitor and all utterances were recorded and time-stamped automatically to files. A questionnaire was given to the participants to find out whether they believed they were conversing to a computer system or to a human. None of those 5 participants had realized they were conversing with a human.

3.1.4 Transcription and Coding of the Dialogues

In the spoken face-to-face dialogues, the guidelines by Thompson (1980) and Trawick (1983) were followed in segmenting the dialogues into sentences or utterances. The spoken face-to-face dialogues contained between 255 and 450 utterances. This difference represents mainly the extent to which the participant needed help to learn how to use the statistical package. About 57% of the utterances were from the user and the rest from the advisor. The average users' utterance length was seven words.

In the typed Wizard-of-Oz dialogues, we used periods or the end of a message to segment the dialogues into sentences. The average users' sentence length was nine words and the average advisor's sentence length was sixteen words. The dialogues were composed of an average of about 44 utterances, 36% from the users. An excerpt from a typed Wizard-of-Oz dialogue is given in Appendix I.

The following is a summary of Section 2.2. The first step was to perform a task analysis. The coders then subdivided each of the user-advisor dialogues into subdialogues which appeared to be the execution of a plan or prerequisite of a plan in the task structure. In addition to segmenting the dialogue into subdialogues, the hierarchical relations between subdialogues were determined by "inserting" the subdialogues into their appropriate location in the task structure. The resulting dialogue structure was hierarchical though subdialogues could be discontinuous in time, that is, subdialogues could be temporarily left out and returned to later.

The interrater reliability estimate on the coding of the dialogues and the generation of the dialogue structures was calculated for each user-advisor dialogue this way: 1) the number of subdialogues produced by rater 1 was added to the number of subdialogues produced by rater 2; 2) the number of differences between raters 1 and 2 was counted (i.e., differences in subdialogue boundaries and labelling) and multipled by two; and 3) the value obtained in step 2 was divided by the value obtained in step 1. From this proportion measuring disagreement, the percentage of agreement was calculated. The obtained interrater reliability was between 72% and 100% over the user-advisor dialogues. The two judges then resolved their differences and agreed on a dialogue structure. The fact that interrater reliability in identifying dialogue structures can be as low as 72% suggests that deriving dialogue structures can be computationally quite difficult, as it relies on recognizing users' goals and transition in these goals and mapping them on a task structure.

3.2 Results

We performed a task analysis and derived a task structure. We then used the task structure to segment and organize the dialogues into subdialogues, deriving a dialogue structure. We know from previous psychological research and linguistic studies (see Sections 1.4 and 1.5) how the antecedents of pronominal and non-pronominal noun phrases should be distributed in dialogues relative to subdialogue boundaries and the hierarchical structure of the discourse. Pronominal anaphors are used to indicate topic continuity (see Givon, 1983; Grosz, Joshi, & Weinstein, 1983), and as a consequence, their antecedents should be mainly discourse entities that are in focus. In other words, their antecedents should be mainly located in the current subdialogue, in the parent subdialogue, and in the top-level subdialogue. Non-pronominal noun phrases are partly used to indicate change of topics or to introduce new topics. Moreover, non-pronominal anaphors contain more semantic information than pronominal anaphors to describe their antecedents. As a consequence, the distribution of the antecedents of non-pronominal anaphors should be more widespread in the dialogue than the distribution of the antecedents of pronominal anaphors.

However, as was pointed out by Fox (1984) such distributions may vary as a function of the genre of the discourse. Following this logic, we hypothesize that the distributions of antecedents of anaphors may vary across communicative contexts. The observed antecedent distributions will be described in terms of the relative position between the sub-dialogue in which an anaphor is located and the subdialogue in which its antecedent is located, as shown in Figure 3-1. The subdialogues were indexed as follows. The current subdialogue, labelled N, is the location of the anaphor to be resolved. The node N-1 immediately dominates N, the node N-2 dominates N-1, and so on. The nodes subordinate to each of the nodes dominating N are indexed beginning with the left-most node and proceeding rightward. Thus, if N-1 is the first node dominating N, the left-most node subordinate to N-1 will be N-1/L1 and each sibling to the right will be N-1/L2, N-1/L3, etc. The nodes subordinate to this level are indexed again beginning left-most and proceeding rightward. For example, the children of node N-1/L1 are, from left to right, N-1/((L1)1), N-1/((L1)2), N-1/((L1)3), and so on. An example of a configuration at a particular node N in the dialogue is shown in Figure 3-1. In this example, the node N-3 is the root, but this is not always the case.

Other analyses were performed on the dialogues but are not reported here. For further analyses and more detail, consult Guindon, Brunner, and Conner (1987) and Guindon, Shuldberg, and Conner (1987a, 1987b).

3.2.1 Spoken Face-To-Face Dialogues

In Table 3-1, the location N-1 indicates the parent subdialogue, **b** the first sentence of the parent subdialogue, **e** the last sentence, and **m** the 1 to 8 intermediate sentences pooled together. The column **I-1** includes all siblings L1, L2, (L1)1, (L2)2, etc., under N-1. N-2, N-3, and N-4 include their corresponding node and their children nodes. Root stands for important concepts introduced at the beginning of the session, mostly the statistical package.

First, 37% of the anaphoric noun phrases were pronominal and 63% were non-pronominal. In Table 3-1, N represents the current sub-dialogue, and **s** the current sentence, **s-1** the sentence preceding **s**, **s-2**

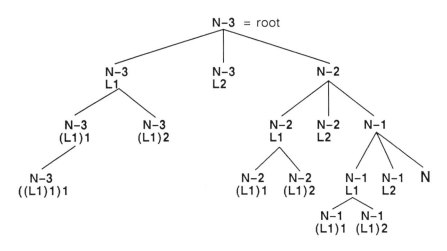

Figure 3-1: Indexing of the subdialogues

Table 3-1: Percentage of antecedents per noun phrase type
in spoken subdialogues

	Location of Antecedents												
	N					N-1				N-2	N-3	N-4	Root	Total
				i>3										
	s	s-1	s-2	s-3	s-i	b	m	e	l-1					
Pron. NP	30	22	11	6	1	7	6	7	2	2	0	0	6	100
Non-Pron. NP	22	19	6	3	2	11	9	12	6	6	0	2	2	100

the sentence preceding **s-1**, and so on. As can be seen in Table 3-1, the frequency of antecedents in the current subdialogue (N) decreases monotonically (e.g., 30, 22, 11, 6, 1) as the distance in number of intervening sentences increases for both types of noun phrases. Therefore, recency determines an order of search for an antecedent in the current subdialogue.

In the parent subdialogue (N-1), the antecedents of anaphors in sub-dialogue N are found most frequently in the first sentence (b) and in last sentence (e) of the subdialogues, and least frequently in all the 1 to 8 intermediate sentences cumulatively pooled together (m), for both types of anaphors. The first and last sentence in paragraphs have been shown, in memory tests, to frequently introduce the most important concepts, in other words, to describe the main elements of the macrostructure of the paragraphs (Guindon & Kintsch, 1984). Moreover, the last sentence may play the role of setting the stage for a new subtopic to be elaborated in the next subdialogue. A related observation is that the pronoun *it* was used throughout the dialogue to refer to the statistical package (i.e., in root) even though the statistical package had not been mentioned directly for many sentences, replicating the findings of Grosz (1977).

These findings are consistent with the expected distribution of antecedents based on recency and on topicality, as expressed in the hierarchical structure of the dialogues. The criteria of recency and topicality are based on psychological findings from text comprehension models and studies (Kintsch & van Dijk, 1978). A parent subdialogue describes information that is topically related and important to the information described in a subordinate subdialogue. We found that this information, as antecedent to an anaphor, was likely to be in the first or last sentence of the parent subdialogue. Moreover, the antecedent *statistical package* which was located in the root subdialogue of the dialogue structure was referred to mainly with the pronoun *it* throughout the dialogue. In other words, it was one of the most important concepts mentioned in the dialogue and because of its importance always stayed in the user's and advisor's working memory (Kintsch & van Dijk, 1978; Guindon, 1985). Recency plays a role mainly in the current subdialogue by the monotonic decrease of occurrence of antecedents given the recency of the sentences in subdialogue N. Topicality plays a role mainly by the relatively large frequency of occurrence of antecedents in the first and last sentence in the parent subdialogue and by the occurrence of antecedents in the root subdialogue. Topicality is determined by the goal-subgoal relationships in the task structure.

As an aside, these findings corroborate an hypothesis of Fox (1987). She observed that a model of conversations must take into account that their production and comprehension happen in real time. Naturally occurring conversations often contain segments that are retroactively reinterpreted, as new information indicates that their initial interpretation was incorrect. Such a phenomenon requires that conversants can have easy access, in their memory, to previous utterances or segments, for longer than one or two sentences and even across subdialogue boundaries. The finding that antecedents in the current subdialogue are likely to refer to important discourse entities in the parent subdialogue, in the first and last sentence, and in the root subdialogue suggests that these discourse entities are more accessible in conversants' memory than other entities across subdialogue boundaries. This would enable easy retroactive interpretation of some of the utterances in the discourse.

Returning to the main hypotheses, Table 3-2 gives the percentages of antecedents located in the current subdialogue (N), in the other subdialogues pooled together (N-1/4), and in the root. A statistical analysis on Table 3-2 reveals a significant chi-square, $\chi(2) = 28.5$, $p < .05$. The following a priori specific comparisons were tested using Ryan's procedure (1960). Antecedents of pronominal noun phrases should be found mainly in the subdialogue containing the anaphor, that is, N, while the antecedents of non-pronominal noun phrases should be more widespread in the dialogue, that is, they should occur more evenly in N and N-1/4. This is supported by a significant chi-square, $\chi(1) = 19.89 > 4.54$, $p < .05$. Moreover, the most important concept, the statistical package, even if introduced only at the beginning of the dialogue, should be referred to more frequently with pronominal noun phrases than non-pronominal noun phrases compared to other concepts in subdialogues N and N-1/4 pooled together. This is supported by a significant chi-square, $\chi(1) = 6.7 > 4.54$, $p < .05$.

To summarize, the distributions of antecedents of pronominal and non-pronominal noun phrases follow an expected pattern which is consistent with the dialogue structure derived on the basis of task structure. This supports the hypothesis that task structure can be used to model dialogue structure. These distributions are also consistent with psychological findings on the use of working memory during discourse

Table 3-2:   Percentage of antecedents per noun phrase type in current vs. other spoken subdialogues

	Location of Antecedents		
	N	N-1/4	Root
Pronominal Noun Phrase	70	24	6
Non-Pronominal Noun Phrase	52	46	2

comprehension, based on recency and topicality. These data are also consistent with a focusing theory of anaphora resolution, as described in computational linguistics. Moreover, these data provide an order of search for antecedents of pronominal anaphors: first, in the current subdialogue in order of recency, second, in the parent subdialogue, in the first and last sentence, and third, in the other sentences.

3.2.2 Typed Wizard-Of-Oz Dialogues

Table 3-3:   Percentage of antecedents per noun phrase type in typed subdialogues

	Location of Antecedents													
	N		i>3			N-1				N-2	N-3	N-4	Root	Total
	s	s-1	s-2	s-3	s-i	b	m	e	l-1					
Pron NP	31	39	3	0	0	0	2	0	0	0	0	0	25	100
Non-Pron NP	34	26	3	1	0	3	6	9	4	2	1	0	11	100

First, fewer noun phrases were pronominal, 20%, than non-pronominal, 80%. As can be seen in Tables 3-3 and 3-4, the antecedents of pronominal noun phrases occur almost exclusively in the current sub-dialogue (73%), except for the root (25%). Moreover, contrary to the spoken face-to-face dialogues, the antecedents of pronominal and non-pronominal noun phrases, if in the parent subdialogue, do not tend to be located in the first or last sentences. Topicality, as expressed in the dialogue structure based on task structure, does not seem to play as important of a role in the typed dialogues than in the spoken face-to-face dialogues.

Table 3-4: Percentage of antecedents per noun phrase type in current vs. other typed subdialogues

	Location of Antecedents		
	N	N-1/4	Root
Pronominal Noun Phrase	73	2	25
Non-Pronominal Noun Phrase	64	25	11

A statistical analysis on Table 3-4 reveals a significant chi-square, $\chi(2) = 11.8$, $p < .05$. The following a priori specific comparisons were tested using Ryan's procedure (1960). Antecedents of pronominal noun phrases should be found mainly in the subdialogue containing the anaphor (N) while the antecedents of non-pronominal noun phrases should be more widespread in N and N-1/4. This is supported by a significant chi-square, $\chi(1) = 6.2 > 4.54$, $p < .05$. The hypothesis that the most important concepts, that is, in root, should be referred to more fre-quently with pronominal noun phrases than non-pronominal noun phrases compared to the other concepts in N and N-1/4, is not sig-nificant, $\chi(1) = 3.82 < 4.54$. Again, topicality does not seem to play as important of a role in determining antecedent distribution in the typed dialogues than in the spoken face-to-face dialogues.

3.2.3 Differences in Antecedent Distributions Between the Types of Dialogues

So far, the analyses were applied to the antecedent distributions for different noun phrases separately in each communicative context. To look at the relationships between the three independent variables, a three-way chi-square analysis was performed. In a three-way chi-square, four null hypotheses are tested. Three of the null hypotheses state that there is no association between the independent variables taken two at a time. The fourth null hypothesis states that the relationship between any two independent variables is the same for the different levels of the third independent variable.

The three two-way chi-square analyses are significant. The first chi-square tests the association between the types of dialogues (typed or spoken) and the types of noun phrases. The proportion of pronominal anaphoric noun phrases in the typed subdialogues is significantly less than in the spoken dialogues, $\chi(1) = 14.6$, $p < .05$. The second chi-square tests the association between types of dialogues and location of antecedents, which is significant $\chi(2) = 30.1$, $p < .05$. Two specific a priori comparisons are tested. The first one compares the antecedent distribution in subdialogues N and N-1/4 in the different types of dialogues. Antecedents of anaphoric noun phrases tend to be more localized in the current subdialogue in the typed dialogues than in the spoken dialogues, $\chi(1) = 10.4 > 4.54$, $p < .05$. The second one compares the antecedent distribution in the root subdialogue to the other subdialogues pooled together. The proportion of noun phrases referring to concepts in the root subdialogue (i.e., the statistical package) is greater in the typed than in the spoken dialogues.

These three results in the typed user-advisor dialogues - the infrequent occurrence of pronominal anaphors, the locality of the antecedents in the current subdialogue, and the frequent explicit reference to the statistical package - show that users do not rely extensively on context for the production and interpretation of their utterances and referring expressions. In the typed Wizard-of-Oz dialogues, users believe they are talking to a computerized advisor. We hypothesize that users believe there is poor shared context between themselves and the advisor. This belief would be based on the lack of shared physical context, that is, the advisor is not sitting nearby as in the spoken face-to-face dialogues. In the spoken face-to-face dialogues, users are able to rely on gestures or gazes to refer to the statistical package (e.g., by just pointing to or looking at the monitor) because users and advisors share a common physical context. In the typed dialogues, they have to refer explicitly to the statistical package. The belief in poor shared context could also be due to the lack of a good model of what is a "computerized advisor". Requesting on-line help to an advisory system is a first time experience for these users. The users might not know whether the advisor is capable of keeping track of the previous utterances in the dialogue. Therefore, the users prefer non-pronominal noun phrases, which are very descriptive, to pronominal phrases. Moreover, the cost of repairing misunderstandings can be very large: typing additional utterances, waiting for the advisor's reply, and entering incorrect commands to the statistical package. The users might subjectively estimate that the cost of such misunderstandings outweighs the cost of using longer-to-type non-pronominal noun phrases. Another likely cause for the little reliance on context is the slow interaction between users and advisor. The interaction between users and advisor is slow because 1) utterances need to be typed, and 2) the users tend to perform operations with the statistical package immediately after a request for help as opposed to ask for more information as in the spoken dialogues. The mere act of requesting help by typing could effect context shifts. In fact, antecedents of anaphors are almost exclusively found in the current subdialogue, especially for pronominal anaphors, as one would expect if typed user-advisor dialogues resemble independent queries more than cohesive discourse.

A few additional analyses reinforce the interpretation of these findings. Figure 3-2 is used to describe one of these analyses. The first analysis supports the interpretation that dialogues in the typed Wizard-of-Oz setting resemble independent queries more than cohesive discourse. Figure 3-2 shows a part of the task structure with the consecutive subdialogues (e.g., shown as **Sub1** and **Sub 2**) inserted in their appropriate location in the task structure, for the beginning of a spoken dialogue and a typed dialogue. Nodes in the task structure without a subdialogue are subtasks which do not have any corresponding subdialogue in the user-advisor dialogue. A distance value was assigned to each link in the task structure, 1 at the top-level, .5 at the next level, .25 at the next, and so on. The decreasing of the distance values captures the fact that the tree represents the task structure at decreasing levels of abstraction. Using the task structure in Appendix II as an example, there is intuitively a larger semantic distance between Task 2.1 (Obtain Data Structure Index) and Task 2.2 (Create Unsorted Vector) than between Task 2.1.1.1 (Enter File Specification) and Task 2.1.1.2 (Press "Enter"). The distance in the task structure between consecutive subdialogues in the spoken and typed conditions are calculated. The average distance between consecutive subdialogues in all the spoken face-to-face condition is .35, and in all the typed Wizard-of-Oz is .71. The subdialogues in the typed dialogues are less clustered with each other and they represent more distant tasks in the task structure than in the spoken dialogues. To summarize, the dialogues in the typed Wizard-of-Oz condition resemble a sequence of independent queries more than a cohesive discourse.

Part of the derived dialogue structure for a spoken dialogue

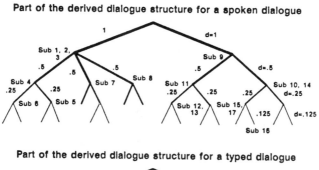

Part of the derived dialogue structure for a typed dialogue

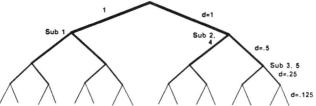

Figure 3-2:   Illustration of the distance between subdialogues in the task structure in the spoken and typed dialogues

A grammatical analysis of the typed user-advisor dialogues in the Wizard-of Oz condition also supports the interpretation that users rely little on context in phrasing their utterances. There is a very high percentage of utterances with prepositional phrases, and about 70% of them in complex nominals (see Guindon, Shuldberg, & Conner, 1987a, 1987b, for a detailed report of this analysis). Users prefer the more descriptive, though longer to type, complex nominals (e.g., *the file with the data about cars*) to the more cryptic but shorter pronominal noun phrases (e.g., *it*), even though there is strong evidence that users are producing language under real-time production constraints. In other words, users in the typed Wizard-of-Oz dialogues produce very precise descriptions of the objects they are referring to.

These last two analyses reinforce the interpretation given to other findings: users in the typed dialogues do not rely extensively on discourse context in generating anaphors. As a consequence, few pronouns are used and most antecedents are located in the current subdialogue. Users do not rely extensively on discourse context possibly because they believe there is poor shared context between user and advisor or because the typed user-advisor dialogues are more like independent queries than cohesive discourse due to the slowness of the interaction.

The three-way chi-square, testing the interaction effect, is not significant, $\chi(2) = 2.82$, $p > .05$. The associations between variables revealed by the significant two-way chi-squares do not vary as a function of the levels of the other variable.

4. Design Implications for Natural Language Front-Ends to User-Advising Systems

Most studies of user advising and tutoring dialogues have concentrated on the problem of identifying, representing, and processing the knowledge necessary for recognizing users' goals and correcting users' misconceptions (e.g., Carberry, 1983, 1984; Woolf & McDonald, 1984; Cohen, 1984). Very few studies have actually collected comprehensive user-advisor dialogues to guide the design of natural language interfaces to advisory systems, except for studies such as Grosz (1977) and

Cohen (1984).   Thompson (1980) collected information retrieval dialogues, as opposed to user-advisor dialogues, and analyzed them at the sentence level only. In Grosz' (1977) study, user-advisor dialogues were either spoken face-to-face or the user would say aloud her utterances which would then be typed by another person to what the user believed was a computerized advisor. Her study did not address the case where the user herself is typing the help-seeking utterances. Cohen (1984) reported analyses of user-advisor dialogues by telephone or typed with "linked" CRTs, where the subjects knew their conversants to be another person. He did not include a case where the users believed they were conversing with a computer. While Cohen's analyses of the dialogues concentrated on the need to recognize users' intent in identifying referents of anaphors, they did not emphasize the structure of the task the users were attempting to perform. Pollack (1985) collected actual user-advisor dialogues between two humans, though occurring through electronic mail. To summarize, while many studies have looked at user-advisor dialogues, none of them have looked at typed user-advisor dialogues in a situation that simulates an interaction with an advisory system - an interaction between a user and a software system providing on-line help. Moreover, their emphasis was often at the sentence level rather than at the dialogue structure level.

In this study, we compared user-advisor dialogues in their most frequent form, spoken face-to-face, to a form that will exist in dialogues between users and on-line advisory systems, typed. This comparison is for the purpose of gathering data to guide the design of natural language front-ends to advisory systems. We have found that typed dialogues to advisory systems resemble a sequence of independent queries more than a cohesive discourse. Users avoid pronominal noun phrases. Instead, users describe carefully what they refer to by using complex nominals. In typed user-advisor dialogues, most antecedents of pronominal noun phrases are found in the current subdialogue, more precisely, in the sentence containing the anaphor or in the previous sentence. Even the distribution of antecedents of non-pronominal noun phrases is more localized in the current subdialogue for the typed dialogues than for the spoken face-to-face dialogues. Moreover, the content of users' requests for help tend to be more independent of each other than in the spoken face-to-face dialogues.   The average distance in the task structure between consecutive subdialogues in the typed dialogues is greater than in the spoken face-to-face dialogues. Finally, topicality, as expressed in the hierarchical dialogue structure, does not seem to play as important of a role in the typed dialogues than in the spoken dialogues. Antecedents of anaphors, especially pronominal anaphors, did not tend to be located in the first and last sentence of the parent subdialogue, contrary to what was observed in the spoken dialogues.

Users rely little on linguistic context in phrasing their utterances in the typed dialogues. This is shown by the infrequent occurrence of pronouns and the very frequent occurrence of complex nominals, by the great locality of the antecedents in the current subdialogue, by the frequent explicit reference to the statistical package, and by the large task distance between subdialogues in the task structure. These findings suggest that users believed the advisor could not build or use an adequate model of dialogue context in interpreting users' utterances in the typed Wizard-of-Oz dialogues. This belief might have arisen from the lack of shared physical context or poor model of the knowledge of the advisor. As a consequence, the users did not rely on context in phrasing their utterances. Another possible cause for the little reliance on context is that the dialogues were not highly interactive because of the long time it took to type in utterances. Each new request for help would effectively produce a context shift, discouraging the use of pronominal noun phrases. An unfortunate consequence is that users cannot take advantage of faster-to-type pronouns in a situation where real-time production constraints are already high, that is, requesting help by typing utterances (see Guindon, Shuldberg, & Conner, 1987a, 1987b, for evidence of real-time production constraints). A fortunate consequence is that the low frequency of pronouns and the extreme locality of their antecedents in the typed dialogues render unnecessary the need to develop a complicated anaphora resolution mechanism based on focusing. A simple search for antecedents of pronominal noun phrases in order of recency will locate most antecedents as being within the current or previous utterance in typed user-advisor dialogues. As far as the non-pronominal noun phrases are concerned, since a great percentage of them were complex nominals providing very precise descriptions of their referents, the need for a focusing mechanism for anaphora resolution is also diminished. Consequently, providing a model of the dialogue structure based on the task structure in natural language front-ends to advisory systems does not seem required.

On the other hand, users phrase their utterances taking into account dialogue structure in spoken face-to-face dialogues, in other words, when users believe that there is good shared context between users and advisors or when the dialogue can be highly interactive. In the spoken dialogues the distributions of noun phrases and of antecedents of anaphors are sensitive to subdialogue boundaries established on the basis of task structure. This appears to be due to a good shared context between user and advisor, due to shared physical space, and to the high level of interaction in the spoken dialogues. These encourage the use of pronominal noun phrases to indicate topic continuity. These also encourage the use of non-pronominal noun phrases to indicate topic shifts. However, since the current technological advances do not yet allow speech input to freely communicate with advisory systems, language understanding systems and anaphora resolution mechanism cannot yet take full advantage of the task structure as model of the dialogue structure.

This study demonstrates that important characteristics of user dialogues are determined by the context in which the interaction takes place. In particular, communicative context parameters such as modality, interaction level, and degree of shared context affect the structure of user-advisor dialogues and the distributions of antecedents of pronominal and non-pronominal noun phrases. This finding is also consistent with another study of typed user-advisor dialogues. Guindon, Shuldberg, and Conner (1987a, 1987b) show that in typed user-advisor dialogues, users are operating under real-time production constraints which induce users to generate syntactically very simple language. Real-time production constraints are associated with language produced to perform another primary task, such as to solve a problem, and where little time is available to plan the utterances. Natural language interfaces to different applications should be designed to take into account and capitalize on the constraints naturally imposed on users' language by the communicative context.

Acknowledgements

We gratefully acknowledge the help of Hans Brunner for helping with the collection and analysis of the data, Sherry Kalin from Control Data Corporation for helping with the collection of data, and Paul Sladky for helping with the analysis of the data. Also, many thanks to Joyce Conner for collecting and analyzing data and for reviewing and editing this chapter. Jeff Conklin, Patrick Lincoln, Nancy Pennington, and Elaine Rich have provided many useful comments on an earlier version of this chapter.

References

Carberry, S. (1983). Tracking user goals in an information-seeking environment. *Proceedings of the American Association for Artificial Intelligence Conference* (pp. 59-63). Washington, D. C.

Carberry, S. (1984). Understanding pragmatically ill-formed input. *Proceedings of the International Conference on Computational Linguistics* (pp. 200-206). Stanford, California.

Card, S. K., Moran, T. P., & Newell, A. (1983). *The psychology of human-computer interaction.* Hillsdale, New Jersey: Lawrence Erlbaum Associates.

Chapanis, A., Ochsman, R. B., Parrish, R. N., & Weeks, G. D. (1972). Studies in interactive communication: I. The effects of four communication modes on the behavior of teams during cooperative problem-solving. *Human Factors, 14,* 487-509.

Chapanis, A., Parrish, R. N., Ochsman, R. B., & Weeks, G. D. (1977). Studies in interactive communication: II. The effects of four communication modes on the behavior of teams during cooperative problem-solving. *Human Factors, 19,* 101-126.

Cohen, P. R. (1984). The pragmatics of referring and the modality of communication. *Computational Linguistics, 10*(2), 97-125.

Colby, B. (1972). *A partial grammar of Eskimo folktales* (Working Paper). Irvine: School of Social Sciences, University of California.

Crowder, R. G. (1976). *Principles of learning and memory.* Hillsdale, New Jersey: Lawrence Erlbaum Associates.

Fox, B. A. (1984). *Discourse structure and anaphora in written and conversational English.* Doctoral dissertation, University of California, Los Angeles.

Fox, B. (1987). Interactional reconstruction in real-time language processing. *Cognitive Science, 11,* 365-387.

Givon, T. (Ed.). (1983). *Topic continuity in discourse*. Amsterdam: John Benjamins.

Grosz, B. J. (1977). *The representation and use of focus in dialogue understanding* (Tech. Rep. 151). Artificial Intelligence Center, SRI International.

Grosz, B. J., & Sidner, C. L. (1985). Discourse structure and the proper treatment of interruptions. *Proceedings of IJCAI 85* (pp. 832-840). Los Angeles: IJCAI.

Grosz, B. J., Joshi, A. K., & Weinstein, S. (1983). Providing a unified account of definite noun phrases in discourse. *Proceedings of the 21st Annual Meeting of the Association for Computational Linguistics*. Association for Computational Linguistics.

Guindon, R. (1985). Anaphora resolution: Short-term memory and focusing. *23rd Annual Meeting of the Association for Computational Linguistics* (pp. 218-227). University of Chicago, Association for Computational Linguistics.

Guindon, R., & Kintsch, W. (1984). Priming macropropositions: Evidence for the primacy of macropropositions in memory for text. *Journal of Verbal Learning and Verbal Behavior, 23*, 508-518.

Guindon, R., Brunner, H., & Conner, J. (1987). *Indicators of goal transitions in user-advisor dialogues* (Tech. Rep.). Austin, Texas: Microelectronics and Computer Technology Corporation.

Guindon, R., Shuldberg, H. K., & Conner, J. (1987a). Grammatical and ungrammatical structures in user-adviser dialogues: Evidence for the sufficiency of restricted languages in natural language interfaces to advisory systems. *Proceedings of the 25th Annual Meeting of the Association for Computational Linguistics* (pp. 41-44). Standford University, CA: ACL.

Guindon, R., Shuldberg, H. K., & Conner, J. (1987b). *Empirical evidence for the sufficiency of very restricted subsets of English for interfaces to advisory systems* (Tech. Rep.). Austin, Texas: Microelectronics and Computer Technology Corporation.

Guindon, R., Sladky, P., Brunner, H., & Conner, J. (1986). The structure of user-adviser dialogues: Is there method in their madness? *Proceedings of the 24th Conference of the Association for Computational Linguistics*. New York, New York: Columbia University.

Kintsch, W., & van Dijk, T. A. (1978). Toward a model of text comprehension and production. *Psychological Review, 85*, 363-394.

Lakoff, G. (1972). Structural complexity in fairy tales. *The Study of Man, 1*, 128-50.

Mandler, J. M., & Johnson, N. S. (1980). On throwing out the baby with the bathwater: A reply to Black and Wilensky's evaluation of story grammar. *Cognitive Science, 4*, 305-312.

Miller, G. A. (1956). The magical number seven, plus or minus two:

Some limits on our capacity for processing information. *Psychological Review, 63*, 81-97.

Pollack, M. E. (1985). Information sought and information provided: An empirical study of user/expert dialogues. In Lorraine Borman & Bill Curtis (Eds.), *CHI '85 Proceedings* (pp. 155-159). San Francisco, California.

Propp, V. (1968). *Morphology of the folktale.* Austin: University of Texas Press.

Reichman, R. (1981). *Plain speaking: A theory and grammar of spontaneous discourse* (Tech. Rep. 4681). Cambridge, Mass.: Bolt, Beranek, and Newman, Inc.

Rumelhart, D. E. (1975). Notes on a schema for stories. In D. G. Bobrow & A. M. Collins (Eds.), *Representation and understanding: Studies in cognitive science.* New York: Academic Press.

Ryan, T. A. (1960). Significance tests for multiple comparison of proportions, variances, and other statistics. *Psychological Bulletin, 57*, 318-328.

Sanford, A. J., & Garrod, S. C. (1981). *Understanding written language.* New York: Wiley.

Sidner, C. L. (1983). Focusing in the comprehension of definite anaphora. In M. Brady & R. Berwick (Eds.), *Computational models of discourse.* Cambridge, Mass.: MIT.

Simon, H. A. (1974). How big is a chunk? *Science, 183*, 482-488.

Thompson, B. H. (1980). Linguistic analysis of natural language communication with computers. *Proceedings of the 8th International Conference on Computational Linguistics* (pp. 190-201). Tokyo: COLING 80.

Thorndyke, P. W. (1977). Cognitive structures in comprehension and memory of narrative discourse. *Cognitive Psychology, 9*, 77-110.

Trawick, D. J. (1983). *Robust sentence analysis and habitability.* Doctoral dissertation, California Institute of Technology, Pasadena.

van Dijk, T. A., & Kintsch, W. (1983). *Strategies of discourse comprehension.* Academic Press.

Woolf, B., & McDonald, D. D. (1984). Building a computer tutor: Design Issues. *IEEE Computer,* Vol. *Sept 84.*

Appendix I: Excerpt From a Typed Dialogue

U: how to get the list of autos

A: The contents of any file, vector, or variable can be listed simply by typing the name of the entity. Auto names are stored in auto.rowlab. Auto features are stored in auto.collab.

U: how to get the average price

A: Computing the average price involves two steps. First, you must create a vector, or copy, of the prices out of auto.stats. Then, you compute the mean of this vector with the "mean" function of the statistical system.

U: how get mean

A: The statistical system's function for computing the mean is called "mean" with the format: variablename_mean(vector)

U: which column has the price

A: The columns for the different auto features can be determined from auto.collab. The order of the features (from left to right) listed in that file corresponds to the left-to-right order of the columns in auto.stats.

U: how create vector

A: The command form for creating vectors is: vectorname_auto.stats[,n] where "n" is the number of the column in auto.stats containing the values that you desire.

U: what is vector

A: A vector is a subset of values form the original body of auto statistics. It can be thought of as a simple list of numbers.

Appendix II: Part of a Task Structure with Inserted Subdialogues

TASK STRUCTURE

- Plan:1 - List Data Description File (DDF)

U: how to get the list of autos
A: The contents of any file, vector, or variable can be listed simply by typing the name of the entity. Auto names are stored in auto.rowlab. Auto features are stored in auto.collab.

    *   Plan:1.1 - Enter File Specification

        - Action:1.1.1 - Type Filename Root
        - Action:1.1.2 - Type Period
        - Action:1.1.3 - Type Filename Extension

    *   Action:1.2 - Press "ENTER"

- Plan:2 - Compute Mean Price; All Cars

U: how to get the average price
A: Computing the average price involves two steps. First, you must create a vector, or copy, of the prices out of auto.stats. Then, you compute the mean of this vector with the "mean" function of the statistical system.

    *   Plan:2.1 - Obtain Data Structure Index (DSI)

        - Plan:2.1.1 - List Data Description File (DDF)
          *   Plan:2.1.1.1 Enter File Specification
            - Action:2.1.1.1.1 - Type Filename Root
            - Action:2.1.1.1.2 - Type Period
            - Action:2.1.1.1.3 - Type Filename Extension
          *   Action:2.1.1.2 - Press "ENTER"
        - Action:2.1.2 - Determine Data Access Index

U: which column has the price
A: The columns for the different auto features can be determined from auto.collab. The order of the features (from left to right) listed in that file corresponds to the left-to-right order of the columns in auto.stats.

    *   [Plan: 2.2 - Create unsorted vector]

U: how create vector
A: The command form for creating vectors is:
vectorname_auto.stats[,n] where "n" is the number of the column
in auto.stats containing the values that you desire.
****
U: what is vector
A: A vector is a subset of values from the original body of auto
statistics. It can be thought of as a simple list of numbers.
****

     -   Plan:2.2.1 - Enter Vector Specification

         * Action:2.2.1.1 - Type Vectorname
         * Action:2.2.1.2 - Type Underscore
         * Action:2.2.1.3 - Type DSI

     -   Action:2.2.2 - Press ENTER

     -   [Plan:2.2.3 - List Result of Computation]

         * Action:2.2.3.1 - Type Variablename
         * Action:2.2.3.2 - Press Enter

    *   Plan:2.3' - Apply Mean Function; DSI

U: how get mean
A: The statistical system's function for computing the mean is
called "mean" with the format: variablename_mean(vector)

     -   Plan:2.3'.1 - Enter Function Specification

        - Action:2.3'.1.1 - Type New Variable Name
        - Action:2.3'.1.2 - Type Underscore
        - Action:2.3'.1.3 - Type Mean Function Name
        - Action:2.3'.1.4 - Type Left Paren
        - Action:2.3'.1.4 - Type DSI
        - Action:2.3'.1.6 - Type Right Paren

     -   Action:2.3'.2 - Press "ENTER"

5
SemNet: Three-Dimensional Graphic Representations of Large Knowledge Bases

KIM M. FAIRCHILD
STEVEN E. POLTROCK
GEORGE W. FURNAS

In the last decade, computers have increased the information available to people by many orders of magnitude. The rate of this information explosion is continuing to increase, straining the ability of computer users to comprehend or manage the available information. To help users interact with immense knowledge bases, we propose SemNet, a three-dimensional graphical interface. SemNet presents views which allow the users to examine local detail while still maintaining a global representation of the rest of the knowledge base. SemNet also provides many semantic navigation techniques such as relative movement, absolute movement, and teleportation. SemNet is an exploratory research vehicle to address questions such as: How should large data bases of knowledge be presented to users? How should users explore, manipulate, and modify these knowledge bases? Alternative answers to these questions were implemented in SemNet and informally evaluated by using SemNet as an interface to large knowledge bases.

1. Introduction

In a few decades, computers have increased the information available to people by many orders of magnitude. The rate of this information explosion is continuing to increase, straining the ability of computer users to comprehend or manage available data. Fifth-generation computers are expected to intensify this problem, but simultaneously help manage the information. With their ability to quickly access and manipulate a large amount of symbolic knowledge, fifth-generation computers should revolutionize problem solving and data management. But symbolic knowledge is also a kind of information, different from numeric data, and poses new problems for computer users. How should large data bases of symbolic knowledge (i.e., knowledge bases) be presented to users? How should users explore, manipulate, and modify these knowledge bases? SemNet has been developed to address these questions.

SemNet is an exploratory research project undertaken to advance understanding of the problems facing both users and developers of large knowledge bases. The immediate objective of the SemNet project is to identify important problems and a collection of possible solutions to these problems. The problems and solutions that have been investigated, reflecting the disciplines of the authors, derive from the convergence of computer science, measurement and scaling, and cognitive psychology. Because this research explores uncharted territory, our emphasis is on identifying and informally evaluating many alternatives instead of conducting formal evaluations of a few alternatives. A longer term objective is to develop a generic approach to knowledge-base browsing and editing by combining and optimizing the best solutions.

The major problem addressed in the SemNet project is how to present large knowledge bases so they can be comprehended by a user or developer. To comprehend a knowledge base, we hypothesize, a user must recognize (1) the identities of individual elements in the knowledge base, (2) the relative position of an element within a network context, and (3) explicit relationships between elements. Consequently, research has been focused on ways to represent elements and their interrelationships within the context of a large knowledge base.

SemNet represents knowledge bases as directed graphs in a three-dimensional space (Fairchild, 1985; Fairchild & Poltrock, 1986). SemNet represents knowledge bases graphically because knowledge bases represent information about relationships between symbolic entities, and graphics are an effective way to communicate relationships among objects. Furthermore, we want to exploit the skills that people have already developed for recognizing visual patterns and moving in three-dimensional space.

Figure 1-1 shows how SemNet represents part of a knowledge base containing Prolog rules. SemNet represents elements of the knowledge base as labeled rectangles connected by lines or arcs. The arcs are color coded to represent specific kinds of relationships between the knowledge-base elements. (The color information is not available in any of the figures in this chapter). In Figure 1-1 the rectangles represent Prolog modules (set of rules) labeled with the module names. The arcs show the modules that each module can cause to execute. The knowledge base is explored by traveling through the three-dimensional space. A user of SemNet manipulates information in the knowledge base by direct manipulation of knowledge-base objects, either the rectangles or the arcs, or by manipulation of tools, which are the (blue) rectangles at the top and bottom of Figure 1-1.

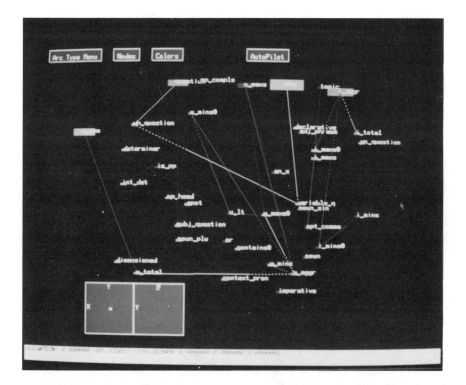

Figure 1-1: Part of a knowledge base consisting of Prolog modules

Three-dimensional graphic representations of knowledge bases, such as the one shown in Figure 1-1, can help reveal the organization of the knowledge base. However, graphic representations do not automatically solve all problems associated with exploring, manipulating, and modifying very large knowledge bases. They simply transform very large knowledge bases into very large directed graphs. The major emphasis of research with SemNet has been to investigate solutions, or partial solutions, to the problems that arise when working with three-dimensional graphic representations of large knowledge bases. In this chapter, the major problems are defined, some potential solutions are explored, and the particular solutions implemented in SemNet are described. Another approach to management of large amounts of information is presented in the chapter on the Memory Extender by Jones.

2. SemNet's Implementation

SemNet is intended to be a general purpose tool for exploring and manipulating arbitrary knowledge bases represented as directed graphs. SemNet can be used as an interface, or part of an interface, to arbitrary knowledge-base applications. This section describes how applications communicate with SemNet, how different kinds of knowledge bases may be represented, and the hardware required for SemNet.

Figure 2-1 shows the components of the SemNet system. These components are implemented on two machines, a Silicon Graphics IRIS Workstation and a machine containing the application program and the knowledge base. In the IRIS, the SemNet user-interface layer, written in C, controls the display and allows the knowledge base to be explored and edited through direct manipulation of graphic objects. In the application machine, the SemNet knowledge-base interface layer, written in LISP, connects arbitrary LISP applications and knowledge bases to the SemNet user-interface layer through a control language. These two layers (the user-interface layer and the knowledge-base interface layer) comprise a general purpose system, and may be attached to arbitrary knowledge-base applications.

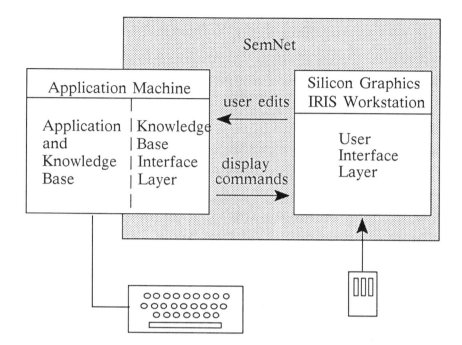

Figure 2-1: Conceptual architecture of SemNet

When the system is initialized, pointers to every element of the knowledge base are sent by the knowledge-base application to the knowledge-base interface layer. The knowledge-base interface layer constructs a description of each of the elements and their interconnections and sends these descriptions via ethernet or a serial connection to the SemNet user-interface layer. The user-interface layer generates the SemNet graphical display. The user, via the mouse, edits the graphic representation as desired. The resulting changes are sent to the knowledge-base interface layer, which in turn passes them to the application for interpretation. The resulting knowledge-base modifications are then sent back through the knowledge-base interface to the SemNet user-interface layer for modification of the graphic display.

All the components shown in Figure 2-1 are required to use SemNet with arbitrary knowledge-base applications. However, for many purposes the SemNet user-interface layer can be used in a stand-alone mode. The SemNet user-interface layer can read a file containing descriptions of the knowledge base like the descriptions generated by the interface layer. The user can browse and manipulate the graphic representation of the knowledge base, but all editing functions that require the application are disabled. This stand-alone mode is useful for training new users, investigating new graphic techniques, and for demonstrations.

When SemNet is integrated with a knowledge-base application, a mapping must be defined between elements of the knowledge base and the graphical objects that represent these elements in SemNet. This mapping defines a graph structure representation of the knowledge base. For a knowledge base represented using frames, this mapping is straightforward. Each frame is represented as a labeled rectangle (the nodes of the network) and slots of the frames are represented as lines (or arcs), color coded to indicate slot type. For a knowledge base represented using rules, defining the mapping requires some ingenuity and analysis of the task to be performed using SemNet. For example, the nodes of the network could represent the antecedents and consequents of rules with arcs representing implication.

SemNet has been used by linguists in the Natural Language Project at Microelectronics and Computer Technology Corporation (MCC) (Slocum & Cohen, 1986) to debug the morphological analyzers that they are developing. These morphological analyzers are knowledge bases expressed as rules organized into groups. SemNet represents each group as a node. The arcs connecting the groups represent paths for messages passed between the groups. Messages passed from one rule group to another are represented as labeled objects that travel along the arcs connecting nodes, providing a dynamic simulation of the morphological analysis. A formal evaluation of SemNet was conducted in this setting (Shook, 1986) and served as the foundation for many of the evaluative statements that follow.

3. Positioning Knowledge Elements

A principal reason that SemNet represents a knowledge base as a graphical network is to reveal the organization or structure of the knowledge base. One of the obstacles to comprehending the organization of the knowledge base is the large number of arc crossings in any large knowledge base. An arbitrary graph cannot, in general, be embedded in a plane without some arcs intersecting. In a flat display, such intersections impede the eyes' efforts to trace interconnections, and crossing points may also be visually confused with nodes. Fortunately, if three dimensions are available, nodes can always be assigned to positions such that no arcs intersect. Of course, arcs still intersect in two-dimensional views of the knowledge base, but when the viewpoint moves, users perceive a three-dimensional space, and the arcs no longer appear to intersect. The resulting visual simplification of the structure was one of the primary motivations for choosing a three-dimensional representation for the SemNet interface.

The positions of the knowledge elements in three-dimensional space also influence how effectively the knowledge base organization is revealed. In Figure 1-1 the assigned positions do not seem too important because relatively few nodes are displayed; Figure 1-1 shows only a small part of a much larger knowledge base. The entire knowledge base is displayed in Figure 3-1 with each knowledge element randomly assigned to a position. In Figure 3-1 the labels have been removed from the nodes and the node size has been reduced. No clear organization emerges in Figure 3-1; randomly assigned positions cause a dense maze of interconnections and obscure relationships among the elements.

The problem is how to assign positions to knowledge elements so that the organization or structure of the knowledge base is maximally apparent to the user. A general solution to this problem probably does not exist; the optimal method of position assignment for one knowledge base may be totally inappropriate for another. Some knowledge bases may contain information that can be used to compute effective positions. For other knowledge bases, the user may have information that is not stated explicitly in the knowledge base, and this information may allow the user to assign effective positions.

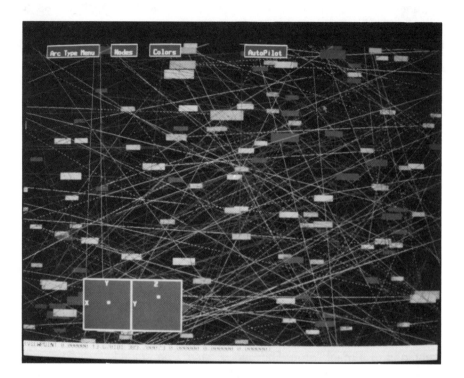

Figure 3-1: The complete knowledge base of Prolog modules with
nodes assigned to random positions

Three potential sources of information for determining the positions of
knowledge elements have been explored in SemNet. First, the positions
of knowledge elements can be based on their properties through
mapping functions, described below. Second, the connectivity between
knowledge elements can be used to assign related elements to adjacent
positions. Third, the user can assign knowledge elements to positions
based on information that is not represented in the knowledge base.

3.1 Mapping Functions

In many cases, the elements of a knowledge base have properties that can be mapped to positions in three-dimensional space, establishing a spatial representation of the knowledge base organization. Suppose, for example, that SemNet was used to browse a semantic network describing the properties of all mammals. Rips, Shoben, and Smith (1973) found that people organize animals along three principal dimensions: size, predacity, and domesticity. If these three properties are defined in the knowledge base, or can be computed from other properties in the knowledge base, then these properties can be transformed into x, y, and z coordinates. The result should be a spatial representation of the knowledge base that closely corresponds to the user's conceptual representation. Hamsters and tigers would be assigned opposite values on all three dimensions of this space. In a large knowledge base there may be many dimensions that could be used to organize the knowledge base, depending on the user's task. In SemNet, the user may select the dimensions from a predefined list.

To use mapping functions in SemNet, the application knowledge base must contain a set of ordering functions, each of which produces an ordering of all knowledge elements. The names of these ordering functions are passed to the SemNet user-interface layer (see Section 2). When a user accesses the *MappingFunctions* tool, SemNet presents a list of the ordering functions. The user indicates which functions should correspond to each of the three display dimensions. SemNet sends these selections to the application, which returns normalized coordinates for each knowledge element.

3.2 Proximity Based Functions

In many knowledge-base applications, the relationships between knowledge elements may provide the key to understanding the knowledge-base organization. These relationships are easier to perceive if related knowledge elements are close together and unrelated knowledge elements are far apart. Several techniques have been explored in SemNet for determining knowledge element positions from the relationships between knowledge elements.

3.2.1 Multidimensional Scaling

One technique uses multidimensional scaling to assign positions to elements so that two elements directly connected by an arc are closer together than elements with no direct connections. (The chapter by McDonald and Schvaneveldt in this volume presents in detail proximity scaling techniques such as multidimensional scaling.) If two elements can be connected by more than one arc, the technique assigns positions so that the distance between two elements decreases as the number of arcs connecting them decreases. A test of this technique was conducted using a knowledge base of 53 elements that all had connections to other knowledge elements.

The first step in this technique is to construct a matrix summarizing the interconnections among the knowledge elements. The entry for row i and column j of the matrix is the number of slots in element i that point to element j. This matrix is made symmetric by summing across the diagonal (the element in row i, column j is added to the element in row j, column i). The symmetric matrix represents the number of interconnections between elements without regard to the direction of the connection.

The positions of the knowledge elements are defined by nonmetric multidimensional scaling applied to this symmetric matrix. This scaling technique yields a three-dimensional solution such that the distance between elements is monotonically related to the number of interconnections between the elements, to the extent that is possible. In our test, the KYST program (based on Kruskal, 1964a, 1964b, and described in Kruskal, Young, & Seery, 1973) with monotone regression and a Torsca starting procedure was used to perform this analysis. The choice of a starting procedure is important because the program iteratively adjusts the elements' positions and may reach a local optimum or saddle point from poor initial values. After 50 iterations the stress was 0.02, which indicates a good fit to the requirement of monotonicity, and changes in the position of elements were in the third decimal place. The final, three-dimensional solution was rotated to principal components.

To test the effectiveness of this technique, SemNet was initially given random positions for the 53 elements of the knowledge base. Qualitatively, this representation of the knowledge base was unaesthetic and confusing. Many of the arcs connecting the knowledge elements were long, and the arcs nearly obscured the knowledge elements. Then the elements were moved to the locations determined by the multidimensional scaling analysis. The results were striking. Not only were both ends of most arcs visible on a single screen, but since the arcs tended to be short, they were easier to trace, and even their two-dimensional projections had fewer crossings. It became apparent for the first time, for example, that our set of test nodes was in fact two disconnected subsets. There were further beneficial effects: Interesting subsets of interconnected nodes became visible, highly connected nodes took central positions, and more isolated nodes moved to the periphery.

Applying this multidimensional scaling technique to large knowledge bases poses some problems. Iterative nonmetric multidimensional scaling programs are slow, and therefore inappropriate for real-time analysis of very large knowledge bases. This problem may not be insurmountable, however. The analysis could be performed off-line (overnight, for example), and simple heuristics could be used to position new knowledge elements as they are defined. For example, an element connected to more than one other element could be positioned at the centroid of all the elements' positions.

3.2.2 Heuristics

Other techniques use heuristics to move related knowledge elements closer together. These heuristics require an initial position for every element, possibly a randomly chosen position, and a specified minimum distance between any two knowledge elements. This minimum distance ensures that nodes remain far enough apart to be discriminable. The heuristics define a new position for each element of the knowledge base, one at a time, and are applied iteratively until the knowledge elements no longer move noticeably.

The centroid heuristic defines the new position of a knowledge element as the weighted mean of the positions of all related knowledge elements, with each position weighted by the number of arcs that directly connect the elements. Because of these weights, a knowledge element moves closer to those knowledge elements with which it shares the most relationships. This heuristic could assign different weights to different kinds of relationships, accommodating differences in relationship importance. If the computed centroid is too close (less than the specified minimum distance) to any knowledge element, a new position is found along an arc between the original position and the centroid.

The centroid heuristic is fast and could readily be used in conjunction with the multidimensional scaling approach described above. The solution obtained is, however, strongly dependent on the initial positions. In tests we conducted with a large knowledge base, the centroid heuristic improved the original random positions significantly, but never untangled the complex web of interconnections.

An annealing heuristic was motivated by recent research on simulated annealing[1] (Kirkpatrick, Gelatt, & Vecchi, 1983). This technique is slower than the centroid heuristic but more successful at untangling the interconnections. A new position for each element is computed by adding a vector of random orientation and length to the current position. A scale factor controlled by the user determines the maximum length of the random vector. The element is moved to the new position if it is closer than the current position to the centroid, but not too close to any other element. By setting the scale factor high initially, knowledge elements can be moved large distances, potentially untangling the interconnections. When new positions are no longer found, the scale factor is gradually reduced until the changes in positions are acceptably small. Like the centroid heuristic, the annealing heuristic is sensitive to initial positions, but it yielded solutions that were judged substantially more effective than the solutions of the centroid heuristic. To illustrate the reduction of complexity that can be achieved by the annealing heuristic, Figures 3-1 and 3-2 show the same knowledge base with positions assigned randomly in Figure 3-1 and positions adjusted by the annealing heuristic in Figure 3-2. An organization of the knowledge base is clearly visible in Figure 3-2, making the knowledge base appear smaller and more comprehensible.

---

[1]The annealing heuristic is not strictly an example of simulated annealing, but it is similar in that a scale factor serves a role similar to temperature in annealing, which produces stable molecular structures by slowly decreasing the temperature from a high initial value.

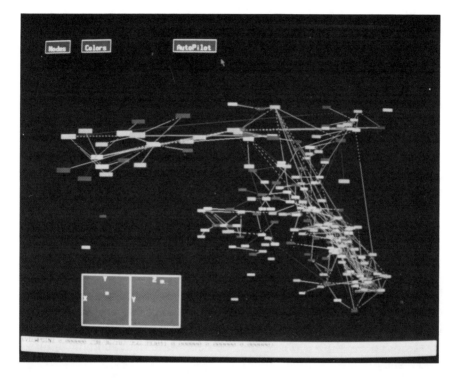

Figure 3-2: The complete knowledge base of Prolog modules with node positions determined by the annealing heuristic

3.3 Personalized Positioning

In some cases, the user may have information that is not in the knowledge base but should be considered when assigning positions to the knowledge elements. The user can simply move the knowledge elements to these positions and leave them there. This is the location method we use in our daily lives: We put things where we want and expect them to be there the next time we look for them. This method can be combined with other positioning techniques. For example, the user can fix the positions of certain knowledge elements, then let all others be adjusted by the annealing or centroid heuristic. These heuristics will

treat the fixed positions as *anchors*, and all connected knowledge elements will be grouped around these anchors. For example, a linguist
could fix one *verb* analysis node and one *noun* analysis node at opposite
ends of the space. Then the annealing or centroid heuristic could be
used to pull apart the remaining noun and verb nodes.

4. Coping with Large Knowledge Bases

Whatever strategies are used to organize the display of a graph, the
number of nodes and arcs can eventually be overwhelming. Two limitations affect performance with large knowledge bases. First, the graphic
hardware is limited in the speed with which it can compute and display
information. As the number of objects to be displayed increases, the
system's responsiveness decreases, degrading the real-time user interaction. Second, humans are limited in their ability to discriminate and
attend to objects on the display.

Somehow, the total amount of information must be reduced. We addressed this issue in SemNet by inventing ways to find and display useful subsets of the knowledge base. The simplest methods involve selection by the user. More sophisticated methods were derived from Generalized Fisheye Views (Furnas, 1986).

When knowledge elements are of different types and not all types are of
current interest, a simple subset-by-type strategy can be adopted. The
user initiates this strategy by simply identifying which type of element
should be displayed. For example, a user could specify that only mammals should be displayed in a knowledge base about animals. This
capability has not been fully implemented in SemNet, but can be accomplished through interacting with the application program.

The underlying spatial metaphor of SemNet allows several strategies for
dividing the knowledge base into subsets using spatial criteria. One
strategy is a natural consequence of the three-dimensional graphics
hardware, which shows only the part of the knowledge base within a
restricted viewing angle when looking in a particular direction from the
viewpoint. This allows the user to concentrate on the subset of nodes

within this viewing angle. Moreover, the perspective view makes objects nearer the viewpoint appear larger, helping the user to examine local neighborhoods more effectively.

These local neighborhoods will be comprehensible only if related elements are within the same neighborhoods. In other words, proximity in euclidean space should correspond to proximity in the graph structure. In general, however, it is not mathematically possible to achieve perfect correspondence between proximity in arbitrary graph structures and proximity in three-dimensional euclidean space, so SemNet provides a *view_neighbors* tool that temporarily pulls all the nodes adjacent to any selected node into view. The *view_neighbors* tool is described in more detail in Section 5.2.4.

4.1 Fisheye Views

In addition to spatial subsets, SemNet's underlying spatial metaphor also supports more sophisticated information reduction strategies called Generalized Fisheye Views (Furnas, 1986). These strategies display details near a focal point and only more important landmarks further away. Such views attempt to give a useful balance of local details and surrounding context. Conceptually, these views are implemented by computing a degree-of-interest value for every object, then displaying only those objects that have a degree-of-interest value greater than a criterion. The degree-of-interest value for any object increases as the a priori importance of the object increases, and decreases as distance increases from the object to the point where the user is currently focused. The following sections discuss several generalized fisheye viewing strategies, two of which, one explicit and one implicit, are currently implemented in SemNet.

4.1.1 Fisheye Views from Clustering

Construction of a fisheye view requires that (1) interactions can be characterized as focused at a point in a reasonably static structure, (2) there be a notion of distance, and (3) there be a notion of differential a priori importance of objects. The first two prerequisites were readily

satisfied in SemNet. The knowledge base is the stable structure, the focal point is a location in three-dimensional space, and distance can be
defined as euclidean. Notions of differential importance, however, were
more elusive. One might consider nodes with more incident arcs to be
more important. Or perhaps the semantics of the domain might associate importance with some other feature of the network. For example,
in a knowledge base, nodes higher in an *ISA*-sublattice might be
considered more important. Or there might be purely non-structural
application-specific importances (e.g., creation date). Any of these definitions of importance could be used in a standard fisheye strategy that
eliminates less important nodes as distance increases. However, while
all these definitions seem reasonable for particular applications, none
seems sufficiently general.

The absence of satisfactory explicit notions of differential importance has
led us to pursue new kinds of generalized fisheye views, all based on
somehow identifying implicit notions of differential importance and
making these notions explicit. For example, even though no individual
knowledge-base element may be more important than others, *sets* of
elements may exist that are more important than individual elements. If
we could find a way to identify such sets, then an implicit structure could
be made explicit by (1) introducing new *cluster-objects* that represent
sets, and (2) assigning greater importance to these cluster-objects than
to individual elements.

Consider the consequences that would emerge if we succeeded in finding ways to identify important sets of elements. Every element could be
assigned to a unique set represented by a cluster-object, then every set
could be assigned to a superset represented by another kind of cluster-
object, and so on. The result would be a new hierarchical structure, with
knowledge-base elements at the bottom and with successive layers of
cluster-objects above the objects that they contain. In this metastructure,
importance corresponds to height in the hierarchy even though no
general definition of differential importance was available in the original
structure. Furthermore, successively higher layers of the metastructure
have fewer and fewer objects in them, allowing a fisheye strategy to be
implemented by displaying knowledge elements near the focal point but
only cluster-objects further from the focal point. As distance from the

focal point increases, the displayed cluster-objects correspond to higher levels of the metastructure. The user can concentrate on knowledge elements in the neighborhood of the focal point in the global context of sets of elements represented by cluster-objects.

How should these cluster-objects be represented? They should probably be discriminable from individual knowledge elements, so that the user can understand the distortion or transformation of the view introduced by the fisheye process. For example, they may be represented by a special cluster icon carrying some identifying information. This information might indicate the level of the cluster and some sort of label. They might be labeled by an explicit cluster-name (if one is available), or labeled by example, that is, displayed with a short list of some knowledge elements inside the cluster, either randomly or systematically chosen (cf. Dumais & Landauer, 1984). Alternatively, one might try to make semantically appropriate pictographs for each individual pseudo-object, but this seems difficult to automate.

Recognizing the advantages of identifying important sets of elements, we have required a method for assigning the elements to these sets. In SemNet, euclidean neighborhoods have been used to assign elements to sets, which again emphasizes the importance of the positions assigned to elements. If semantic information is used to assign positions to the elements, then these euclidean neighborhoods may approximate meaningful subdivisions of the elements. Simple hierarchical clustering has been imposed on the nodes by dividing the space in half along the x, y, and z axes. Each of the resulting eight sub-regions has been itself similarly subdivided, and so on recursively down three levels. This successive octal subdivision yields a rooted 8-ary tree, with the SemNet objects partitioned among its leaves. The internal nodes of the tree are the cluster-objects.

Figure 4-1 shows the resulting SemNet display for one view of the same knowledge base depicted in Figures 3-1 and 3-2. The objects that are displayed in this fisheye view depend on the position of the viewpoint, which the user controls using the mouse. In the middle of the display, knowledge-base elements, such as *yesno* and *quantify*, are visible because these elements are in the same subdivision as the viewpoint. The large (green) rectangles, such as *pt* and *is*, are cluster-objects that represent the subdivisions adjacent to the subdivision containing the viewpoint. The (orange) rectangles, such as *terminal*, are cluster-objects representing sets of four subdivisions that are further away from the current subdivision. This fisheye technique of representing the more remote regions in correspondingly larger chunks essentially reduces the number of objects to be displayed on the screen logarithmically, yet preserves a balance of local detail and global context. A (blue) band at the bottom of each cluster-object represents the proportion of the knowledge base located within the volume represented by that icon. Each cluster-object is positioned at the center of the volume it covers and labeled with the name of its most highly connected node (a label-by-example heuristic).

Note that tree distance is used to determine the degree-of-interest value for all the objects. Cluster objects are interesting because they have high a priori importance, but knowledge-base elements in one subdivision are interesting because they are all equally close (in tree distance) to the viewpoint. Although the tree is based on a subdivision of euclidean space, tree distance is not identical to distance in euclidean space. Tree distance was chosen because the subdivision structure is static and easily computed, and the algorithms for what to display in any tree-structure fisheye are very fast. However, tree distance has several drawbacks. First, when the viewpoint is moved, the objects that are displayed change abruptly at (invisible) subdivision boundaries. This distracting effect is ameliorated by using euclidean distance to tell when a boundary is being approached, then highlighting the clusters that are about to change. For example, in Figure 4-1 the *is* and *pt* cluster objects have light green borders, indicating that the viewpoint is near the boundaries of those subdivisions. If the viewpoint moves much closer, the knowledge-base elements in one of those subdivisions will be exposed and the current subdivision will be represented by a cluster object. A second drawback of tree distance is that the subdivision structure is very heterogeneous with respect to the embedding euclidean space. As a result, a small motion crossing a low-level subdivision boundary has a much smaller effect than a similar motion crossing one of the highest level subdivisions (in which case everything changes). We were unable to fix this problem since, as far as we know, it can be remedied only by adopting some other metastructure (e.g., a non-hierarchical clustering model).

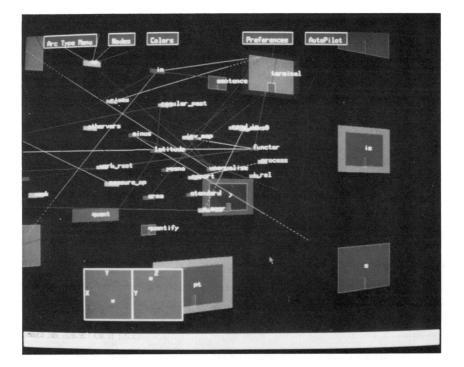

Figure 4-1: A fisheye view of the complete knowledge base of
Prolog modules

We have already noted that the subdivision strategy for assigning
knowledge-base elements to sets increases the importance of the positions assigned to the elements. In order for any spatial subdivisions to be
meaningful, elements must first be placed in the space so that nearby
elements are closely related. Otherwise the content of the spatially
defined clusters will be essentially random, and the resulting metastructure will not have captured the implicit importance structure. The fisheye
view would not make sense. Thus, either very meaningful mapping functions or proximity-based node placement techniques must be used. Furthermore, the octant subdivision strategy implicitly assumes that cuts
perpendicular to the x, y, and z axes are the most appropriate. This may

be defensible when coordinates come from mapping functions that make these axes meaningful. When object positions result from proximity-based techniques however, the final orientation of the cloud of points is typically arbitrary[2] , so the cuts will be similarly arbitrary. One possible solution would be to do the clustering more intelligently, based on the distribution of the nodes and not simply on nested, binary, orthogonal subdivisions.

4.1.2 Fisheye Views from Three-Dimensional Point Perspective

The SemNet interface contains another strategy for managing size. It comes naturally from the way three-dimensional graphics are used, and it exemplifies another generalized fisheye strategy for worlds that do not have explicit differential a priori importance. A balance of local detail and global context arises automatically from the geometry of point perspective in three dimensions: A few nearby points loom large and those further away appear smaller and smaller. We argue that this is not trivial -- an orthogonal projection of three-dimensional space would not achieve this fisheye-like balance, and would be correspondingly less useful. This ability of a movable perspective viewpoint in three-dimensional space to help deal with size and complexity through a combination of geometric subsets and fisheye views was the original motivation for its use in the SemNet interface.

It is useful to analyze this fisheye effect, not in terms of the geometry of projection, but in terms of a general metastructure strategy. This time, however, the metastructure is not a hierarchy of clusters. Instead, each

---

[2]Many proximity scaling packages, like KYST or MDS, rotate to some canonical orientation, such as principal components. While such orientations are well defined they are rarely semantically interpretable, so cuts based on halving the canonically oriented axes are also unlikely to be semantically sensible. The problem really is that the current subdivision scheme is blind; it is totally oblivious to the configuration of points, and any natural structure (e.g., natural clustering) they might have. That is, of course, why the technique can be so simple and so fast. An alternative is to use subdivision techniques, like agglomerative clustering, that more tediously (e.g., O(n#)) construct a hierarchy that reflects the detailed positions of points. The hope would be that it would thereby make semantically sensible clusters.

SemNet object is associated with a continuous set of graphic representations that differ only in size. These graphic representations are the same as those that result from perspective geometry. Combining these sets with the original knowledge-base structure yields a metastructure with a new size dimension orthogonal to the original structure. Now assume that the a priori importance of a graphic representation is inversely related to size: Smaller images of each object are more important than larger images. This assumption may seem counterintuitive, but reflects the intuition that it is more important that an object be represented, even if it is small, than not represented at all.

The fisheye view that results from this elaborated importance structure and euclidean distance is equivalent to the view that results from perspective geometry. Since the higher level graphic representations are smaller, the resulting views are reduced compared to a non-fisheye view (such as would result from an orthogonal projection). The geometric knowledge embedded in the three-dimensional graphics hardware selects the correct size for each object in the view quickly and automatically.

Theoretically, this fisheye conceptualization supports other transformations of the objects' representations. For example, the objects could change in form as well as size. The most detailed representation of an object (for use at close range) might be an icon containing the node's full English title and perhaps other useful information. Next might be a smaller box containing only the node's title, next only a small unlabeled box, and finally just a small point. The fisheye view would select the appropriate form and size for each knowledge-base element by first computing degree-of-interest values from distance and a priori importance, then displaying the representations with values closest to the criterion. At present, we simply make use of the IRIS hardware and the geometric fisheye; consequently, objects change only in size.

4.1.3 Fisheye Views from Sampling Density.

In addition to the two fisheye strategies currently implemented, there is at least one other strategy that we could have used that does not depend on explicit values of differential a priori importance. Consider a structure whose layout exhibits a kind of graded spatial autocorrelation between the objects: Only small changes happen from neighbor to neighbor in the space; major changes happen only gradually. In pictures, for example, local changes usually just delineate small details. In such a case, sampling density can be used to make explicit the distinction between major and minor features. In a picture, the image would be sampled very densely near the point of interest to give high resolution and detail. Regions successively further away would be sampled less and less densely, and only major changes in the image would be visible. This corresponds exactly to what the human retina does to achieve information compression. In SemNet a comparable strategy could be implemented since a proximity-based node layout should give the right kind of autocorrelational structure. Thus, one would sample the three-dimensional space densely near the current point of view, showing all objects. Further away, only a correspondingly smaller proportion of the objects would be permitted in the view -- only a coarse sampling to give the gist of the more remote regions.

4.2 The Display of Arcs

Two issues arise in the display of arcs. First, if not all nodes are visible, which arcs should be shown? In SemNet a simple strategy was adopted: Show a directed arc if and only if its origin node was explicitly visible.

A second problem, one we did not address, involves what to do when the number of arcs, not the number of nodes, is extremely large. This problem can be solved by following a similar approach. First, strategies for dividing the arcs into sets are needed. If, as in a knowledge base, the arcs are of different types (e.g., different semantic relations), those arcs corresponding to types that are not of current interest may be deleted. Fisheye strategies are also possible if arcs have differential importance; for example, in a knowledge base about animals, the user may determine that the ISA and EAT relationships are more important than the CREATOR-OF and DATE-OF-EXTINCTION relationships. Then less important arcs would be deleted as distance increased.

5. Navigation and Browsing

To explore graphical representations of large knowledge bases, such as those shown in Figures 3-1 and 3-2, the user must be able to move the viewpoint or move the entire knowledge base. Suppose, for example, a user needs to inspect a particular knowledge element and all its connections in Figure 3-2. This task could be accomplished by moving the viewpoint close to that element, restricting the view to the small set of elements in a local region. Although this technique provides a powerful method for coping with the size and complexity of the knowledge base, it raises a new set of problems associated with navigating in a virtual three-dimensional space. These problems can be decomposed into two aspects of navigation: recognizing locations and controlling locations.

5.1 Recognizing Locations

How does the user know where the current viewpoint is in a complex knowledge space? One solution is to provide navigation aids similar to those found in the real world. For example, when traveling in a foreign city, people use abstract scale models or maps to discover where places are in relation to each other and how to get to new places. Landmarks, both natural and man-made, often help to identify the current position. SemNet provides tools similar to maps that show the current position of the viewpoint in the x-y and the x-z planes. Structures similar to landmarks may occur naturally when knowledge elements form structures that, with experience, become recognizable.

When following a complex path in the real world, people sometimes leave marks so the path can be retraced later. This approach could be adopted in SemNet, allowing the user to place identifiable markers on each section of the knowledge; for example, an icon for an elephant could represent information about large African animals. In addition, SemNet could show the path that was followed to reach the current location and provide automatic means for retracing it. Path retracing could have the added benefit of helping to re-establish the context that led to the current position. These capabilities do not currently exist in SemNet.

From our experiences with navigating through a three-dimensional knowledge space, the single most important feature of the interface is to make the user experience a *real*, three-dimensional space. diSessa (1985) terms such a user a *naive realist* - that what the user sees and manipulates on the display screen is the knowledge itself, rather than simply an interface to actions that manipulate an invisible system. The same control movements the user already makes to control the real world should map directly into the virtual world. One important component of this is the quality of the three-dimensional imagery (Poltrock et al., 1986). Real-time movement of graphical objects, motion parallax, graphic depth cues, and stereopsis will enhance this display.

Many cues help a user to recognize the current static position of the viewpoint. The organization of the knowledge base and features of the graphical objects provide perceptual information about the viewpoint position. For example, objects near the viewpoint are larger than objects far from the viewpoint. Other ways that graphical objects communicate location were described in Section 4. A map of the space is provided by an *Absolute Positioning* tool (the (blue) rectangle at the lower left in Figures 1-1, 3-1, and 3-2) , which shows the current position of the viewpoint.

Because the space is three dimensional, the relative depth of objects is important too. When the viewpoint is stationary, however, the knowledge base looks flat because there are few effective cues to depth. Two methods were explored for enhancing the depth effects in a static display. One method is to vertically oscillate the viewpoint, creating the impression that the knowledge base is rocking around the x axis. Although this method improves perception of depth, linguists in MCC's Natural Language Project found it distracting. The second method is to make small random movements of the viewpoint. This method appears to be as effective as vertical oscillations and is more pleasant to watch.

5.2 Controlling Location

How should the user control the position of the viewpoint, thereby determining the portion of the knowledge base that is displayed? Five different methods have been explored for either moving the viewpoint in a complex three-dimensional knowledge space or moving the knowledge base itself.

5.2.1 Relative Movement

The first method implemented in SemNet evolved from past experience with real-time visual simulation systems for training pilots to fly helicopters. This method provides independent controls for three orthogonal rotations of the viewpoint and movement forward and backward along the line of sight. This movement method is accessed by selecting the helicopter flight option on SemNet's main system menu. A submenu allows the user to select roll, pitch, yaw, or forward and backward movement. Tools for adjusting the velocity of movement and rotation are also provided.

This relative movement method has proven difficult to use for several reasons. First, changes in orientation are confusing, perhaps because there are no visual cues such as the gauges provided in helicopters and airplanes to indicate the current orientation. Consequently, users quickly become lost and disoriented. To help users recover their orientation, functions were added to the flight menu that return the viewpoint to the center of the space and level off the orientation. Second, the relative movement method is slow and awkward to use. Users must often iteratively adjust one control after another to reach a location that is readily visible on the display. Characteristics of the available control devices (i.e., the mouse and keyboard) may be largely responsible for these problems. If the user had a joystick and accelerator that could be manipulated simultaneously, the helicopter model would probably be an effective method for controlling viewpoint. Some of the three-dimensional control devices that are becoming available commercially may provide acceptable substitutes for an accelerator and joystick.

5.2.2 Absolute Movement

With a map of the three-dimensional knowledge space, the user can point to the desired viewpoint location. One kind of map used in SemNet is shown in Figures 1-1, 3-1, and 3-2. Because the space is three dimensional, the map shown in the figures has two two-dimensional parts, one representing the x-y plane and the other representing the y-z plane. The position of the viewpoint in the three-dimensional knowledge space is represented by an asterisk in each plane of the map. The user manipulates the position of the viewpoint by moving the asterisk in one plane at a time using the mouse. A filter ensures that the viewpoint moves smoothly, retaining the experience of travel through a three-dimensional space.

This absolute movement method is quicker and easier to use than the relative movement method described above. It poses new problems however. First, viewpoint positioning is not very accurate; it is easy to move rapidly to an approximate position but difficult to adjust the viewpoint precisely. This problem could be solved by allowing the user to adjust the filter so the viewpoint moves more slowly. The second problem is that using two-dimensional maps of a three-dimensional space imposes an extra cognitive demand on the user, forcing the user to determine which map to use and which direction to move the mouse to cause desired movements. Moving the mouse up and down in the x-y plane or left and right in the y-z plane causes the viewpoint to move along the y axis. It is easy to confuse these motions and difficult to determine the correct mouse movements required to move the viewpoint toward a particular object. This unnaturalness may be solved when three-dimensional control and display devices are available, allowing a direct coupling of the user's actions and the display consequences.

Two different absolute movement tools have been implemented in Sem-Net to explore alternative ways of controlling three-dimensional movement in two-dimensional maps. One tool, shown in the figures, displays two maps; the other tool shows three maps corresponding to the x-y, y-z, and z-x planes. The third map is, of course, redundant; it provides no information that is not available in the other two maps. More importantly, users rarely used the z-x map, but restricted their attention to the other two maps.

The tool with three maps also presented a miniature version of the knowledge base, which was expected to help the user navigate. Any advantage of this information was overwhelmed, however, by the heavy processing load that it imposed on the computer. Movements were less smooth because of processing required to maintain the map images.

5.2.3 Teleportation

Teleportation, a movement method based on cache table principles, works nicely with other movement methods. Once the user has been to a location in the knowledge space, the chance of needing to go back to that same location increases dramatically. Typically, when entering new information into a knowledge-base, a user will find information that is similar to the piece to be entered, make a copy, and edit it. Teleportation allows the user to pick a recently visited knowledge element from a two-dimensional list (a menu) and instantly move to the location of the knowledge element. By selecting options from this menu, the user could pop to a location, make a copy of a knowledge element, then pop back to the original location to continue editing. This concept can easily be extended to create various types of bookkeeping lists that store concepts to be added, locations of interesting places, and concepts to be tested.

5.2.4 Hyperspace Movement

Browsing a knowledge base typically involves examining knowledge elements one at a time, observing which knowledge elements are related to the one under examination, then following a selected relationship to examine another knowledge element. The hyperspace movement method facilitates this kind of browsing. It is particularly useful in a large knowledge base in which the relationships among knowledge elements are not easily recognized and in situations in which a user is searching for an element similar to one that has been found. In a knowledge base about animals, a user could follow the *eats* relationship from *tiger* to *mongoose* to *snake* to *hamster*, thereby traveling from one end of the knowledge base to the other.

Hyperspace movement is accomplished by first selecting a function called *view_neighbors*. This function temporarily moves all the nodes connected to the selected knowledge element, positioning them around it. When this function is de-activated, or when a new node is selected, these nodes snap back to their original positions. If the next node selected is one of the moved nodes, the viewpoint follows this node back to its original position, the newly selected node is in the center of the display and all related nodes are distributed around it.

The hyperspace movement method is particularly useful when clustering methods are used to compress the information in the knowledge base (see Section 4). If an element is related to an element in another cluster, this method can be used to pull the connected element from the cluster. If the user decides this element is important, a single keystroke will move the viewpoint to this new element.

5.2.5 Moving the Space

All the movement methods described above involve moving the viewpoint through a static knowledge space. It is not clear that this is the best way to represent the movement task. Perhaps movement control would seem more natural to a user if it was conceptualized as manipulating the position of the knowledge base instead of manipulating the viewpoint. In support of this alternative, research has shown that when children are asked to describe how a structure would appear after some movement, they are more accurate if they are asked to imagine that the structure is rotated than if they imagine themselves moving to another viewpoint (Huttenlocher & Presson, 1979). Three SemNet tools allow the user to set the attitude or orientation of the knowledge space while keeping the viewpoint fixed. Initial findings suggest that this movement method is effective but it has not yet been systematically compared with the other methods.

6. Showing Dynamic Execution of a Knowledge Base

After a knowledge base has been entered, the user must test and debug it. Typically, the user makes a query or an assertion to the knowledge base, which processes this input and possibly makes internal changes to the data, usually returning a text string. To debug this process, the user needs a history of the nodes that were visited and the paths that were taken. In the past, this history was obtained by printing the current execution state as each node was visited. For complex knowledge bases this debugging trace may be hundreds of pages long, overloading the user.

The approach taken in SemNet is to show dynamically the changes that result from knowledge-base processing. During knowledge-base execution, when one node completes its processing and passes its result to another node, an object called a *sprite* travels down arcs between the nodes to show the progress of the execution. Attached to the sprite is a label showing the current value of the computation. In the Natural Language Project application, this label is the piece of the word the system is analyzing.

Since the knowledge base executes much faster than a human can follow, the speed of the sprite is under the user's control. To show the history of knowledge-base execution, both arcs and nodes have three color-coded states: background, active, and relaxed. Initially, all objects are set to the background color. When the sprite traverses an arc, the color of the arc and its connected nodes change to active. Both the nodes and the arc change to the relaxed color when the sprite has moved on to other arcs and nodes. By examining the color of the nodes and arcs, the user can determine which nodes have executed, which helps to localize errors.

When the user has determined that a particular region of the knowledge base is responsible for an error, extra debugging aids can be requested for the nodes in that region. When one of these nodes is encountered, a temporary fixed menu appears, which contains the rules that the node represents. Highlighting is used to show how each rule in the menu responded to the input.

7. Conclusion

As knowledge bases become larger, more powerful semantic and syntactic techniques will be required for exploring and manipulating the knowledge. SemNet offers a syntactic approach to solving this problem. SemNet's representation of a knowledge base is based entirely on the names and positions of the knowledge elements and the connections among them. SemNet demonstrates how major problems in knowledge-base management can be solved, or partially solved, with only this syntactic information. Of course, semantic information available to the application program could be used in conjunction with SemNet's syntactic techniques to achieve a more effective solution.

The positions of the knowledge elements greatly affect comprehension of the knowledge base structure. The application program assigns initial positions, allowing use of semantic information that is unavailable to SemNet. Alternatively, positions can be determined by heuristics designed to put knowledge elements close together spatially if they are neighbors in the graph structure formed by their interconnections. These methods for assigning positions become increasingly important and increasingly less effective as the knowledge base increases in size, pointing to the need for further research on this problem.

An important issue has been how, using only syntactic information, SemNet can reduce the displayed information by presenting less information about those knowledge elements unimportant to the user's immediate concern. To some extent, this information reduction is accomplished automatically by the three-dimensional graphic hardware if proximity-based positioning has been used. Objects near the viewpoint, which is assumed to represent the region of immediate interest, are displayed at full size. Object size diminishes as distance from the viewpoint increases, and objects outside the field of view are not displayed at all. The result is a fisheye view based on three-dimensional perspective. This method has been made more effective by combining it with a fisheye view based on clustering. All knowledge elements within local regions of euclidean space have been assigned to clusters, neighboring clusters have been assigned to higher level clusters, and so on. Only knowledge elements near the viewpoint are presented; further from the viewpoint, cluster-objects are displayed that represent all the knowledge elements in a region of the space. The combination of these two methods greatly reduces the displayed information while providing both local details and global context.

SemNet has been an exploratory project to investigate alternative solutions to problems endemic to large knowledge-base systems. SemNet
was never intended to provide solutions to all knowledge-base problems.
However, SemNet was intended to help users recognize and understand
the structure or organization of a large knowledge base. To achieve this
understanding, we hypothesize, the user must recognize the identities of
knowledge-base elements, explicit relationships between elements, and
the relative position of elements within the knowledge base. To expand
an old aphorism, SemNet attempts to reveal the structure of the forest,
not details about trees.

The details of the knowledge-base are de-emphasized and the structure
is emphasized by representing the elements of the knowledge base as
simple, labeled rectangles and the relationships between elements as
color-coded arcs. Navigation tools enable a user to explore the structure,
view different parts of it, and follow relationships from one element to
another. Positioning heuristics and fisheye techniques are intended to
ensure that the view presented to the user communicates the logical
structure of the knowledge base.

Although SemNet has been an exploratory research project, an outcome
of the project is a system that can be integrated with a wide range of
applications. SemNet solves some but not all problems that are commonly encountered in knowledge-base applications. Indeed, a single
system cannot address all knowledge-base problems because they
depend on the application and the tasks that are to be performed. Consequently, SemNet is intended to be used in conjunction with an application program that would provide access to the contents of the
knowledge-base elements. In the Prolog example shown in Figures 1-1
and Figures 3-1 to 4-1, SemNet shows the relationships among Prolog
modules, while an application program would display the contents of
these modules and support module construction and editing. The MCC
Natural Language Project accomplished a tighter marriage of SemNet
with the application program. When a linguist debugs a rule system using
SemNet, the nodes represent collections of rules responsible for analyzing morphemes that visibly travel from one node to another. When an
error is isolated to a node, the linguist can request a display of the rule
collection, which SemNet obtains from the application program. Other

potential applications of SemNet are: communicating the structure of large projects, debugging object-oriented programs, browsing through hypermedia documents, and representing connectionist models.

Acknowledgements

We would like to thank two of our colleagues, Jonathan Slocum and Jonathan Grudin for their intellectual support in the development of Sem-Net and the preparation of this paper. We also would like to acknowledge the contribution of Vernor Vinge, author of "True Names", for his visionary support of our work and other artificial realities.

References

diSessa, Andrea A. (1985). A principled design for an integrated computational environment. *Human-Computer Interaction, 1*, 1-47.

Dumais, S. T. & Landauer, T. K. (1984). Describing categories of objects for menu retrieval systems. *Research Methods, Instruments and Computers, 16*, 242-248.

Fairchild, K. M. (1985). *Construction of a semantic net virtual world metaphor* (Tech. Rep. No. HI-163-85). Austin, TX: Microelectronics and Computer Technology Corporation.

Fairchild, K. M., & Poltrock, S. E. (1986). *SemNet* [Videotape]. Presented at CHI'86 Human Factors in Computing Systems, Boston, 1986, and (Tech. Rep No HI-104-86), Austin, TX: Microelectronics and Computer Technology Corporation.

Fairchild, K. M., & Poltrock, S. E. (1987). *Soaring through knowledge space: SemNet 2.1* [Videotape]. Presented at CHI'87 Human Factors in Computing Systems, Toronto, 1987, and (Tech. Rep. No. HI-104-86, Rev. 1), Austin, TX: Microelectronics and Computer Technology Corporation.

Furnas, G. W. (1986). Generalized fisheye views. *Proceedings of CHI'86 Human Factors in Computing Systems*, 16-23. New York: ACM.

Huttenlocher, J., & Presson, C. C. (1979). The coding and transformation of spatial information. *Cognitive Psychology, 11*, 375-394.

Kirkpatrick, S., Gelatt, C. D., & Vecchi, M. P. (1983). Optimization by simulated annealing. *Science, 220*, 671-680.

Kruskal, J. B. (1964a). Multidimensional scaling by optimizing goodness of fit to a non-metric hypothesis. *Psychometrika, 29*, 1-27.

Kruskal, J. B. (1964b). Non-metric multidimensional scaling: A numerical method. *Psychometrika, 29*, 28-42.

Kruskal, J. B., Young, F. W., & Seery, J. B. (1973). *How to use KYST: A very flexible program to do multidimensional scaling* (Technical Memorandum). Murray Hill, NJ: Bell Laboratories.

Poltrock, S. E., Shook, R. E., Fairchild, K., Lovgren, J. E., Tarlton, P. N., Tarlton, M., & Hauser, M. (1986). *Three-dimensional interfaces: The promise and the problems* (Tech. Rep. No. HI-291-86). Austin, TX.: Microelectronics and Computer Technology Corporation.

Rips, L. J., Shoben, E. J., & Smith, E. E. (1973). Semantic distance and the verification of semantic relations. *Journal of Verbal Learning and Verbal Behavior, 12*, 1-20.

Shook, Robert E. (1986). *SemNet: A conceptual and interface evaluation* (Tech. Rep. No. HI-320-86-P). Austin, TX: Microelectronics and Computer Technology Corporation.

Slocum J., & Cohen, R. (1986). *NABU documentation, Natural Language Processing Project* (Tech. Rep. No. AI-228-86-Q). Austin, TX: Microelectronics and Computer Technology Corporation.

Vinge, V. (1981). *True names.* Dell Books.

6
"As We May Think"?:[1]
Psychological Considerations in the Design of a Personal Filing System

WILLIAM P. JONES

An understanding of people and the problems people encounter in tasks of information processing can guide us not only in the design of the interface to a computing system but also in the initial selection of this system's application. Additional possibilities for an interplay between basic research into human information processing and applied efforts to build more useable (and useful) computing systems may exist to the extent that there is a similarity of task considerations. In this chapter we explore some of the task considerations that are in effect in the operation of a personal filing system and we note their similarities to considerations surrounding the actions of human memory. The possibility is raised that many constructs found in models of human memory may have application in computer-based systems of information retrieval. In the other direction, it is possible that insights gained from efforts to build better computer-based systems of information retrieval may increase our understanding of human memory.

1. Introduction

Computers have come to play a major role in our world. We speak of the rise of the computer and of a computerized society. However, this is symmetrically viewed as a rise of the computer user and of a computer-literate society. The time has long since passed when computers were the exclusive tool of a small, dedicated cadre of programming elite. A broad class of users now exists of varying backgrounds and needs.

---

[1]This segment originally appeared as the title of an article by Vannevar Bush, *Atlantic Monthly*, July, 1945, 101-108.

Most of these users have neither the time nor the inclination to master a computing system in all of its potential complexity.

Simon's (1981) characterization of an artifact gives us three general areas of concern in the design of any computing system:

1. The *outer environment* of the system, in which it must operate to accomplish its goals (i.e., its functionality or purpose);

2. The *goals* of the system; and

3. The *inner environment* of the system consisting of mechanisms (e.g., programs, electronic circuitry) that are the means by which the system accomplishes its goals.

Today's broad base of users has produced a dramatic change in the computer's outer environment such that, increasingly, its success in meeting its purpose, indeed the very selection of its purpose in the first place, is (or ought to be) determined by user considerations. Beyond this, an increasing emphasis on systems capable of providing human-like assistance can be expected to influence the inner environment of a system as well. Roughly corresponding to the three areas of a computing system as an artifact, therefore, are three potential applications of psychology:

- *At the* **interface** - When a computing system's outer environment is determined in large part by the user population it services, then its success in meeting its goals will heavily depend upon its ability to communicate with its user population. As an act of communication, for example, the success of the human/computer interaction depends upon a common language that can be spoken and understood by both the user and the system.

- *Back to the initial* **application selection** - An understanding of the problems people encounter in their attempts to process information (in a variety of task situations) may suggest new and creative applications for the computer. The computer, as a processor of information, can be used to extend and complement a person's own capabilities. In the movement from text processors to "idea processors", for example, we are asking the computer to play an increasingly significant role in our efforts to express and communicate our ideas to others. How do people go about the task of writing and what kinds of problems do they encounter? Even partial answers to these questions may help us to design systems of dramatically improved usefulness. The importance of psychological considerations then goes far beyond the interface to the initial selection of a system's purpose and functionality.

• ... *And on to the* **application system's design** - Many aspects of the way people process information may be worthy of simulation on the computer. The interest is then not only in those things that go wrong in human cognition (i.e., its limitations) but also on the many other things that go right. Underlying this possibility is the notion that the nature of the information processing task may do much to determine the inner environment of any system that would accomplish this task, regardless of the physical medium (e.g., person or computer) within which the system is realized (see Newell, 1970; Simon, 1981).

This three-fold relevance of psychology is illustrated in this chapter by looking at considerations that apply to the design of information retrieval systems and, in particular, to the design of a personal filing system. This exercise is instantiated through an examination of the Memory Extender (ME) personal filing system (Jones, 1986). The ME system is designed to improve the user interface to a personal database by actively modeling the user's own memory for files and for the context within which these files are used. The ME system is similar, in many respects, to current spreading activation network models of human information processing (e.g., Anderson, 1976, 1983). The ME system is currently implemented in Zetalisp and can run on any 3600 series Symbolics Lisp Machine. It is integrated into the ZMACS text editor and essentially "piggy backs" the variety of filing systems (e.g., Tops 20, VMS, Unix) that currently serve a Symbolics Lisp Machine.

The ME system is an actual running, working system and has been released to MCC shareholders as such. However, although anecdotal accounts of the ME system have been very positive, no evaluation yet exists to support the contention that the ME system is better (or worse) than other filing systems. The primary purpose of this chapter's discussion of the ME system, then, is not to extol the system's virtues. Instead, discussion of the ME system provides a useful framework within which to examine some of the considerations that apply to the design of a filing system. Any filing system is imperfectly decomposed into a set of interlocking components and we cannot meaningfully discuss these components without some sense of the ways in which these components fit together. Along with our examination of the ME system approach we will also explore alternatives that are found in more conventional systems of information retrieval.

We will see that many constructs of a computer-based information retrieval system have their analogues in models of human memory where they realize a similar purpose. The argument is advanced that this results from a similarity of considerations. A strong version of this argument asserts that the basic nature of an information retrieval task does much to determine the design of any system that would accomplish this task - whether the system is realized in the human brain or in an a digital computer (Newell, 1970; Simon, 1981) . To the extent that this is true, we profit, in our efforts to design better systems of information retrieval, from our understanding of the workings of human memory.

1.1 Why Study the Design of a Personal Filing System?

From the theoretical perspective of a researcher who is studying human memory, the question, "Why study the design of a personal filing system?", is answered through a direct extension of the arguments advanced above. To the extent that there is similarity in the tasks of information retrieval involving the computer (e.g., through use of its filing system) and the human brain, and to the extent that this similarity gives rise to a similarity of task considerations, then researchers of human memory may stand to benefit from the lessons learned by designers of computer-based information retrieval systems.

From an applied perspective, we note that the advantages of on-line information storage and retrieval are enormous and largely unrealized. Some of these advantages derive from the application of computing power (e.g., calendars can remind, text can be formatted in a variety of ways, data can be analyzed) and some derive from the speed of electronic transmission (e.g., we now speak of the portable, electronic office). The cost of electronic storage, moreover, continues to decline. We can, therefore, anticipate that the number of files in the average user's directory will increase substantially - these may someday number in the thousands or perhaps even the hundreds of thousands.

A question now arises: How is a user to keep track of all these files? It is quite possible that fundamental limitations in the use of electronic storage may be psychological rather than economic. Moreover, problems in the use of a filing system, unlike many problems in the use of a computer, may actually increase with expertise. Growth in expertise is generally accompanied by a growth in the size of the user's filing system. As more and more files are entrusted to electronic storage devices over longer and longer periods of time, the user's accessibility to a particular desired file is likely to decrease.

Filing systems, in addition to being a worthy subject of study in their own right, also provide a useful microcosm for a study of the general problem of *object reference* which is especially problematic in the user/computer interaction (Furnas, Landauer, Gomez, & Dumais, 1983). Effective use of any computer system requires a knowledge of the mapping between the objects of the computer (e.g., functions, commands, personal files, etc.) and the computer's interface representation of these objects. Most conventional computing systems have a name-oriented approach resulting in a largely one-to-one mapping between objects and their interface representations (i.e., their names). The user's attempt to traverse such a mapping in either direction results in two basic problems:

- recall problems - "What name is that object called by anyway? I can't remember."

- recognition problems - "What is the purpose/use/contents of this object? I can't tell from its name".

These are general problems of object reference which are made more concrete in this chapter through our look at the design of a personal filing system.

1.2 Psychology in the Design of a Personal Filing System

The general areas for the use of psychology in computer system design, as discussed above, all readily apply to the design of a personal filing system:

- *At the* **interface** - Many problems in the use of a filing system can be viewed as problems of communication between the user and the computer. Consider, for example, the problems of recall and recognition that arise in the use of a conventional name-oriented filing system. In one direction, few of the many features a user may be able to recall concerning a desired object (i.e., a file) are likely to be understood by the computer in the sense that these can be used to delimit the computer's search for the object. The computer, for example, typically has no means of directly connecting terms in an expression such as "the accounting dataset created last Tuesday" to an appropriate file. In the other direction, the computer's representation of an object (especially if it is only a single name) is often not understood by the user in the sense that it is descriptive of the object's function. Given a representation such as "smith.let", for example, I may be able to infer that the associated file contains a letter. But is it a letter to, from, or perhaps about, Smith? And what else can I determine regarding the letter's contents from this single-name description?

- *Back to the initial* **application selection** - Why do we use a filing system in the first place? In part we use a filing system as an external memory that serves to extend, complement, and overcome the limitations of our own internal memories. Much initial time and effort must be invested to integrate a piece of information into internal memory - both to insure its immediate comprehensibility and to insure its accessibility at a later point in time. Moreover, this information, once acquired, is often partially or wholly inaccessible at a later point in time (i.e., it is distorted or forgotten). Electronic storage, by contrast, has an initial property of *impressibility* permitting the rapid transcription of detailed information and a subsequent property of *indelibility* promoting the preservation of this information, in its exact form, for long periods of time. Unfortunately, in our attempt to overcome limitations of human memory through our use of a conventional filing system, we also sacrifice many of the advantages of human memory as well ...

- ... *And on to the* **application program's design** - In its capacity for the storage of vast quantities of information in a readily accessible form, human memory is magnificent. Ideally, a personal filing system should give us the best of both worlds, i.e., the filing system should help us to overcome some of the limitations of human memory while at the same time preserving many of the benefits of human memory. Our chances of success in this endeavor are improved to the extent that we are able to determine what these benefits of human memory are and how they are realized.

With respect to this last point, we can contrast the name-oriented, one-to-one mapping of conventional computing systems with the distributed, many-to-many nature of conceptual representations in an associative network depiction of human memory such as that of Figure 1-1.

Features   Concepts

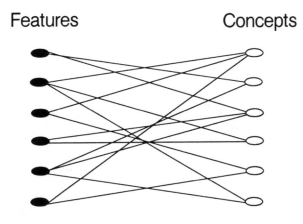

Figure 1-1: A depiction of the distributed, many-to-many mapping between concepts and their representations (i.e., the features, and perhaps other concepts, to which they are connected) hypothesized in human memory.

In one direction, the representation of a given concept can be distributed across a network through its associations to various features (or other concepts). In the other direction, a given feature (or a concept) may participate in the representations of several concepts in the network.

We might wish for a computing system with a representational mapping more like that of a person - in particular, a person who both understands our own use of terms and can express the functionality of an object in these terms. For example, the potential advantages of a mapping such as that depicted in Figure 1-1 become apparent if we replace the word "concept" with the word "file" and the word "feature" with the word "term" (or "name"). In one direction, this mapping gives the user several ways to specify a particular file. In the other direction, this mapping gives the system a variety of terms by which to describe a particular file to the user. However, the effective use of such a many-to-many mapping depends upon our ability to answer a number of questions including the following:

- How does the system arrive at a useful many-to-many mapping?

- How does the system make appropriate modifications to this mapping to reflect corresponding changes in the way objects are referred to by a user or user group?

- In the recall direction, how does the system disambiguate a user reference? When a term is associated to several objects, its specification alone is generally not sufficient to distinguish between a desired object and other objects in the database.

- In the recognition direction, what part of an object's representation should the system display so that the user can best determine whether the object meets the user's needs? A given object, through its various uses, may be associated to many different terms, not all of which are equally informative at a given point in time.

These and related questions can be translated into questions concerning the way people function. How do we arrive at, maintain, and adaptively modify our representations of the world around us? How do we disambiguate incoming information? And how do we go about deciding what first to say about a particular object when describing it to others?

These are some of the questions driving basic research into human information processing and the skills of inter-personal communication. This chapter advances the possibility that the psychological insights gained from these basic research efforts can be translated into applied prescriptions for system design.

As has already been noted, the design of the ME system freely borrows from constructs found in models of human memory (and, more generally, models of human information processing). Specifically, the ME system represents the adaptation of an associative, spreading activation approach (Anderson, 1976, 1983; Collins & Quillian, 1969, 1972; Collins & Loftus, 1975). Clearly, this is only one of many approaches to the modeling of human memory and it is beyond the scope of this chapter to adequately examine all the alternatives. However, we explore some of the more salient alternatives in Section 3 as part of a discussion dealing with analogues to ME system constructs in models of human memory. But first the ME system and its use are described in Section 2. As part of this description, ME system constructs are compared with those of conventional filing systems and of information retrieval systems.

2. The ME System

What follows is only a partial description of the ME system. (For a more complete description of the ME system, see Jones, 1986.) First we look at the ME system's representational scheme. This is followed by a look at some of the ways in which the ME system can be used. Finally, three important processes of the ME system are discussed in turn:

- its means of adaptation through the *exchange of representational information*
- its application of *decay mechanisms* as a means of reducing representational inertia
- its *spreading activation matching algorithm.*

2.1 The Representational Scheme

Objects in the ME system are represented in an associative network of weighted term links. A word about this article's terminology is in order:

- *Objects* in the ME system are a class of nodes that the user can reference and manipulate. Files are ME system objects with contents that the user can retrieve into the text editor and modify. A "context" is also an object in the ME system with its own set of properties and its own set of permissible user actions. More generally, the documents of a public information retrieval system and the commands, functions, and procedures of a computing system can all be regarded as objects.

- The *representation* of an object refers to its set of out-links, i.e., the set of links extending from the object to terms in the database. The representation of an object will sometimes also refer to the set of terms at the other end of these out-links.

The representation of an object should be distinguished from related notions of an object's *display* and *indexing*:

- An object's *display* is what the user sees (and what the computer presents) on the terminal screen. The ME system, through various display modes, offers the user different views of a given object. Object representations form the basis of several display modes.

- An object's *indexing* is its set of in-links, i.e., the set of links extending from terms in the database to the object. The indexing of an object may also refer to the terms of these in-links. Since all links involving a file object are bi-directional, a file's in-links and its out-links are one and the same, in the ME system. Consequently, a file's indexing is equivalent to its representation. This is not true for context objects. A context object in the ME system has a representation (it has out-links leading to terms) but no indexing (no in-links). Note that a file's representation/indexing is not the same as its contents.

2.1.1 The Representation of Files

A file is represented, i.e., indexed, in the ME system by a set of variably weighted term links (see Figure 2-1). These links are bi-directional in the sense that, for every link pointing from a term to the file, there is a corresponding link pointing from the file back to the term.

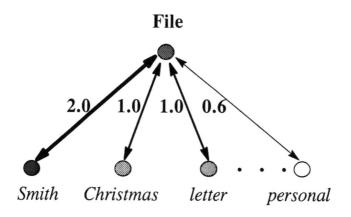

Figure 2-1:   A sample representation of a file in the ME system

From the user's perspective, bi-directionality carries both a recall and a recognition function. In one direction, the user can directly access (i.e., recall) a file through a specification of some of its associated terms. In the other direction, the computer can represent the file to the user, thus enabling its recognition (as distinct from other files), through a presentation of its associated terms.

The variable weighting of terms provides a basis by which to order files according to the likelihood of their reference (see Furnas, Landauer, Gomez, & Dumais, 1983) and so aids in file recall.   With reference to Figure 1-1, for example, variable weighting might enable the system to generate an educated guess regarding the likely referent (e.g., a file) of an ambiguous reference (e.g., a term with links to several files). Such a weighting scheme might also be used to improve a file's recognizability. For example, the system can order the terms in a file's representation on the basis of their weights before presenting these terms to the user.[2] In both its recall and recognition functions, therefore, a variable weighting scheme promises to realize benefits that are not found in conventional keyword representations with all-or-none (i.e., binary) weighting schemes.[3]

It is not intended that users will ever have to directly concern themselves with the manipulation of term weights (although the ME system does give users an option to do so if they choose). The assignment of term weights and their modification is a system's responsibility and the user need never do more than simply specify a given term. Moreover, the ME system processes frequently make even the user specification of terms unnecessary. The system, for example, is able to determine its representation of a file, in part, from a consideration of the contexts within which the file is used.

2.2 The Representation of Context

In the ME system, context, like other objects, is represented by a set of variably weighted term links.[4] Through its term links, the context object can be viewed as expressing a set of givens that hold across a series of file transactions. Since the context object is often used as a query to generate a set of partial file matches, it can also be seen to define and represent a working set of files. Among its many uses, the context object can form the basis of a query during retrieval attempts and it can form the basis of a newly created file's representation.

---

[2]Such an ordering is motivated by an assumption that the weight of a term in a file's representation is correlated with the term's importance as a descriptor of the file's contents or purpose. In this chapter's discussion of context, we explore the notion that the descriptive value of a term in a file's representation is heavily dependent upon the context within which the file occurs.

[3]In the ensuing discussion it will become apparent that, although a link has only one associated weight, the interpretation of this weight in the ME system is *node relative* and so depends upon direction from which the link is traversed.

[4]In contrast to a file's representation, however, these links are uni-directional: A link can be traversed from the context object to its associated terms, but traversal in the reverse direction is not possible (i.e., it is not possible to "retrieve" the context).

To the extent that the user and the computer share such a common context, exchanges can be simultaneously brief and precise. Consider a very simplified filing situation involving a many-to-many mapping in which all combinations of letter type ("business", "birthday", "Christmas", ...) and letter recipient ("Jones", "Smith", "Brown", ...) are realized. A user's attempt to retrieve a letter through specification of the term "Smith" is then ambiguous unless it is understood that the user is working with a series of "Christmas" letters. A shared context thus obviates the repeated specification of the term "Christmas" with each new retrieval attempt. More generally, a shared context enables the user to realize advantages associated with the potential accessibility of objects in a large filing system together with the advantages of abbreviated com-munication that are possible in a small filing system. A shared context between user and computer can also be used to reduce the amount of information a user must specify regarding the representation of a newly created file for purposes of storage. In a context of Christmas letters, for example, a newly created letter might reasonably "inherit" the term "Christmas." The chapter by Guindon in this volume shows, in the con-text of user-advisory systems, that users will naturally resort to longer, more descriptive expressions to refer to objects when the users believe that there is poor shared context between users and advisor.

The ME system's representation of context can be contrasted with the hierarchical approach of a system such as UNIX. In a file system hierar-chy, a context, of sorts, is established through the specification of a "path" leading to a "working directory." This path is then prepended to user-generated file names, both during storage and retrieval attempts.

Several problems are generally associated with the use of a file hierarchy:

- *lack of expressive power* - Since a context (i.e., a working directory) must correspond to a non-terminal node (i.e., a directory/subdirectory), a hierarchy's ability to represent the context of the user/computer interaction is extremely limited.

- *brittleness* - The hierarchy is static and cannot be recon-figured except through explicit, often laborious, input from the user.

- *all-or-none file inclusion* - Files are either in a directory or they are not; gradations in the relative importance of files (in the context of the directory) cannot be reliably represented.

- *order-dependent directory specification* - A change of working directory or the retrieval of a file that is not in the current working directory requires a complete specification of a path and the components of this path must be specified in their proper order.

- *name-oriented file specification* - Retrieval of a file that is in the current working directory is name-oriented and so, subject to problems of recall and recognition as these were discussed earlier in this paper.

In contrast to the hierarchical approach, the ME system's representation of context promises to be at the same time more flexible and more precise. An analogy can be drawn between the current working directory of a hierarchical system and the set of partial file matches that is generated when the context object forms the basis of a query in the ME system. Unlike the working directory, however, this is a set with no sharp boundaries - files in the database receive a graded preferential treatment during retrieval attempts according to their representational similarity to the context. The number of ways a filing system can be partitioned in this manner is limited only by the representational richness of the files involved.

2.3 Use of the ME System

The upcoming section on the ME system adaptivity will discuss the means by which a file's representation - in particular, a newly created file's representation - is automatically enhanced by contextual information. Also discussed in that section and the immediately following section on decay mechanisms, are the ways in which the ME system can arrive at and adaptively modify a representation of the context while keeping the need for direct user intervention to a minimum. But first, we will look at some of the ways in which the ME system can be used.

Figure 2-2 illustrates a situation in which the user has initiated the formation of a list of files that partially match the current context. The

```
current context:
    mail      pdp        nov

matching files:
  RULES      | linguists  connection exchange  | mail      pdp        nov
  SIGNATURE  | address    email      template  | mail      nov
  GOLDEN     | decision   error      statistics| mail      pdp
  DESCENT    | descent    misha      pavel     | pdp
  TRANS      | printer    mail3      info      | mail      nov
  DREYFUS    | perceptron rosenblatt simon     | pdp
  INFO       | release    info       hawaii    | mail      nov
  MAIL2      | mailrc     info       tmp       | mail      nov
  SCHVAN-REV | boulder    schvan     review    | mail
  HERRING    | prinz      sl         jep       | mail      nov
  MAIL-INFO  | ir         parity     info      | mail      pdp
  RELEASE    | software   norman     release   | mail      pdp
  TMP        | submission hawaii     paths     | nov
  USER-GUIDE | release    temp       letter    | mail   ┌Available Actions┐
  AUTO-INDEX | ijmms      auto       index     | mail   │  retrieve file  │
  PENZIAS    | 2nd        order      problem   | mail   │  create version │
  PARITY     | parity     discussion connection| mail   │  specify terms  │
  GAINES-SPE | ijmms      review     doc       | mail   │  erase links    │
  NOV-85     | old        85         status    | nov    │  delete file    │
  HERO-86    | milestones hero       letter    | mail   │  file views     │
  PRINZ-10-2 | prinz      sl         jep       | mail   │  save file      │
                                                        └─────────────────┘
command pane
click here to change the display mode
click here to exit

inactive█

input pane
erase all term links in this file's representation
```

Figure 2-2:   An example of the "current context match menu"
(the context and files are each represented in
an ordered line of terms).

current context is represented in its own display line in the top pane.
About 25 matching files are represented in an ordered listing of display
lines in the much larger pane. (The user can scroll downwards to view
more file matches.) Context in this instance serves as a query. The user
can change the composition and ordering of the partial match list by
mousing the context line and then selecting a "specify terms" option.
Newly specified context terms are added to the context's display line and
also dynamically effect a reconstitution of the partial match listing.

The user can also initiate various file-oriented operations by mousing on
a file's display line. The user can, for example, modify a file's indexing
and representation through the specification of terms. The specification
of file terms, like the specification of context terms, brings about a
dynamic reconstitution of the partial match listing.

In Figure 2-2, a file's display line is divided into three sections. In the leftmost section is the file's "label". A file's label is simply one of the file's associated terms (which may, in fact, occur elsewhere in the display line as well) that has a reasonably strong connection to the file and reasonably few, competing connections to other files in the database.[5] To the right of the file's label in the display line is a section of terms in the file's representation that distinguish it from the current context. This ordered list of terms (with the most distinguishing terms occurring leftmost in the display) is constructed by first normalizing context and file representations so that each forms a vector with a block metric length of 1.0 (i.e., the sum of weights in each vector equals 1.0). The context's vector is then essentially subtracted from the file's vector. In a similar manner, the representation of the current context is used to construct a set of ordered terms that account for the file's rated similarity to the current context. These terms are presented in the rightmost section of a file's display line.

The ME system's representation of context can thus be seen to carry both a recall function, through its use in the construction of a partial match ordering of files, and a recognition function, through its use in the construction of a file's display line. Implicit in the presentation of distinguishing terms is a context-dependent definition of the term *significance* similar to that put forth by Meadow (1973): "Words are significant as subject descriptors, then, in proportion to the difference between their actual and expected frequencies." In Olson's (1970) paradigm case, a speaker must communicate to a listener the location of a gold star that has been placed under a small, white, round, wooden block. Olson observes that the content of the speaker's utterance is likely to depend upon the context in which the block occurs. In Case 1, a second, small, BLACK, round wooden block is present and, therefore, the speaker is likely to say "It's under the WHITE one". In Case 2, a second, small, white, SQUARE block is present. Now the speaker is likely to say "It's under the ROUND one". In Case 1, the features of roundness, smallness, "woodenness", and "blockness" are givens of the situation and are, therefore, not informative with respect to the block in question. Likewise,

---

[5]The system assigns a file's label on the basis of the file's associated information. This can then be overridden by the user.

the features of smallness, whiteness, woodenness, and blockness are the givens in Case 2.

Many of the givens in a ME system partial match listing are represented in the query (e.g., the current context).[6] As the rightmost sections in the file display lines of Figure 2-2 illustrate, terms in the query are likely to occur with high frequency across files in the partial match listing - especially those near the top of the listing. These terms, then, are not, by the definition given above, very significant or distinguishing (in the context established by the query). Why then do we bother to present similar terms in the rightmost section of a file's display line? In fact, the display mode illustrated in Figure 2-2 is only one of many.[7] If the user selects a "different terms" display mode, the middle and rightmost sections of a file's display line in Figure 2-2 would be replaced with a single section presenting an ordered listing of terms in a file's representation that distinguish it from the representation of the query. However, the representations of files can overlap with the query's representation in a variety of ways. The "different/similar" display mode in Figure 2-2 attempts to give us the best of both worlds by telling us not only how files in the match window differ from the query but also what accounts for the rated similarity of these files to the query.

2.3.1 File Retrieval

With reference to Figure 2-2, specification of terms, whether file or context, dynamically causes a readjustment in the partial match listing. Files may move up or down in this listing and the position of terms within a line representing a file or the current context may change depending upon

---

[6]We will see that the query of a partial match window need not necessarily be the current context. As an alternative, for example, the ME system allows us to use a selected file's representation as the query of a partial match window. We might do this in order to initiate a sort of query by example.

[7]A user may pick from among several display modes, including: 1. *strongest terms* - A file's terms are ordered in its display solely on the basis of their relative strength without regard to the current context; 2. *different terms* - Only those terms that distinguish a file from the current context are presented; 3. *similar terms* - Only those terms that account for the file's similarity to the current context are presented.

the change in their relative weights. The user is thus given direct feedback on the effect of his/her input to the system. The prescribed strategy for file retrieval is to modify the current context through the specification of terms that are associated to the desired file. This can be an iterative procedure that continues until the file's representation is recognized somewhere on the list.

If users do not want to base a retrieval attempt on the current context, they can choose from among several alternatives. For example, the user can request a partial match listing to a file. This is essentially a retrieval-by-example (i.e., "show me files that are similar to this one") in which the representation of a specified file replaces the representation of the current context as the query of a partial match listing. The user can also request a partial match listing to a null object. This is analogous to a temporary "return to the home directory" in a hierarchical filing system such as that of UNIX. In addition, the user can erase the current context or reinstate the representation of an old, previously saved context before initiating the formation of a context partial match listing.

2.3.2 File Storage

If the user initiates the formation of a list of partial matches to a specified file, the format of this presentation is identical to that of Figure 2-2 except that the wording "current context" is replaced by "current file." This listing permits the user to retrieve or otherwise work with files that are related to the specified file. The use of the listing in this manner constitutes a form of retrieval-by-example. The listing also helps the user to determine whether the representation of the current file is sufficiently distinct from that of other files in the database. This can be done prior to the file's storage in order to insure its subsequent retrievability.

There is, therefore, an essential symmetry between the actions of storage and retrieval. In both cases, the attempt is to disambiguate through the elaboration of a query - whether this is a file or the current context. As part of a retrieval action, the partial match listing can be viewed as a system response that effectively asks "Do you want this file or this file or ...?" As part of a storage action, the partial match listing can be viewed as a system response that effectively asks "How is this file (the query) different from these other files?" - in a sense, the system is being "reminded" of these other related files.

2.3.3 Putting Some of This Together - An Example

The following example helps to sketch out some of the features of the ME system. In the coming sections we will look in greater detail at the ME system constructs that underly these features. Suppose a user named Henry is writing a series of Christmas letters to friends. This being the case, it is likely that the terms "Christmas", "letter", and "friend" are already part of the ME system's representation of the current context. Now Henry wants to create a new file to contain a "Christmas letter to John Smith in Toledo". Henry does not need to explicitly associate the terms "Christmas", "letter", and "friend" to the newly created file. Instead, this is automatically done in the ME system through a process of information exchange (to be discussed shortly). Suppose Henry then explicitly associates the term "Smith" to the file but neglects to associate the term "John".

Now Henry completes the composition of the letter and is ready to store the file for subsequent printing. Preliminary to this act of file storage, Henry elects to form a partial match listing to the file's representation. This listing makes it apparent that Henry has already created a Christmas letter to another friend named Smith. Fortunately, the listing also makes it possible for Henry to directly modify the representations of both the new and the old files. Henry elects to associate the term "Toledo" to the new file and the term "Topeka" to the old file (to represent the other Smith's current city of residence).

Now, at some point several months later, Henry wants to write another letter to "John Smith in Toledo" but, preliminary to this, Henry wants to retrieve the Christmas letter in order to determine what was most recently sent to John Smith. To effect this retrieval, Henry might specify the term "John" to be included in the current context's representation. Unfortunately, the resulting partial match listing does not bring up the old Christmas letter file because Henry neglected to associate this term to the file at the time of its creation. Henry does finally retrieve the file through specification of the terms "Smith" and "Toledo". Now the process of information exchange acts to strengthen the terms "Smith" and "Toledo" in the file's representation. Moreover, this process also acts to automatically include the term "John" in the file's representation. This error correction facility increases Henry's chances of retrieving the file using the term "John" the next time around. Finally, when Henry creates the new file to Smith, the terms "John", "Smith", and "Toledo" will all be automatically associated to this file through the information exchange process.

2.4 The Learning Process

To the extent that the ME system can make appropriate modifications in its representations, the need for the direct intervention by the user is lessened. In this regard, the ME system acquires a limited degree of adaptivity through its attempt to capitalize upon a very important interplay that exists between the files of a database and the context within which these files are used.

In one direction, representational similarities among the files a user is working with (or has recently worked with), can be used to define, at least partially, the current context. Context so defined, will necessarily change, however slightly, with each new file that is retrieved.

In the other direction, a file's representation can be defined, at least partially, by the various contexts in which it has been used. The representation of a file, at least in the user's memory, can be expected to change, however slightly, each time it is used. At the very least, the user will have formed incidental, episodic associations between the file and the files that immediately preceded and followed it in an interactive sequence with the computer. Beyond this, it might be assumed that feature commonalities among these "surrounding" files express something substantive about the file's use that should be incorporated into its representation.

The ME system tracks this context/file interplay through a process of *representational information exchange*. After it has been determined that a newly retrieved (or created) file is in fact desired,[8] the context's representation is modified in the following manner:

$$C_n = C_{n-1} + rF_{n-1}.$$

In this equation, r is a constant $(0 < r < 1)$, F_{n-1} is the file's representation, C_{n-1} is the context's representation before the exchange of information, and C_n is the context's representation after the exchange. (For purposes of the equation, all file representations are expressed as vectors of term weights.)

Similarly, the file's representation is modified in the following manner:

$$F_n = F_{n-1} + sC_{n-1}.$$

In this equation, s is a constant $(0 < s < 1)$, C_{n-1} is the context's representation, F_{n-1} is the file's representation before the exchange of information, and F_n is the file's representation after the exchange. (Again, for purposes of the equation, all file representations are expressed as vectors of term weights.) Currently both r and s have the somewhat arbitrary value of .2. Considerations surrounding the selection of these and other parameter values of the ME system will be discussed in greater detail later in this chapter. These operations are similar to the document retrieval operations of *relevance feedback* and *dynamic document vector alteration* (Ide & Salton, 1971; Salton & McGill, 1983).

A sort of one-sided exchange of information also takes place when a new file is created from the current context. In this case, the file's initial representation is identical to that of the current context,[9] but the representation of the current context remains unchanged (since the new file has no information to give in return).[10] In this manner, the new file inherits representational givens of the current situation.

---

[8]The user can explicitly state that a file is desired or the system can infer this from user-initiated operations such as file storage/modification.

[9]Terms extracted from a user-supplied pathname are subsequently added to a newly created file's representation.

[10]Strictly speaking, of course, no file begins its life tabula rasa. At the very least, a new file has a creation date. It may also have initial contents. As an extension to the ME system, this information might be used to partially determine the file's initial representation in the ME system.

More generally, those terms are added to a file's representation (or strengthened) that the user is perhaps least likely to explicate in the current context (see Olson, 1970). To the extent that these contextual givens are the "ground" of the current interaction, the user may not even be aware of them. Nevertheless, these context terms may afford very important routes to the file's subsequent retrieval in other contexts.

As illustrated earlier, another interesting by-product of the information exchange is an adaptive indexing of files (Furnas, Landauer, Gomez, & Dumais, 1983). For example, a user composing a letter to John Smith may have himself associated the term "Smith" to the file at the time of its creation but may have neglected to mention the term "John." A subsequent retrieval attempt that begins by modifying the current context to include the term "John" will then not have the desired results (the file will not receive any activation from this term). However, if the user does eventually get the file in some other way (e.g., by including the term "Smith" in the current context) then the term "John" will automatically be added to the file's representation through the process of information exchange (since it is still a part of the context's representation). This error correcting feature of the exchange process thus acts to decrease the likelihood of subsequent retrieval failures.[11]

The ME system applies the process of representational information exchange in the interests of reaching and maintaining a representational accord with the user regarding the files of the database and the context within which these are used. It is important to note that this process may enable the ME system to modify its representations over time in order to match corresponding changes in the user's internal representations. The user's representation of a given file is likely to change with each usage.

---

[11]Of course this process of information exchange will sometimes accidentally associate terms to objects. The user in the example above may have mistakenly typed "Dave" instead of "John" and only later realized his error. The accidental formation of a link between a term such as "Dave" and the file that is eventually selected is not a problem for several reasons. First, in the use of the ME system's spreading activation matching algorithm, a file is not penalized for its representational richness. Secondly, accidental associations are typically "washed away" with time through a decay mechanism to be discussed in the next section. Finally, these links may even have some short-term utility. The user may, for example, sometimes want "the file that I worked with yesterday after mistakenly typing the term 'Dave'".

In turn, the user's representation of the current context will likely change with each new file that is specified. Unless these changes are matched by corresponding changes in the computer's own representations, user and computer may eventually cease to share a common field of referents and common language of reference.

2.5 Decay Mechanisms

Context and file representations are "manually" modified through user-initiated operations of term specification and are automatically modified through the adaptive operation of information exchange. Both kinds of operations are cumulative - the "new" is simply added onto the "old".[12] If this cumulative enrichment of object representations were allowed to go unchecked, a sort of "representational inertia" would develop, making the system progressively more resistant to change. From another perspective, the effects of user input or of information exchange would be devalued over the course of the system's use. This problem is countered in the ME system through two important mechanisms of decay.

Each time the current context object is modified, a *context decay mechanism* operates to keep the context object's *strength* - defined to be the sum of its term weights - at or below a constant prescribed value P. Similarly, a *global decay mechanism* periodically operates so that the mean of all file strengths remains constant. (Although the strength of a given file may deviate considerably from this average.)
In both cases a *decay factor* is formed as follows:

$$d = P / A,$$

where P and A are the prescribed and actual strengths (or average strengths), respectively. The weights of all term links involved are then simply multiplied by d (providing $d < 1$). A term link is deleted if its new weight falls below a certain threshold (currently equal to .1). The value of P for purposes of both context and global decay is somewhat

---

[12]For example, when an object's representation is modified through a user-initiated act of term specification, one of two things happens: a) A new link between the object and a specified term is formed and given a weight of one. b) If a link between this object and the specified term already exists, its weight is incremented by one.

arbitrarily fixed in the current ME system at the constant value of 5.0. (Parameter choices of the ME system will be discussed later in this chapter.)

The decay mechanisms, in addition to reducing the system's representational inertia, also have the beneficial effect of "washing away" links whose initial formation was accidental or whose current existence is no longer useful. Since context decay acts to keep the strength of the context object constant, the entry of new terms into the context object's representation will result in the eventual displacement of old terms. (This is dynamically represented in the context object's partial match window.) However, the displacement of context terms happens in a gradual rather than an all-or-none manner.

Although the mean of file strengths (again, a file's strength is defined to be the sum of its weights to terms in the system) remains fairly constant in the ME system, there will generally be considerable variation in the strengths of individual files. In combination with the matching algorithm, to be discussed shortly, this has the generally beneficial effect of giving preferential treatment to files whose use is frequent. On the other hand, if the use of a file is very infrequent, its strength will eventually approach zero, effectively rendering the file unretrievable. The ME system calls the user's attention to files whose strengths have fallen below a certain threshold under the assumption that these files may no longer be needed. The user then has the option either to delete these files or to strengthen their representations. The ME system thus provides a principled means by which to cleanse the database of files whose usefulness has passed. To the extent that the global decay mechanism mirrors a forgetting process in the user's own memory, this facility also serves to remind the user of the existence of "forgotten" files.[13]

---

[13]Note, however, that the strength of unused files in the ME system decays exponentially. In contrast, it appears that long-term forgetting in people is better characterized by a power law function (see Anderson, 1983; Wickelgren, 1976) - a point we return to in the section dealing with human information processing analogues to ME system constructs.

2.6 The Matching Process

The matching process of the ME system is used to order the files of a database according to their representational similarity to a given query (e.g., the context or an active file). In the first stage of the matching process (see Figure 2-3), a single unit of activation A is divided among the terms of the query according to their relative weights. Specifically, a given query term t receives activation,

$$a_t = A * (w_{Qt} / W_Q),$$

where w_{Qt} equals the weight from the query to term t and W_Q equals the sum of the query's associated term weights.

In the second stage of the matching process, the activation received by a given term t in the first stage is further partitioned among each of its associated files so that a given file receives activation,

$$a_F = a_t * (w_{tF} / W_t),$$

where w_{tF} equals the weight from term t to file $\mathbf{F}$ and W_t equals the sum of term t's associated file weights. The activation a given file receives in this manner from several different query terms will sum together. Files can then be ordered in a partial match listing according to their activation levels.[14]

Elsewhere it has been argued (Jones and Furnas, 1987) that this spreading activation process compares favorably with a class of *vector similarity measures* (e.g., the *correlation, covariance, cosine, dot-product, dice,* and *Jaccard* coefficients) that are conventionally used in document retrieval systems (see Salton & McGill, pp. 201-204, for a review of these measures). This comparison holds from the perspective of both computational efficiency and psychological utility. Only the high points of this comparison will be presented here.

---

[14]In a special boolean case in which all links are either zero- or one-weighted and each term has an equal number of one-weighted links, the spreading activation mechanism produces an "and/or" ordering of files: the more terms a file has in common with the query, the higher it is on the partial match list.

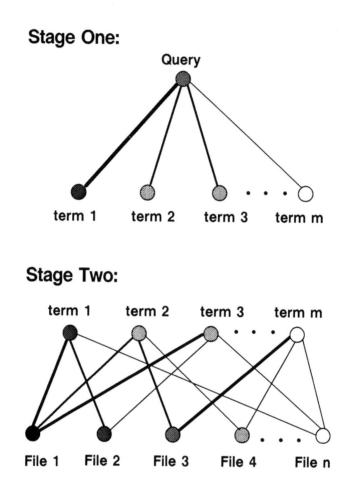

Figure 2-3: The ME system's spreading activation matching algorithm

2.6.1 Computational Efficiency

In large measure, the ME system's spreading activation matching process is efficient because activation travels only a short distance. Activation spread in the ME system is a simple two-stage process: 1. Activation leaving the object to be matched spreads to associated terms. 2. Activation then spreads from these terms to matching objects in the system.[15] Further gains in computational efficiency result from the utilization of:

- *The specificity of term reference* - The ability to traverse links in the term-to-file direction permits the ME system to limit the scope of the matching process to a subset of the files in the database.

- *Incremental matching* - The matching process can often be limited to a computation of changes induced by the current user input on a previous partial match listing. (This listing may be associated either with the context object or with a file the user is currently working on).

In fact, the ME system rarely follows the full-fledged spreading activation matching process outlined at the beginning of this section during a retrieval attempt. Instead, the matching process is limited to currently specified modifications in the representation of the context object. If, for example, a user adds the term "birthday" to a context object currently associated to the terms "letter" and "Christmas", then activation will only spread from the birthday term to associated files in the database. The effects of this activation spread are then essentially "added on" to a partial match listing in which the effects of terms "letter" and "Christmas" have already been computed.[16] A comparable situation holds with respect to modifications of a file. This approach realizes a substantial gain in computational efficiency while sacrificing nothing with regards to the information content of a query.

We would thus appear to have the best of both worlds. Earlier in this chapter, it was noted that the representation of context minimized the user input required to retrieve a desired file. The ME system, through its utilization of incremental matching, translates this benefit of psychological utility into a benefit of computational efficiency as well.

---

[15]We will see that allowing activation to spread farther gives the ME system a limited ability to induce term synonymy (see also Jones, 1986). In limiting the spread of activation, therefore, gains in computational efficiency are realized through the sacrifice of some psychological utility. Nevertheless, even this very restricted version of spreading activation realizes potential benefits of psychological utility that are not found in the use of conventional vector similarity measures.

[16]The situation is slightly more complicated than this, but a more precise discussion of the procedure used is beyond the scope of this chapter.

Implicit in the discussion of term reference specificity is the notion of a *link weight threshold*. Term-to-file links whose weights fall below a certain threshold are not traversed during the second stage of the matching process (see Figure 2-3). This is greater than zero so that zero-weighted links are never considered. Such a threshold can also be applied to the query-to-term links of the first stage of the matching process.

In fact it is likely that the distribution of link weights at both stages of the matching process is very uneven. For example, a comparatively small number p of the most heavily weighted links emanating from the query to be matched may account for a large portion of the total weighting in its link associates. In turn, a comparatively small number q of the most heavily weighted links emanating from a given term may account for a large portion of the total weighting in its link associates. When this is true, the results of the matching process may be much the same when only these $p + p*q$ links are considered (i.e., when activation spreads down these links only).

The only "threshold" actually observed in the current version of the ME system is that activation spreading down a link must be greater than zero, i.e., all links with positive weight are currently considered during the matching process. The ME system's use of incremental matching, together with its current limitation in the distance of activation spread, make the system quite responsive (single-term input from the user is processed in one to two seconds). The speed of the ME system thus obviates the imposition of a stronger threshold which might lead to information loss (however slight).

The spreading activation matching process of the ME system, in combination with its associative, bi-directional representation scheme, makes possible a principled increase in computational efficiency through reductions in p and q. In the parlance of the document retrieval discipline, reductions in p will result in some loss in the precision of a query (some disambiguating information in the query is lost) while reductions in q will result in some loss in the recall rate of the query (some potentially matching files do not receive activation from a term in the query). In the extreme, when $p = q = 1$, we essentially have a name-oriented system. The value of q may be considerably smaller than the number of files in the system set so that only a small subset of the total set of files is considered during any given matching attempt.

In its computational efficiency, the ME system compares favorably with a class of vector similarity measures. All vector similarity measures involve some pairwise consideration of vector strengths; in most of these measures (e.g., the dice, Jaccard, correlation, covariance, cosine, and dot-product coefficients) this consists of a dot product of the two vectors for which a similarity measure is desired. The most straightforward way of generating a listing of partial file matches to a given query using a vector similarity measure involves resolving query and file objects into vectors of m weights each, where m equals the number of terms in the lexicon.[17] A similarity measure would then be successively computed between the query vector and each of n file vectors. Since the time to do this computation increases with m^*n, this straightforward approach is clearly unacceptable when applied to a large and growing database.

In light of the earlier discussion, it is reasonable to suppose that we could save time by matching only the p largest weights in the query vector to corresponding weights in file vectors without serious distortion in the resulting similarity measures. Nevertheless, the computation of similarity under this circumstance still increases with n, the number of files in the database - a relationship to be avoided in a large and expanding database. (Recall, that a time is anticipated when the average user may wish to store several thousand or perhaps several hundred thousand files in a database.)

In public document retrieval systems, the efficiency of a vector similarity matching process can be further increased through the use of file cluster-ing (see Goffman, 1968; Jardine & Sibson, 1968; Salton, 1978; Sparck Jones, 1970). File clustering is a two-step process. First, a pairwise similarity measure among all objects in the system is derived through a vector similarity measure. Second, clusters or classes of related objects are constructed with reference to an object-by-object similarity matrix. A given cluster can be represented by a centroid that reflects the represen-tational similarities among the objects in the cluster. When an object O is

---

[17]Most of these weights would, of course, equal zero.

matched to the centroids of a taxonomy, as opposed to the individual objects, matching time is naturally faster and it no longer necessarily increases with the total number of objects in the system.

The success of such an approach depends upon two important conditions:

> 1) The classification should be *stable* in the sense that small alterations of the data, because of the addition of new items or changes in old ones, should cause only minor alterations in the classification. 2) The classification should also be *well defined* in that a given body of data should produce a single classification or at least one of a small set of compatible classifications. (Salton & McGill, 1983, pp. 215-216.)

Neither of these conditions is likely to be met in the comparatively volatile situation of a personal filing system. A classification scheme can group objects in only one or, at most, a handful of ways. Retrieval that is mediated by a classification scheme thus serves to limit the expressive power of an object's representation no matter how rich this may be. Moreover, in the constantly changing environment of a personal filing system, any classification scheme, no matter how adequate it may have been at the time of its formation, is apt to be quickly rendered obsolete with the introduction of new objects or the modification of old objects.

In a personal filing system, in contrast to a document retrieval system, the intent of the user is more often to retrieve an individual object (as opposed to a class of related objects). It is thus desirable that the representational integrity of objects be maintained as nearly as possible. It should also be noted that the computation of inter-object similarity that forms the basis of a classification scheme can be extremely costly. (At best, the computation time increases with the square of the object set size). Again this is much more of a consideration in a dynamically changing personal filing system than it is in a comparatively static, well-defined document retrieval system.

Problems of computational efficiency in the vector similarity approach derive primarily from a failure to use term-to-object links in a database. We will see that this failure to use term-to-object information produces problems of psychological utility for vector similarity measures as well.

2.6.2 Psychological Utility

As a term is included in the representations of more and more objects of a filing system, its *discriminating value*, i.e., its ability to distinguish among the objects in the filing system is diminished (see Salton & Yang, 1973; Sparck Jones, 1972). A potentially serious problem arises when an information retrieval system fails to take this into account.

This problem is illustrated in the following simplified, but representative scenario: A user named Sally has composed a birthday letter to Fred and has stored the resulting file **a** with an indexing representation characterized by the following list of term/weight pairs: ("Fred" 1.0) ("birthday" 2.0). Note that Sally has inadvertently failed to include the term "letter" in the file's representation[18] (or, alternatively, the file's weight to this term is zero). There is a set **B** of 30 or so other letters in Sally's filing system, each with a representation of the form: (<name> 1.0) ("letter" 2.0). No files besides file **a**, however, have an association to term "Fred."

Later, Sally wishes to retrieve file **a**. However, Sally remembers only that the file contained a "letter" addressed to "Fred" so that the query she generates might look like this: ("Fred" 1.0) ("letter" 1.0). When any of a variety of vector similarity measures are applied, the resulting partial match listing will place all files in set **B** ahead of file **a**. This occurs because files in set **B** have a stronger association to "letter" than file **a** has to term "Fred". Unfortunately, this occurs in spite of the fact that "Fred", since it is uniquely associated with file **a**, has considerably more discriminating power than the term "letter." Thus the effect of these two query terms on the matching process is distorted in a direction opposite to what we want.

In the ME system, a term's discriminating ability is directly computed as part of the spreading-activation matching process. The activation reaching a given term is partitioned among its links according to their relative strengths. Consequently, the more objects a term is associated to, the

---

[18]If the term "letter" were a contextual given, the ME system might have automatically associated this term to the file in any case (through the information exchange process).

less matching activation any one of these objects will receive. When this spreading activation process is applied to the example involving Sally, for example, file **a** now receives considerably more activation than any of the files in set **B**.[19]

With reference to Figure 2-3 it can be seen that the ME system's two-stage spread of activation has the effect of making the matching process sensitive to each of two important sources of information:

- *within-query term relationships* - the relationship holding among the weights of term links emanating from the query

- *between-object term relationships* - the relationship holding among the weights of object links emanating from a given query term.

During the first stage, activation spreads from the query "node" to query terms according to the relative magnitude of their query weights. Clearly then, the more heavily weighted terms in a query will exert a larger influence on the matching process since they receive more activation - which they subsequently send on to database objects. The relative importance of a query term (as expressed by its weight) is thus directly translated into the term's relative influence on the matching process. Perhaps less obvious is that this first-stage partitioning of activation places an upward limit on the effect that any query term can exert upon the matching process; the effect of a query term on the matching process is limited by the amount of activation it receives from the query.

Similarity measures that do not have this "limiting" feature (e.g., the dice, dot product, and covariance coefficients) make it possible for a single query term to exert an undue influence on the matching process (see Jones & Furnas, 1987). Using these measures, for example, an object that has only the least important of the query terms in its representation can still be rated more similar to the query than any other object providing that the weight of its connection to this query term is high enough.

---

[19]File **a** receives 1/2 of the total activation while each of the files in set **B** receives only 1/60 of the total activation.

During the second stage of the ME system's matching process, activation deposited at each of the query terms spreads outward to associated objects in the database. Objects associated to a given query term can be seen to be competing with each other for a limited supply of activation. Objects that are more strongly connected to a query term (and so, presumably, have more "to do" with this term) will receive a larger share of its activation. At this stage, then, the ME system's matching process is sensitive to between-object term relationships.

Some similarity measures (e.g., the cosine and correlation coefficients) do not have this sensitivity to between-object term relationships (see Jones & Furnas, 1987). These measures may rate files **a** and **b** as equally similar to a query even though the strengths of file **a**'s connections to query terms are each twice as strong as the corresponding strengths of file **b**'s connections.

At a general level, the advantages of the ME system's spreading activation matching algorithm derive from the dynamic and automatic way in which its actions are determined by the representational structures involved. The flow of activation leaving a node (e.g., the query or a term) is directly affected by changes in the relative strengths of links involved. In this way the matching process is able to use information regarding the discriminating value of a term, within-query term relationships, and between-object term relationships in order to improve the system's psychological utility. In the next section we explore an additional gain in psychological utility that may result from simply allowing activation in the database to spread a little further.

2.6.3 The Induction of Term Synonymy

The version of the ME system presented thus far is unable to recognize or use relationships that may exist (in the user's mind, at least) among terms in the user/computer dialogue. One important inter-term relationship is that of synonymy. In the extreme, a user may apply two terms interchangeably (e.g., "letter" and "message"), perhaps associating one term to a file during a storage attempt and later attempting to retrieve this file with the second term. The retrieval attempt may then fail unless the system can recognize a relationship between these two terms.

We would thus like a system that knows, or is able to figure out, how similar a term x is to other terms in the lexicon. In the ME system this can be done by simply making term x the query of the matching process, i.e., the starting point of activation spread. This can be understood with reference to Figure 2-3 if we simply interchange the words "file" and "term." Now, in Figure 2-3, activation spreads from a term to its associated files in stage one; in stage two it then spreads from these files to associated terms in the database.

Essentially we are "turning around" the network of object-term links to compute a listing of partial term matches to a given term x. All the advantages of spreading activation apply that were previously discussed with respect to the computation of a listing of partially similar objects. The recall rate of any retrieval attempt involving term x can then be improved by simply substituting term x in a user's query with the partially similar term matches to term x.[20]

This computation of term similarity can actually be an integral part of a *four-stage spreading activation process*. Under the two-stage spreading activation matching process, outlined earlier in this chapter, activation first spreads from the query Q to the set **G** of its term associates and then spreads from these terms to a set **H** of their object associates. Now consider the effect of adding two more stages to this process: 3. Activation now spreads from **H** to the set of their term associates **I**. 4. Activation then spreads from **I** to a set of their object associates **J**. The objects in **J** are now used to form a listing of partial matches to Q. The second and third stages in this process serve to compute the similarity between the terms of the query and other terms in the system. In the final stage of this process, similar terms not in the original query (i.e., terms receiving object-mediated activation from the query terms) are effectively added to the query before a final partial match listing is derived.

Under the four-stage process, information regarding term similarities is inferred from usage patterns in the filing system itself rather than being imported from some external source. This approach is, therefore, more

---

[20]Unless the circumstances are very unusual, term x will be at the top of this listing.

likely to pick up on a user's idiosyncratic use of terms. Note that two terms that are identified as being fairly synonymous by this process might not be regarded as synonymous according to any generally accepted definitions of these terms. However, from a practical standpoint, we are primarily interested in ways of detecting the interchangeable use of terms in situations of ME system use. If a user persistently uses two terms interchangeably, we might reasonably regard them as being synonymous within the world of the ME system.

The ME system approach, with its dynamic search for term co-occurrence patterns across objects of the database, is similar in spirit to Mozer's attempt to apply a connectionist approach to an information retrieval task (Mozer, 1984). Unfortunately, most existing connectionist models, including the one used by Mozer, place extreme demands on the computational resources of a conventional serial computer. In this regard, the computational advantages of the ME system's spreading activation process have already been noted. On the other hand, the ME system is not currently equipped to handle negative information, whether this is expressed in terms of activation or link weights. It remains to be determined whether this poses a serious limitation in tasks of information retrieval.

The ME system approach to term synonymy can also be compared with techniques of *automatic thesaurus construction* that are used in document retrieval systems (Salton & Lesk, 1971; Sparck Jones, 1971; Lesk, 1969; for a review, see Salton & McGill, 1983, pp. 78-81). Automatic thesaurus construction typically involves a two-step process that is virtually identical to that used to cluster files of similar representations. First, a pairwise similarity rating among all terms of the lexicon is established through a vector similarity measure. For the purposes of this measure, a term is represented by a vector reflecting the strengths of its associations to the objects in the system. Second, classes of similar (synonymous) terms are constructed with reference to a term-to-term similarity matrix. These synonymous term classes can then be used to improve the recall rate of a query. Perhaps the most straightforward way of accomplishing this is simply to append the terms of a synonymous class to a query when this query already contains one of its members.

However, the automatic thesaurus approach suffers from limitations that are analogous to those discussed earlier in this article with reference to file clustering:

- *The approach is computationally expensive.* At best, the time to construct synonymy classes increases with the square of the number of terms in the computer's lexicon.

- *The representation of term synonymy is static.* The updating of an automatically constructed thesaurus, to reflect the introduction into the database of new objects or the modification of old objects, is cumbersome and subject to inaccuracies; the complete reconstruction of an automatically constructed thesaurus is computationally expensive.

- *The representation of term synonymy is all-or-none.* Either two terms are in the same cluster or they are not. The approach thus offers only a crude approximation to a reality wherein the similarity of two terms can vary in a more or less continuous fashion.

- *A given classification represents only a single partition of terms.* This differs from a reality wherein a term, in its various senses, may properly belong to several different synonymy classes.

- *Term similarities are computed from a vector similarity measure.* All of the problems of vector similarity measures apply that were previously discussed with respect to the computation object/object similarities.

In each of these respects, the four-stage spreading activation process is superior:

- *The approach is computationally less expensive.* The computational advantages of spreading activation in the ME system, as these were discussed earlier, apply here as well. In particular, costs of the four-stage process can be limited by considering only the strongest links at any given stage in the process.

- *The representation of term synonymy is dynamic.* Since the computation of term similarity is an integral part of the attempt to match a query to objects in the system, its results can dynamically change to reflect the introduction of new objects into the database or the modification of old objects.

- *Term synonymy is represented in a continuous manner.* For example, the influence at stage four of a term not in the original query will vary continuously as a function of the amount of object-mediated activation it receives from terms in the query.

- *A term, in its various senses, can be similar to many other terms in the database.* The extent to which this happens is limited only by term co-occurrence patterns across objects in the database. The term "letter", for example, may co-occur, under different circumstances, with terms "alphabet" and "message".

- *Term similarities are computed using a spreading activation measure.* All of the comparative advantages that this entails have already been discussed.

The four-stage spreading activation process is a simple and direct extension of the two-stage process (activation is simply allowed to spread farther). It is important to note that this approach does not involve an explicit representation of term relationships - the basic representational scheme of the ME system is unaltered by this extension.

However, one caveat should be expressed. As a consequence of this four-stage process some objects will receive more activation than they would have under the simple two-stage process outlined earlier. Conversely, other objects may receive proportionally less of the total activation than they would have under the two-stage process. Objects directly linked to an original query term "letter", for example, may end up with proportionally less of the total activation if the query is expanded, during the four-stage process, to include the term "message". It remains to be seen whether this effect is always positive. Moreover, we can ask what would happen if activation were allowed to spread still farther (e.g., in processes involving six, eight, ten ... stages). This question has a matrix algebraic expression. Unfortunately, except in rare instances, the matrix representation of this situation is asymmetric and, consequently, there is no clean expression (that this author is aware of at any rate) for the asymptotic pattern, if any, that activation will assume in the network if it is allowed to spread indefinitely.

3. Human Information Processing Analogues

The discussion of the previous section focused on the ME system and a comparison of its constructs with those of other information retrieval systems. This was done in order to explicate some of the considerations that apply to the design of information retrieval systems and, more specifically, to the design of a personal filing system. Many constructs of the ME system are borrowed from models of human information processing where they appear to realize a similar purpose. Alternate constructs, found in other applied systems of information retrieval, also have their analogues in models of human information processing. In this section, we examine some of these analogues. This examination advances the argument that correspondences between the constructs of computer-based systems of information retrieval and models of human information processing arise from a similarity of task considerations.

3.1 The Representational Scheme

File representations in the ME system form an associative network of bi-directional, weighted term links. In the field of information retrieval, various vector models (see Salton & McGill, 1983) represent a movement away from binary or keyword indexing schemes towards weighted term representations. Clearly, weighted term representations potentially carry more information than binary term representations. As has already been noted, for example, term weights can indicate the relative importance of terms in a file's representation. (See Jones & Furnas, 1987, for a discussion of the various kinds of information that term weights are capable of expressing).

The ability to move in a term-to-file (as well as a file-to-term) direction, i.e., the feature of bi-directionality, represents another step in the evolution to a network representation. In the previous section we saw that the bi-directional use of weighted terms can serve both a recall and a recognition function. In a recall direction, moving from specified terms to their associated files, the ME system's spreading activation mechanism uses the relative magnitude of link weights as a basis by which to order files in a partial match listing. In a recognition direction, moving from a given file to its associated terms, the ME system can interpret link weights in many ways, some of them context-dependent, with the aim of displaying those terms that are most descriptive regarding the file's purpose.[21] Moreover, with the application of a spreading activation mechanism, it becomes possible, by traversing links in both file-to-term and term-to-file directions, to compute information not directly represented in any given link (term synonymy, for example).

Corresponding to this evolution from binary, keyword indexing schemes, there has been, in proposed models of human memory, an evolution away from feature set models (e.g., Meyer, 1970; Schaeffer & Wallace, 1970; Smith, Shoben, & Rips, 1974) towards associational network models (e.g., Anderson, 1976, 1983; Collins & Quillian, 1969, 1972; Collins & Loftus, 1975; Norman & Rumelhart, 1975). This evolution, moreover, can be driven by many of the same considerations as those used to promote the use of weighted, bi-directional term links in an information retrieval system. Network representations, for example, suggest more clearly how we might go about deriving information regarding a concept that is unlikely to have been included in the concept's immediate representation in memory (e.g., that an aardvark has skin).[22]

3.2 Working Memory and the Representation of the Current Context

Context in the ME system provides a focus of attention in a manner similar to that provided by a person's short-term or working memory. The ME system's representation of context, coupled with its application of contextual decay (aimed at keeping the prescribed length of context

---

[21]Note that the interpretation of a link's weight in the ME system is generally *node relative* and so depends heavily upon the direction of interpretation. Relative to other terms and links in a file F's representation, for example, the weight to the term "letters" may make this term highly significant. Relative to other file links emanating from the term "letters", on the other hand, this same weight may mean that file F is of only moderate importance (i.e., several other file links are more heavily weighted).

[22]Note, however, that feature-set and network representations are formally equivalent in the absence of a specification of associated processes that might act upon these representations (see Anderson, 1978).

constant) has a clear analogue in proposed models of short-term memory in people (see Crowder, 1976, pp. 132-215, for a discussion of some of these models). Terms in the current context's representation that are not periodically strengthened (either through the actions of representational information exchange or through the direct intervention of the user) will eventually fade away as new terms are introduced into the context's representation This is essentially a continuous version of *displacement* theories of forgetting in human short-term memory (Atkinson & Shiffrin, 1968; Waugh & Norman, 1965), i.e., the new pushes out the old (albeit, gradually).

In the current version of the ME system, contextual decay acts to keep the sum of the context's term length weights constant at five. This choice of the context object's prescribed length was a fairly arbitrary one; the optimal length of the context object has yet to be determined. If the context object is too long, it becomes too resistant to change so that the ME system has trouble reacting to changes in the user's focus of attention (whether these are signalled directly or indirectly through the file retrieval). Conversely, if the context object is too short, then the ME system is apt to "forget" important representational givens of the current situation - the user must then respecify these. Again, these questions have their human memory analogues which suggests a new approach to efforts aimed at determining the size of human short-term memory. Research in this area has been almost entirely descriptive in nature, i.e., in a given task, with a given set of materials, according to a given set of criteria, what is the span of short-term memory? (See Broadbent, 1975, for a review.) As an alternative, we might, for example, attempt to understand how variations in the span of short-term memory might affect performance. It may not always be the case that "more is better".

3.3 The Learning Process

The process of representational information exchange provides the ME system with a limited ability to adapt and to learn. In one direction, the representation of the current context is modified to increase its representational similarity to a newly retrieved file. This helps the ME system to keep pace with gradual shifts in the user's focus of attention. In the other direction, the ME system modifies the representation of a newly retrieved file in order to increase its representational similarity to the current context. This has the effect of introducing, or strengthening, associations between the file and context terms so that the file is better able to compete with other files for the activation of these terms on subsequent occasions.

The ME system's process of information exchange is consistent with the Hebbian notion that the simultaneous activity of two elements can lead to the formation of a permanent association between these two elements (Hebb, 1949). The process is quite similar to that used in the *stimulus sampling model* of learning (Estes, 1955, 1959) and it produces analogous predictions. The stimulus sampling model predicts that a *massed presentation* of learning trials over a given association will lead to superior performance on a test trial provided that the test trial and learning trials all occur in roughly the same context. Since changes in context are correlated with the passage of time, this generally means that the test trial must immediately follow the learning trials. However, if a significant change in context occurs between the last learning trial and a subsequent test trial (e.g., if there is a longer interval between these two events), then the stimulus sampling model predicts that a *distributed presentation* of learning trials will produce superior performance. Both of these predictions have received empirical confirmation (Glenberg, 1976).

An analogous situation holds in the ME system. Any attempted retrieval of a file can be viewed as a test trial. The relative success of this trial (for anything short of complete retrieval failure) can be measured in terms of the effort required to bring a file near the top of a partial match listing. At the same time, a successful retrieval can be viewed as a learning trial since associations are formed that increase the ease with which the file is retrieved on successive occasions. In general, the more times a file has been successfully retrieved (the learning trials), the easier it will be to retrieve the file again.

However, the actual ease of a file's retrieval depends upon the composition of the current context object. The more strongly associated a desired file is to the terms in the context object, the higher it will be in the partial match listing and, hence, the easier it will be to retrieve. This means that a file will realize immediate, but short-term gains in retrievability from its repeated retrieval in the current context. However, over a longer run in which the context is likely to change in unpredictable ways, a file's retrievability is better improved by a spacing of successful retrievals.[23] A spaced or distributed occurrence of a file's retrievals will tend to increase the diversity of terms to which the file is associated. This association to a diversity of terms, in turn, will increase the file's general retrievability under some unforeseen future context.

The information exchange process of the ME system has two parameters. One of these governs the extent to which the ME system's representation of the context is modified by a retrieved file; the other parameter governs the extent to which a retrieved file's representation is modified by the current context. The basic question underlying the choice of values for both of these parameters is this: How much learning, i.e., how much representational change, should occur as a consequence of the current interaction? With too little change, the system exhibits too much inertia - it is "stupid". With too much change, the system becomes too erratic; its behavior is unduly influenced by the current situation and it develops a sort of amnesia. The hope arises that parameter choices might be guided by a better understanding of analogous learning processes in people. Suggestive in this regard, in connectionist models of human information processing, is the apparent superiority of the error-correcting delta learning rule to the Hebbian learning rule (see McClelland & Rumelhart, 1985, pp. 165; Stone, 1986).

3.4 Decay Mechanisms

In the ME system, decay plays a very important and beneficial role and may play a comparable role in human memory. Decay operates to reduce and, ultimately, nullify the influence of links whose usefulness has passed. (These links may have been accidentally formed in the first place). In doing so, the decay mechanism gives greater expression to links more recently formed or more frequently strengthened. Without

---

[23]This comparison only holds, of course, when we hold the number of successful retrievals of a file constant and manipulate only the spacing of these trials.

decay, the system would slowly grind to a halt as its representations became progressively more resistant to change.

Again parameter questions arise - this time regarding the extent and time course of decay. The decay mechanisms of the current ME system produce an exponential forgetting function. While such a function produces a good approximation of short-term forgetting in people, its predictions of long-term forgetting are excessive; long-term forgetting is better described by the power law function (Anderson, 1983; Wickelgren, 1976). From this we might infer that an exponential forgetting function is more appropriate for context decay in the ME system than it is for the global decay. Unfortunately, the implementation of a power law function seems to require that each link have a memory not only for the time of its creation, but also for the time of each of its strengthenings; the computational costs of such an implementation seem excessive.

One question of relevance to both human memory and in the ME system is this: How much forgetting is optimal? With too little forgetting, the system's ability to modify its behavior is compromised; with too much forgetting, the system develops amnesia. There is an obvious correspondence between these questions and those discussed in the previous section with respect to learning and information exchange. In fact, some interference theories of human forgetting deny the existence of distinct mechanisms of decay (see Crowder, pp. 217-263); memories do not fade with disuse, rather they are rendered relatively less accessible as a consequence of new memories that are formed during the learning process. Applying this approach to computer-based systems of information retrieval, we might dispense with the need for separate mechanisms of decay through an appropriate selection and parameterization of the learning process.

3.5 The Matching Process

The spreading activation mechanism of the ME system is a limited, more primitive version of a spreading activation retrieval mechanism used in the ACT model of human information processing (Anderson, 1976, 1983). Key to this mechanism's operation is a *node-relative* partitioning of activation: The activation entering a given node at time n is partitioned at time n+1 among the node's out-links (and the nodes at the other end of these links) according to their relative strengths.

3.5.1 Relevant Results From the Fact-Retrieval Paradigm

In the ACT model, the number of a node's out-links is referred to as its *fan*. A node with a high fan generally sends less activation down any one of its out-links (to associated nodes) than does a node with a low fan. In turn, the accessibility of nodes and links in the ACT model is determined in large measure by the amount of activation they receive. The ACT model predicts the basic *fan effect* which has received repeated empirical verification in *fact retrieval* experiments (Anderson, 1974, 1976). Generally speaking, it takes more time to retrieve a trace from memory if the available retrieval cues have been associated to many other memory traces as well. The fan effect can be understood to reflect a decrease in trace availability that accompanies a decrease in the discriminating power of the available eliciting cues. An analogous situation holds in the ME system: As the discrimination value of terms decreases, more of them generally have to be specified (or must already be present in the current context) in order to push a desired file near the top of a partial match listing.

A second, so-called *min effect* (see Anderson, 1976) has also been observed in fact retrieval experiments. When two or more cues are presented at the same time, trace retrieval time is most heavily influenced by the cue with the lowest fan. The ACT model readily predicts such an effect since the cue with the lowest fan will send comparatively more activation to the relevant memory trace. Again, an analogous situation holds in the ME system; when two or more terms are provided by the user during a retrieval attempt, the term with the smallest number of object links will generally have the largest impact upon the ordering of the partial match listing. This has the very beneficial effect of giving preferential treatment to those terms that are most discriminating.

However, other research in human memory indicates that fan effects are reduced and even reversed under certain circumstances (e.g., Jones & Anderson, 1987; Reder & Anderson, 1980; Reder & Ross, 1983; Smith, Adams & Schorr, 1978). Characteristic of studies showing a reduction and sometimes reversal of fan effects is a situation in which experimental subjects must distinguish between a set of elements that share some relation to one another and another set of elements that do not share this relation. In the Reder and Anderson (1980) studies, for example, there was virtually no effect on decision time for the number of facts associated to a fictitious person when these facts were related (e.g., "Steven called to have a phone installed", "Steven unpacked all of his boxes", "Steven mailed out change of address cards") and foils were unrelated (e.g., "Steven wanted to major in psychology").

How do we understand these effects with respect to situations involving the use of a personal filing system? An example will help. Instead of a set of related facts, we might speak of the set of related files, say, all "letters" in the filing system. (In this example "letters" will refer to both a term and the set of this term's associated files.) Instead of unrelated foils, we might envision a situation in which any file in this set will satisfy our needs. Perhaps we are about to write a new letter and we want to retrieve an existing letter to use as a template for purposes of text formatting - any letter file will do. Now, as part of this retrieval process, we specify the term "letters". Since the activation leaving "letters" is partitioned among all of its associated files, less activation will go to any particular file in the "letters" set as its size increases, i.e., we get the basic negative effect of fan.

But there may be a positive effect of fan as well! Keep in mind that the "letters" term is typically added on to an existing context. As the size of the "letters" set increases, the chances increase that one or more of its member files is already near the top of the partial match listing as a consequence of its representational similarity to the current context. And, analogous to a situation in which experimental subjects are tested with unrelated foils, we do not care which file(s) in the "letters" set these are - any one will do. It might then be the case that activation from the "letters" term, even though diluted, is enough to bring one of these files into view for selection.

What, then, is the net effect of fan in a situation such as this? It can be shown that the curve relating the fan of a term (i.e., the number of its links to files) to negative effects will generally be much more negatively accelerated than the curve relating a term's fan to positive effects.[24] When the sizes of the "letters" set (under different conditions of fan) are small in relation to the size of the total set of files, for example, the increase in positive effects of fan may be roughly linear. In this same range, increases in the negative effects of fan will rapidly diminish with increases in fan. Given these relationships, circumstances may arise in which small variations in the size of the "letters" set produce a negative fan effect, but this negative effect is offset, with larger variations, by a positive fan effect that results in a reversal of fan effects. A pattern analogous to this one has been empirically observed in fact-retrieval experiments and it is well accounted for in an ACT-like *indirect-pathway model* of memory retrieval (Jones & Anderson, 1987).

3.5.2 Comparisons to a Discrimination Net Approach

In opposition to spreading activation, network models of human information processing are various *discrimination net* models (e.g., Feigenbaum, 1963; Kolodner, 1983a, 1983b; Simon & Feigenbaum, 1964). The hierarchy of a UNIX-style filing system, such as that depicted in Figure 3-1, is a kind of discrimination net. Each level of a file hierarchy can be viewed as a different test. The user specifies a desired file by filtering through a series of tests corresponding to progressively lower levels in the hierarchy.

Barsalou and Bower (1984) point out a number of basic problems with the discrimination net approach to human information processing which readily translate into problems with the use of a file hierarchy:

- *"Extreme sensitivity to missing or incorrect properties* ... If a property is missing, it may not be possible to search any further in the net ... even when the remaining properties are sufficient for a correct discrimination, they can not converge on the correct action once search has been misdirected."
  (Barsalou & Bower, 1984, pg. 18). Analogously, in a hierarchical filing system, the user must specify an exact path to a desired file and the components of this path must

---

[24]Again, note that we expect positive effects only in circumstances in which any, or almost any, file in the set of a term's associates will meet our needs.

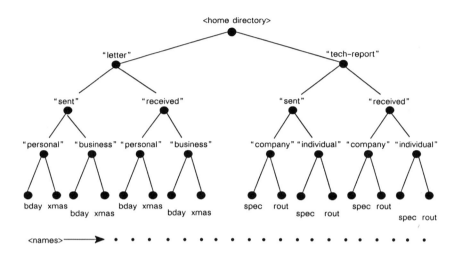

Figure 3-1: An illustration of a file hierarchy

be specified in their proper order. If a path component is forgotten or incorrectly specified, the user is in trouble.

- *"Insufficient sensitivity to the discriminativeness of properties* ... nets always inefficiently test a pattern's shared properties before its unique ones when both kinds are represented" (Barsalou & Bower, 1984, pg. 17). Analogously, in a hierarchical filing system the user must specify first those components to a file's path that, by virtue of their position in the file hierarchy, are apt to be the least discriminating.

- *"Inefficiency in multiple knowledge domains* ... As increasing numbers of properties are shared by subnets within a larger net, the number of nodes needed to represent each additional shared property can increase exponentially" (Barsalou & Bower, 1984, pp. 18). Essentially a discrimination net cannot efficiently represent factorial combinations of properties (or terms). Note the repetition of path component names in Figure 3-1.

All of these limitations are overcome in a spreading-activation, network approach to retrieval - whether this is retrieval from human memory or from electronic storage. In the ME system, for example, a desired file can usually be disambiguated through a specification of any one of a number of different term combinations. Therefore, the user can readily overcome a failure to recall one or more of a file's associated terms. The ME system enforces no particular order of term specification and it enables the user to pursue a strategy of specifying first those terms in a desired file's representation that are most specific to that file and hence most discriminating. (There may be no need to specify any other terms). Finally, the ME system, through its multi-term representation of files, easily handles files that are characterized by various factorial combinations of terms.

4. Conclusion

In any filing system, there is a mapping between files and a representational language (e.g., names, terms); and there are means of traversing and interpreting this mapping. In one direction, the system must use this mapping to generate a set of files that match (perhaps to varying degrees) a user's request. In the other direction, the system must use this mapping to describe a given file in terms that help the user to understand the file's contents and purpose. In both directions, a many-to-many mapping promises to realize benefits that are not found in a conventional name-oriented representational scheme that is essentially a one-to-one mapping between files and terms (i.e., names). In a recall direction, a many-to-many mapping can give the user several retrieval routes to a given file. In a recognition direction, a many-to-many mapping can enable the system to be more descriptive regarding a given file's contents and purpose.

However, the attempt to shift to the use of a many-to-many mapping raises a number of issues. How does the system arrive at and maintain a useful many-to-many mapping? In the recall direction, how does the system disambiguate a user reference? In the recognition direction, what part of an object's representation should the system display so that the user can best determine whether the object meets the user's needs? As noted in the introduction, these and related questions can be readily translated into basic research questions concerning the way people function. How do we arrive at, maintain, and adaptively modify our representations of the world around us? How do we disambiguate incoming information? And how we go about deciding what first to say about a particular object when describing it to others?

The design of the Memory Extender (ME) personal filing system includes the adaptation of a number of constructs found in models of human information processing:

- A weighted, bi-directional term link representation of files that resembles associative network representations of human memory.

- A weighted, term link representation of contextual givens that, in combination with a mechanism of contextual decay, resembles models of human short-term memory.

- A process of representational information exchange that resembles proposed processes of learning in people.

- Mechanisms of decay, contextual and global, that again have their analogues in models of human information processing.

- A spreading activation matching process that is a limited, more primitive version of proposed mechanisms of spreading activation in human information processing.

Constructs of the ME system are intended to realize functions that are quite similar to those realized by their counterparts in models of human memory. But, just as there are a variety of approaches to the modeling of human memory, so too, there are a variety of designs for a computer-based system of information retrieval. As already noted, there is, as yet, no empirical evidence to suggest that the design of the ME system is superior to that of other systems of information retrieval. Moreover, a number of important issues are unaddressed in the current version of the ME system. How, for example, can a system recognize and use higher order terms so that these have influence beyond the mere sum of their parts (e.g., "computer science" as distinct from "computer" and "science")? How can the system make use of syntax in a user's query? How might the system make use of negative information? And the list goes on.

The primary point of this chapter, then, is not to advance the ME system per se, but rather, to use the discussion of the ME system as a framework within which to explore some of task considerations that are in force when we attempt to design a system of information retrieval (e.g., a personal filing system). More importantly, this discussion has identified a similarity between these task considerations and those that apply to situations of human information processing. This similarity of task considerations supports the belief (see Newell, 1970) that increases in our understanding of human information processing may help us design better computer-based systems of information processing - particularly systems in which user considerations are predominant. In turn, it is likely that lessons learned in the attempt to design computer-based systems will be of use in the attempts to model human information processing. Such transfer, for example, may give us an understanding not only for the "what" of human memory but also for the "why" and the "how" of human memory. This argues for a free interplay between basic research in human information processing and applied research to build better computing systems.

Acknowledgements

I would like to thank Ernest Chang, Raymonde Guindon, Sandy Keller, Jim Miller, Don Norman, and Roger Schvaneveldt for comments made on earlier drafts of this chapter.

References

Anderson, J. R. (1974). Retrieval of propositional information from long-term memory. *Cognitive Psychology, 6*, 451-474.
Anderson, J. R. (1976). *Language, Memory, and Thought.* Hillsdale, New Jersey: Lawrence Erlbaum Associates.
Anderson, J. R. (1978). Arguments concerning representations for mental imagery. *Psychological Review, 85*, 249-277.
Anderson, J. R. (1983). *The Architecture of Cognition.* Cambridge, Massachusetts: Harvard University Press.
Atkinson, R. C. & Shiffrin, R. M. (1968). Human memory: A proposed

system and its control processes. In K. W. Spence & J. T. Spence (Eds.), *The Psychology of Learning and Motivation.* New York: Academic Press.

Barsalou, L. W. & Bower, G. H. (1984). Discrimination nets as psychological models. *Cognitive Science, 8,* 1-26.

Broadbent, D. E. (1975). The magical number seven after fifteen years. In R. A. Kennedy & A. Wilkes (Eds.), *Studies in Long-term Memory.* New York: Wiley.

Bush, V. (1945). As we may think. *Atlantic Monthly, 176,* 101-108.

Collins, A. M., & Quillian, M. R. (1969). Retrieval time from semantic memory. *Journal of Verbal Learning and Verbal Behavior, 8,* 240-247.

Collins, A. M., & Quillian, M. R. (1972). Experiments on semantic memory and language comprehension. In L. Gregg (Ed.), *Cognition and Learning.* New York: Wiley and Sons.

Collins, A. M., & Loftus, E. F. (1975). A spreading activation theory of semantic processing. *Psychological Review, 82,* 407-428.

Crowder, R. G. (1976). *Principles of Learning and Memory.* Hillsdale, N.J.: Lawrence Erlbaum Associates.

Estes, W. K. (1955). Statistical theory of spontaneous recovery and regression. *Psychological Review, 62,* 145-154.

Estes, W. K. (1959). The statistical approach to learning theory. In S. Koch (Ed.), *Psychology: A Study of a Science, Vol. II.* New York: McGraw-Hill.

Feigenbaum, E. A. (1963). Simulation of verbal learning behavior. In E. A. Feigenbaum & J. Feldman (Eds.), *Computers and Thought.* New York: McGraw-Hill.

Furnas, G. W., Landauer, T. K., Gomez, L. M., & Dumais, S. T. (1983). Statistical semantics: Analysis of the potential performance of key-word information systems. *The Bell System Technical Journal, 62,* 1753-1806.

Glenberg, A. M. (1976). Monotonic and nonmonotonic lag effects in paired-associate and recognition memory paradigms. *Journal of Verbal Learning and Verbal Behavior, 7,* 311-325.

Goffman, W. (1968). An indirect method of information retrieval. *Information Storage and Retrieval, 4,* 361-373.

Hebb, D. O. (1949). *The Organization of Behavior: A Neuropsychological Theory.* New York: Wiley.

Ide, E. & Salton, G. (1971). Interactive search strategies and dynamic file organization in information retrieval. In G. Salton (Ed.), *The Smart Retrieval System - Experiments in Automatic Document Processing.* Englewood Cliffs, N.J.: Prentice-Hall.

Jardine, N., & Sibson, R. (1968). A model for taxonomy. *Mathematical Biosciences, 2,* 465-482.

Jones, W. P. (1986). On the applied use of computer models of memory: The Memory Extender personal filing system. *Int. J. Man-Machine Studies, 25*, 191-228.

Jones, W. P. & Furnas, G. W. (in press). Pictures of relevance: A geometric analysis of similarity measures. *Journal of the American Society for Information Science.*

Jones, W. P. & Anderson, J. R. (in press). Short- and long-term memory retrieval: A comparision of the effects of information load and re-latedness. *Journal of Experimental Psychology: General.*

Kolodner, J. L. (1983a). Maintaining memory organization in a long term dynamic memory. *Cognitive Science, 7*, 243-280.

Kolodner, J. L. (1983b). Reconstructive memory: A computer model. *Cognitive Science, 7*, 281-328.

Lesk, M. E. (1969). Word-word associations in document retrieval systems. *American Documentation, 20*, 27-38.

McClelland, J. L. & Rumelhart, D. E. (1985). Distributed memory and the representation of general and specific information. *Journal of Experimental Psychology: General, 114*, 159-188.

Meadow, C. T. (1973). *Analysis of Information Systems.* New York: Wiley and Sons.

Meyer, D. E. (1970). On the representation and retrieval of stored semantic information. *Cognitive Psychology, 1*, 242-300.

Mozer, M. C. (1984). *Inductive information retrieval using parallel distributed computation* (Tech. Rep. C-015). La Jolla, CA 92093: Institute for Cognitive Science, University of California, San Diego.

Newell, A. (1970). Remarks on the relationship between artificial intelligence and cognitive psychology. In R. B. Banerji & M. D. Mesarovic (Eds.), *Theoretical approaches to non-numerical problem solving.* Berlin: Springer-Verlag.

Norman, D. A. & Rumelhart, D. E. (1975). *Explorations in Cognition.* San Francisco: W. H. Freeman.

Olson, D. R. (1970). Language and thought: Aspects of a cognitive theory of semantics. *Psychological Review, 77*, 257-273.

Reder, L. M. & Anderson, J. R. (1980). A partial resolution of the paradox of interference: The role of integrating knowledge. *Cognitive Psychology, 12*, 447-472.

Reder, L. M. & Ross, B. H. (1983). Integrated knowledge in different tasks: the role of retrieval strategy on fan effects. *Journal of Experimental Psychology: Learning, Memory, and Cognition, 9*, 55-72.

Salton, G., & Lesk, M. E. (1971). Information analysis and dictionary construction. In G. Salton (Ed.), *The SMART Retrieval System - Experiments in Automatic Document Processing.* Englewood Cliffs, New Jersey: Prentice-Hall, Inc.

Salton, G., & Yang, C. S. (1973). On the specification of term values in automatic indexing. *Journal of Documentation, 29*, 351-372.

Salton, G. (1978). Generation and search of clustered files. *Association for Computing Machinery Transactions on Data Base Systems, 3*, 321-346.

Salton, G., & McGill, M. J. (1983). *Introduction to Modern Information Retrieval.* New York: McGraw Hill.

Schaeffer, B. & Wallace, R. (1970). The comparison of word meanings. *Journal of Experimental Psychology, 86*, 144-152.

Simon, H. A., & Feigenbaum, E. A. (1964). An information processing theory of some effects of similarity, familiarity, and meaningfulness in verbal learning. *Journal of Verbal Learning and Verbal Behavior, 3*, 385-396.

Simon, H. A. (1981). *Sciences of the Artificial.* Cambridge, Massachusetts: Massachusetts Institute of Technology Press.

Smith, E. E., Shoben, E. J., & Rips, L. J. (1974). Structure and process in semantic memory: A featural model for semantic decisions. *Psychological Review, 31*, 214-241.

Smith, E. E., Adams, N., & Schorr, D. (1978). Fact retrieval and the paradox of interference. *Cognitive Psychology, 10*, 438-464.

Sparck Jones, K. (1970). Some thoughts on classification for retrieval. *Journal of Documentation, 26*, 89-101.

Sparck Jones, K. (1971). *Automatic Keyword Classification for Information Retrieval.* London: Butterworths.

Sparck Jones, K. (1972). A statistical interpretation of term specificity and its application in retrieval. *Journal of Documentation, 28*, 11-20.

Stone, G. O. (1986). An analysis of the delta rule and the learning of statistical associations. In D. E. Rumelhart & J. L. McClelland (Eds.), *Parallel Distributed Processing: Explorations in the Microstructure of Cognition, Volume 1: Foundations.* Cambridge, Massachusetts: MIT Press.

Waugh, N. C., & Norman, D. A. (1965). Primary Memory. *Psychological Review, 72*, 89-104.

Wickelgren, W. A. (1976). Memory storage dynamics. In W. K. Estes (Ed.), *Handbook of Learning and Cognitive Processes.* Hillsdale, New Jersey: Lawrence Erlbaum Associates.

7
The Application of User Knowledge to Interface Design

JAMES E. MCDONALD
ROGER W. SCHVANEVELDT

In this chapter we discuss a methodology appropriate for interface *design*, which we define as the process whereby the designer plans and specifies the user interface. The interface designer's objective is to make devices easier and more enjoyable to use, and to make it possible for people to perform tasks which they might not otherwise be able to accomplish. With this objective in mind, we will propose a guiding interface design principle and offer a methodology for applying this principle to different interfaces. We would like to stress at the outset that ours is a methodology under development and that it needs additional empirical support. This approach to interface design is worth considering because it is empirically based, potentially formal, and in concert with current thinking in cognitive science. It is, of course, up to the reader to decide whether or not the arguments and data presented are sufficient to justify such optimism. In the following sections we first discuss some common approaches to interface design in order to place our methodology in perspective. We then present the theoretical motivations for our approach, along with a related discussion of scaling and knowledge acquisition techniques, followed by a review of several applications that illustrate key aspects of our methodology. The last of these studies is an ongoing investigation of UNIX users aimed at improving the on-line documentation system.

1. Interface Design Methods

The most common method used to design interfaces assigns the task of building user interfaces to the engineers or computer scientists responsible for the rest of the system. In many cases the interface is not given any special status, in that it is not treated as a separate component, but simply viewed as another facet of the system hardware and/or software. We and others have argued that this approach is unsatisfactory for both designers and users (Norman, 1982; Schvaneveldt, McDonald, & Cooke, 1985). The approach is unsatisfactory for designers because they must engage in activities for which they are not specifically trained and for which no detailed specifications exist. It is unsatisfactory for users because the resulting interfaces are often idiosyncratic, based on the preferences of designers, and arcane, because the designer's and user's perspectives **are** different (Manheimer, Stone, & McDonald, 1983). Another consequence of this approach is that those responsible for designing interfaces are often inclined to place cost and efficiency above usability when the inevitable cost vs. usability trade-offs must be made.

1.1 Interface Standards and Guidelines

One solution to the problems described above might be to develop interface *standards* and *guidelines* (e.g., the German DIN standards and IBM's UIA guidelines). Such guidelines tend to be loosely organized collections of recommendations based on facts, experimental results, and opinions. Unfortunately, the recommendations in typical guidelines are based on too few facts and experimental results and far too many opinions. Although well motivated, the soundness of the guideline approach must be questioned on several grounds. First, even when supported by data, many of the recommendations made in guidelines are not valid for specific applications. When recommendations are general (i.e., derived from basic research), they are suspect because particular applications are likely to include factors which invalidate them. On the other hand, when the recommendations in guidelines are derived from studies of particular applications (i.e., based on applied research), unique characteristics of these applications make general conclusions impossible and, again, may invalidate the recommendations.

The main supporters of guidelines are labor unions, manufacturers, and engineers, but there are some human-factors practitioners who favor them as well. The supporters seem to be motivated by the belief that, in the absence of knowledge about how to optimally design interfaces, some benefit can be obtained by designing interfaces in a *consistent* fashion. Human-computer interfaces do exhibit surprising variability, even in their most basic characteristics. A notorious example is the placement and meaning of auxiliary keys on keyboards (e.g., shift, return, control, and programmable function keys). Other puzzling inconsistencies, difficult to understand without some knowledge of their evolution, include differences in command naming and syntax. Many computer users are unpleasantly surprised when they attempt to transfer their knowledge from one application to a similar one. For example, someone familiar with a text editor such as *vi*, will have considerable difficulty applying his or her knowledge to a different text editor, such as *emacs*, even when using the same terminal hardware and the same operating system (i.e., UNIX). Even greater difficulties may be encountered if the transfer of knowledge involves different hardware and/or a new operating system (e.g., DOS). Although such difficulties may be explicable from the developers' perspective, they really cannot be justified from the users' standpoint.

It would be a mistake, however, to conclude that standardization is a good solution to the most important interface design problems. More often than not, applications are hard to use because of bad interface design, and standardization would only exacerbate these problems. If, as many believe, *all* current interfaces are less than optimal, then standardization will simply doom us to inferior interfaces for years to come. Emerson observed that "a *foolish* consistency is the hobgoblin of little minds..." It would indeed be foolish to insist on consistent interface design before learning more about good interface design.

A final problem with guidelines is that they do not necessarily accomplish one of their main objectives; they do not necessarily make things easier for designers. Guidelines require interpretation, often by designers unfamiliar with psychological methods or jargon who are therefore ill-equipped for the task. Thus, the guideline approach may still result in inconsistently designed interfaces and actually increase the burden on interface designers by requiring them to consult large collections of ambiguous recommendations.

1.2 Creative Insights

The best interface designs, if critical acclaim is any measure of success, have resulted from the efforts of one or more creative individuals. When such efforts succeed, they appear to result from fundamental insights into the relationships between particular problems and common solutions (e.g., desktops, spreadsheets). At its best, this approach produces highly creative interfaces which retain salient characteristics of the prototype systems while improving on their efficiency and/or power. In many cases it seems that once a metaphor is found, the details of the interface follow quite naturally. Thus, if one uses the metaphor of a paper ledger for an "electronic" spreadsheet, then the notion of a matrix of "cells" as the interface logically follows. Our analysis is not meant to trivialize such achievements. On the contrary, we are among those who believe that the best human-computer interfaces have thus far resulted from clever ideas and not formal methodologies. However, much of the credit for such successes must go to "flashes of insight" into similarities between apparently different systems and how these similarities might be exploited. Furthermore, this approach seems to work well for some applications (e.g., spreadsheets) and not others (e.g., operating systems). It is simply not a general approach to interface design.

We have thus far dismissed guidelines as unsupported by data and of little value for specific applications, and creative insights as unreliable. What are the alternatives? We contend that the strengths of scientific disciplines, such as cognitive psychology, lie in their use of theories and methodologies. Empirical methodologies have the dual characteristics of *generality*, meaning they can be applied in a wide range of situations, and *validity*, meaning the answers produced by their application are legitimate for the situations to which they are applied. Thus, we propose a methodological approach to interface design.

1.3 Representing Models in the Interface

Although not directly related to any particular psychological theory, the interface design methodology we propose is most compatible with information processing theories that stress the importance of knowledge. In its present form it does not constitute a theory of user psychology or even a comprehensive set of guidelines. However, our methodology does seem suited to a wide range of applications and its basic premises can be clearly and succinctly stated:

1. Users develop conceptual models of devices (systems) through use of or from experience with related systems or tasks.

2. Experienced users' conceptual models can be characterized as memory schemata that can be elicited and represented using an empirical methodology.

3. Interfaces that reflect experienced user knowledge will facilitate learning and increase productivity for users at all levels of expertise.

A major theme of our work is that effective human-computer interaction depends on the communication of the structure and organization of computer systems via the interface. The user needs a model of the computer system that accurately represents its structure. Our research is concerned with the development and evaluation of methods for eliciting, representing, and communicating appropriate models of systems.

1.3.1 User's Models of Systems and Tasks

Models are frequently employed as explanatory constructs in an effort to clarify the process of designing and using devices. Norman (1986) distinguished two types of conceptual models, designer and user models, and contended that the user interface serves as a physical model of the system (i.e., the *system image*). Designers' models consist of those plans that designers attempt to embody in systems they build, whereas users' models are mental representations of the systems formed by users through experience. The user interface, consisting of all aspects of the system that the user comes into contact with -- "either physically, perceptually, or conceptually" (Moran, 1981) -- serves as a physical bridge between these two types of conceptual models. We have been concerned with methods for obtaining and representing users' models of systems and tasks. Our goal is to incorporate such models into the user-system interface (the system image). In short, we propose to base designers' models on users' models.

A number of theories have been offered about the nature of users' mental models of devices. Young (1983) discussed eight types of device models ranging from strong analogy (metaphor) to commonality. Metaphors are perhaps the most common type of model proposed, and they have been exploited in several systems. The frequent use of metaphors in the user-computer interface (e.g., the desktop metaphor) stems from the belief that metaphors provide useful, ready-made models for users of new systems. More importantly for users without previous task knowledge, metaphors may provide new applications with coherent frameworks.

The degree to which interfaces rely on metaphor varies, with some computer-based applications strongly exploiting existing task knowledge. Continuing our previous example, spreadsheet programs are a rather direct form of metaphor. However, this analogy only carries the user so far. Electronic spreadsheets have several capabilities that are only indirectly related to the use of paper spreadsheets. For example, the capabilities of placing formulae in cells, rather than simple values, and moving cells from one location to another are quite indirectly related to the corresponding qualities of paper spreadsheets. Similarly, the use of the typewriter metaphor in word-processor training is of questionable value. Once again, a suitable metaphor exists because the designer's model of the system was based on an existing device (the typewriter). However, beyond communicating to the novice that she can type on the keyboard and letters will appear on the CRT as if it were paper, little is actually gained. This metaphor may also help the user understand why letters disappear when the backspace key is pressed, if the user is familiar with "correcting" typewriters, but may lead to confusion as to why the left cursor key doesn't perform similarly. In short, there is much new knowledge that must be acquired in learning to use a word processor, and an individual who continues to use one like a typewriter will probably fail to see the value in it. To suggest that a new device is like a familiar one because they both share a set of basic characteristics implies that they share other characteristics as well, possibly limitations.

Another difficulty with using metaphors for interface design is that there is currently no methodology for finding them. In fact, it is unlikely that suitable metaphors exist for complex systems (cf. Norman, 1986). When metaphors are found, they are usually suitable for simple systems or parts of complex systems, and collections of suitable analogies do not suitably represent systems. Thus, to explain that the heart is like a pump may prove useful in conveying important information about how the heart functions. It might also be appropriate to compare the hand to a pair of pliers and the eye to a camera. However, it is highly unlikely that the pump-pliers-camera model conveys anything salient about how the human body works. Thus, metaphors may not be extensible and ex- planations at one level of abstraction may not hold at other levels (cf. Halasz & Moran, 1982). The methodology we propose provides coherent frameworks for interface design that are inherently extensible by capitalizing on users' task-related knowledge.

1.3.2 Empirical Coherence Models

We contend that users' conceptual models, or system-related knowledge structures, can be characterized as "schemata" in which parts of the sys- tem are associated because they are functionally related or because they have other common characteristics (Young, 1983). During the development of these conceptual models, individual facts about the sys- tem are either made to fit into the framework provided by the schema or are excluded and forgotten. Knowledge about systems or tasks can be obtained from users, or potential users, with the methodology we propose. Furthermore, this knowledge can be represented, using various scaling techniques, and serves as the basis for interface design. As we will show in this chapter, there are reasonably well-developed techniques for eliciting users' system- or task-related knowledge, as well as for representing such knowledge in the form of coherence models.

As a physical model of the system, the user interface should only represent those aspects of the system that are relevant to users. Other aspects, such as the particular way in which functions are implemented, are not relevant and should not be represented. Ideally, an interface should project a consistent whole that facilitates the accomplishment of tasks using the system. Relationships among aspects of the system can be emphasized by: (a) organizing interface components such that strongly associated components are physically close together, whereas weakly associated components are physically far apart, (b) using different colors to identify members of groups or categories, (c) graphically "linking" related components together, (d) restricting access to components according to associations thereby creating "modes," or (e) using similar names or shapes (icons) for related components.

In short, the user interface should provide a complete and coherent view of the structure of the system from the user's perspective. System designers should be concerned with developing systems around coherent structures, and interface designers should be concerned with communicating these structures to users. In addition to other relationships, the user interface should convey: (a) the types of data structures embodied in the system or application program, (b) the way in which the data structures depend upon each other, and (c) the data needed and produced by each program. One challenge for research in this area is to identify the appropriate levels of abstraction for conveying these aspects of systems to users and to develop effective means for communicating them. We hypothesize that user interfaces that embody coherence models will facilitate the development of users' mental models and that such models offer advantages over those based on metaphor. In this chapter we focus on the use of scaling techniques to derive coherence models.

2. Proximity Scaling Techniques

Psychological scaling techniques provide several potentially useful methods for measuring and representing users' mental models. These representations can then be used as the basis for coherence models of systems. The techniques can be subdivided into two major classes, those that yield continuous models of mental structure and those that yield discrete models.

The methods to be discussed all rely on some measure of psychological distance (or dissimilarity) among the entities to be scaled. The methods take pairwise distances as input and produce spatial or graph-theoretic representations as output. The pairwise distances can be obtained from several sources such as psychological judgments, frequency of co-occurrence, confusability, correlations, temporal distance, or spatial distance. Generally there are two goals shared by most psychometric methods: (1) to reduce a large number of pairwise distances to a simpler representation, and (2) to give some insight into the organization underlying the pairwise distances. Let's examine some of these methods in some detail.

2.1 Continuous Models

Continuous, or spatial, models represent entities as points in a multidimensional space. These models usually provide some global information about the entities represented in that the dimensions of the space often correspond to abstract dimensions underlying the variations among the entities. Multidimensional scaling (MDS) is a term used for a variety of specific techniques that represent the scaled entities as points in multidimensional space (Kruskal, 1964, 1977; Shepard, 1962a, 1962b, 1963). Essentially the techniques attempt to find a spatial layout of the points that best corresponds to the given pairwise distances. This generally requires some iterative procedure (e.g., the method of steepest descent) that may lead to inappropriate representations if local minima are encountered. There are methods for protecting against such problems, however. Shepard (1974) is an excellent source of information about potential problems associated with MDS and ways of dealing with them.

The various MDS techniques differ in the exact method used to iterate over various spatial layouts and the criteria used to determine the fit between the spatial representation and the original pairwise distance estimates. Nonmetric MDS attempts to fit the order of the distances estimates, and thus, only requires ordinal measurement. Three-way MDS makes use of several sets of distance estimates (usually from different people) and yields information about the weights attached to each dimension of the space by each set of estimates.

There are several advantages to be gained from MDS analysis. MDS can represent large amounts of data in a form that is more amenable to interpretation. Dimensions of the space can represent important aspects underlying the mental representation of the scaled entities. In some of the applications we will discuss later, MDS provides a means for defining a spatial layout which is based on users' knowledge of concepts in a domain.

There are also some characteristics of MDS that fail to capture important aspects of the psychological organization of certain domains. If the domain consists of a very heterogeneous collection of concepts, a spatial representation may require several dimensions to capture the many ways in which the concepts vary. But many dimensions can be difficult to interpret and difficult to represent. There are also some problems that naturally follow from spatial representations. Tversky (1977) discusses the observation that the psychological interpretation of the relations between two entities may be asymmetrical. For example, Cuba seems to be more similar to Russia than Russia is to Cuba. Such asymmetries are not compatible with spatial representations, although some efforts have been made to cope with asymmetric data within the MDS framework (Constantine & Gower, 1978; Harshman, Green, Wind, & Lundy, 1982; Krumhansl, 1978).

As MDS attempts to find a spatial representation to account for the pairwise distances given as input, each of the distances plays an equal role in constraining the solution. In one sense, the equal weighting of the distances may be seen as a strength of the method. The entire data set determines the representation. However, when MDS is used to scale psychological similarity or psychological relatedness, equal weighting of the judgments may not be appropriate. It may be more important to capture the relations among the more related concepts. Equal weighting of related and unrelated concepts may lead to distortions in the representation of the related concepts to accommodate those that are not related. Because relations are represented by distance in spatial representations, this problem is difficult to resolve.

2.2 Discrete Models

Several psychometric methods derive from the mathematical theory of graphs, structures consisting of *nodes* and *links* connecting some pairs of nodes (Carre, 1979; Christofides, 1975; Gibbons, 1985; Harary, 1969). A *graph* can be displayed by a diagram in which nodes are shown as points, and links are indicated by lines connecting appropriate pairs of points. In general, a direction is associated with a link so that one can distinguish its initial and terminal endpoints (nodes). Directed links are called *arcs*. In a symmetric graph, for every arc there is another arc that connects the same pair of nodes in the opposite direction. Such graphs may be referred to as undirected because a pair of arcs can be represented by a single *edge* without direction.

A *path* is a sequence of links such that the initial endpoint of each link in the sequence (except the first) is the same as the terminal endpoint of the preceding link. The initial endpoint of the first link and the terminal endpoint of the last link of a path are, respectively, the initial and terminal endpoints of the path. A path can also be specified by the sequence of nodes which it visits. A path with the same initial and terminal endpoints is a *cycle*. A path (or cycle) is *simple* if it does not traverse any arc of a graph more than once. A path (or cycle) is *elementary* if all the initial endpoints (or all the terminal endpoints) of the arcs in the path are distinct. We will use the terms path and cycle to refer to elementary paths and cycles, respectively.

In applications of graphs, each node represents an entity, and the links represent pairwise relations between entities. Because a set of nodes can be connected by links in many possible ways, a wide variety of structures can be represented by graphs.

Trees are the basis of such psychometric methods as hierarchical cluster analysis (Johnson, 1967), weighted free trees (Cunningham, 1978), and additive similarity trees (Sattath & Tversky, 1977). A *tree* is a graph with no cycles. An undirected connected tree has exactly *n-1* edges where *n* is the number of nodes. In connected trees there is exactly one path connecting two nodes. Links may have weights (distances or costs) associated with them, in which case the graph is known as a *network*. In a network, the length of a path can be computed by summing the weights associated with the links in the path. The geodetic distance between two nodes is the length of the minimum length path connecting the nodes. The minimal spanning sub-tree (Kruskal, 1956) of a network consists of a subset of the links in the network such that the sub-graph is a tree and the sum of the link weights is minimal over the set of all possible sub-trees.

Hierarchical cluster analysis provides a set of nested (hierarchical) groupings of the entities which should correspond to meaningful categories. Different hierarchical clustering methods use different definitions of the distance between a category (once formed) and the other entities and categories. The single link method uses the minimum of the distances between the entities in a category and the entities in other categories. The complete link method uses the maximum distance. A less common variation uses the average distance between entities in different categories. As we will see later, there are some close connections between hierarchical clustering and minimal spanning trees. The value of hierarchical cluster analysis lies in its potential for revealing the underlying categorical structure for a set of entities. One problem often encountered stems from the necessity for clusters to be nested, which means that an entity can only belong to certain clusters.

Additive clustering (Shepard & Arabie, 1979) is a method for producing overlapping clusters so that an entity may belong to more than one cluster. The clusters are not necessarily nested so that non-hierarchical characteristics can be seen. Such a representation violates the constraints on a tree structure and, thus, corresponds to a more general graph. The theory underlying additive clustering assumes that the entities have associated sets of features and that the clusters correspond to shared features among the entities. One value of the method lies in its ability to suggest the underlying features.

Other methods derive from the assumption that the appropriate representation for the entities under study is a network (Dearholt, Schvaneveldt, & Durso, 1985; Feger & Bien, 1982; Hutchinson, 1981; Schvaneveldt & Durso, 1981; Schvaneveldt, Durso, & Dearholt, 1985). These methods assume that the pairwise distances given as input represent an underlying network. The output is the network corresponding to the distances.

2.2.1 Pathfinder

The method we have investigated most closely is realized in an algorithm (Pathfinder) which is based on the idea that a link is present in the output network if and only if that link is a minimum length path between the nodes connected by the link in the (complete) network corresponding to the input distances. Links are given weights corresponding to the pairwise distances given as input, and the length of a path is a function of the weights on links in the path. Generalizing beyond the usual definition of path length as the arithmetic sum of the link weights, Pathfinder defines the length of a path, L(P), consisting of k links to be:

$$L(P)=(w_1^r+w_2^r+...+w_k^r)^{1/r}, \text{ where } w_i \text{ is the } i^{th} \text{ link weight and } r \geq 1.$$

This adaptation of the Minkowski r-metric to the measurement of path length allows Pathfinder to accommodate different assumptions about the level of measurement associated with the distance estimates. Ordinal level measurement requires r to be infinity in which case L(P) is equivalent to the maximum weight in the path. Ratio-level measurement allows any value of $r \geq 1$, and the particular value selected can be determined by the desired density (number of links) of the network (see below) and/or the interpretability of the solution.

Another parameter used by the Pathfinder algorithm is q, the maximum number of links in paths searched in defining the minimum path lengths for all pairs of nodes. The q-parameter is useful from two different perspectives. First, there may be some limit on the number of links that could be meaningfully involved in connections between nodes in a particular domain. This limit can be imposed with q. Second, there is a computational advantage that follows from limiting the number of links in paths which can be significant when working with large numbers of nodes. Meaningful values of q range from 2 to the number of nodes minus one (n-1).

Let us call a network generated from the Pathfinder algorithm a PFNET(r, q), indicating that the particular PFNET was generated using a particular value of the r-metric and a particular value of q. There are systematic inclusion relationships between PFNETs generated with different values of r and q. We define inclusion of networks as follows: PFNET' is included in PFNET if and only if PFNET' and PFNET have the same nodes and every link in PFNET' is also a link in PFNET. Then PFNET(r_1, q_1) is included in PFNET(r_2, q_2) if and only if $r_1 \geq r_2$ and $q_1 \geq q_2$.

These inclusion properties mean that PFNET($r=\infty$, $q=n-1$) is the least dense of the alternative PFNETs, and it is included in all other PFNETs. As r or q decrease, additional links may be added to the PFNET, increasing the density of the network. PFNET($r=\infty$, $q=n-1$) is the union of the minimum-cost spanning trees for all possible PFNETs generated from a particular data set. PFNET($r=\infty$, $q=n-1$) will be the unique minimum-cost spanning tree when there is such a unique tree. The PFNET($r=\infty$, $q=n-1$) allows a construction of the single-link hierarchical clustering solution (minimum method). Essentially this construction involves grouping nodes according to the links between nodes starting with the minimum link weights and proceeding in order through all of the links. It is not possible to derive the PFNET from the hierarchical scaling scheme (HCS) solution. The HCS solution does not provide sufficient information to recover all of the PFNET links.

Networks provide for a natural separation of structural and quantitative information. Structure is determined by the particular set of links in a network and quantitative information is contained in the weights associated with links. Many of our applications of Pathfinder have focused on the structure of PFNETs without regard for the link weights (even though link weights in the form of pairwise distance estimates are used by Pathfinder to construct the PFNET).

PFNETs often have informative structures and substructures such as trees, chains of links, cycles, star structures, and many others. These substructures may have meaningful psychological interpretations (cf. Schvaneveldt, Durso, & Dearholt, 1985). We have also analyzed the link structures of novices and experts (computer programmers and Air Force fighter pilots) to identify systematic differences in their conceptual organizations (Cooke, 1983; Schvaneveldt, Durso, Goldsmith, Breen, Cooke, Tucker, & DeMaio, 1985). In addition we have found that the information contained in the link weights of PFNETs predicts recall orders in free recall (Cooke, Durso, & Schvaneveldt, 1986). The link weights are also used in a measure of node centrality (the degree similarity product) by Dearholt, Schvaneveldt, and Durso (1985).

Some of the properties of PFNETs that contrast with other methods for representing the structure in psychological distance data are:

1. PFNETs can directly model asymmetries in psychological distance because two nodes can be connected by 0, 1, or 2 links. If two links connect the nodes, they can have different weights.

2. PFNETs emphasize pairwise relations between entities. The structure of PFNETs is mainly determined by the closeness of more similar entities and is relatively unaffected by the distance of distant entities. MDS, in contrast, usually weights all pairwise distances equally in determining the spatial representation of the entities. It is possible to vary the weight of each data point in an MDS solution, but this feature is rarely used in practice.

3. PFNETs are capable of representing structures for relatively heterogeneous sets of entities. The PFNETs will capture local structure among related entities and are capable of producing disconnected networks when some of the distance estimates are infinite. When heterogeneous sets of entities are connected, there will often be only a single connection from an entity in one homogeneous subset to an entity in another homogeneous subset.

4. PFNETs are capable of preserving the "nearest neighbor" relations in a set of distance estimates which is not always possible with spatial representations (cf. Tversky & Hutchinson, 1986).

3. Methodological Considerations

One of the first steps in applying our methodology is obtaining the estimates of distance necessary for scaling analysis. All of the techniques we discuss require as input a matrix of distance estimates for all pairs of items in the set. In general, such matrices may be symmetrical (i.e., the distance from A to B is equal to the distance from B to A) or asymmetrical (i.e., the distance from A to B is not necessarily equal to the distance from B to A) although only Pathfinder makes use of asymmetries.

3.1 Eliciting Concepts

In order to develop effective models of the systems as viewed by users, all important actions, objects, concepts, tasks, etc., must be included in the set of items. For some applications this is a deceptively straightforward process. If one is designing a menu system containing *n* items, then the *n* items themselves will undoubtedly be in the set. However, it is seldom clear what constitutes a sufficient set of concepts for many domains, and even when an obvious set of concepts does exist, applications may require models with multiple levels of abstraction (e.g., higher level categories), and these abstractions may not be readily available. We will discuss one approach to defining category abstractions in describing our work on the UNIX *man* system.

Recently, Cooke (1987) conducted a study in which she compared four techniques (concept listing, interview, step listing, and chapter listing) on the number and types of concepts elicited. She identified seven categories of concepts: (1) explanations, (2) general rules, (3) conditional rules, (4) pure concepts, (5) procedures, (6) facts, and (7) other. The interview and chapter listing techniques elicited the largest number of concepts, although they also produced the largest amount of redundancy. The four "idea" elicitation techniques also varied in the types of knowledge elicited (e.g., the step technique elicited procedures and general rules, whereas the chapter technique elicited concepts). Cooke (1987) listed several factors that should be considered in selecting a particular technique, such as (1) the type of knowledge desired, (2) the detail or complexity desired, (3) the importance of eliciting as much knowledge as possible, (4) the importance of irrelevancy and redundancy, and (5) the man hours available to perform the task. She also concluded that, if possible, several different techniques should be employed in order to insure more complete coverage of the domain.

3.2 Sources of Knowledge

It is generally held that novice and experienced users have different schemas for the domain in which expertise is measured. However, it is not clear how their schemas differ. It may be that experienced and novice users share a "core" schema, but that experienced users have more elaborate knowledge structures with extensions to the basic core (cf. Rosch & Mervis, 1975). Alternatively, experience may cause even the core schema to be reshaped, making the experienced user's view of the system quite incompatible with that of the novice.

Although there may be occasions when using novice schemas for interface design is desirable, expert schemas are generally preferable, particularly when novices are expected to become more expert. Theoretically, novice schemas are simpler and potentially easier for other novice users to learn, but they are also less stable. This characteristic of novice schemas, compared to those of experts, is exhibited in the high degree of variability obtained from judgments of relatedness. Furthermore, experts' schemas can be simplified if simpler models are required, while still preserving important aspects. This approach also results in models that are extensible and capable of being adapted to changing levels of expertise. Deciding to use experts is not enough, however, because there may be many kinds of expertise within a particular domain (e.g., general knowledge about a broad range of functions versus a great deal of specific knowledge about a narrow range). In any case, it may be useful to compare novice and experienced users' schemas in order to construct models which emphasize these differences, because they may represent novice user misconceptions (Cooke, 1983). It is also important to remember that a design engineer's view of a system is likely to be different than an experienced user's model (Manheimer et al., 1983). A final note: it is important to remember that subjects *will* provide distance estimates if asked to do so, even if they are unfamiliar with the concepts. It is a good idea to determine each subject's familiarity with the concepts to be rated in order to avoid incorporating such "noise" in the proximity matrices.

3.3 Obtaining Estimates of Distance

3.3.1 Instructions

Once a set of items to be rated has been selected, several problems associated with obtaining estimates of distance remain. One of the first decisions to be made concerns the instructions to give raters. General relatedness instructions are commonly used under the assumption that raters will choose the most relevant dimensions on which to compare the items. We have observed, however, that this lack of guidance can lead to difficulties when the data are scaled (e.g., uninterpretable dimensions using MDS), or even later when the results of the scaling analyses are applied to interface design. For example, if raters are asked to judge the relatedness of a set of items that occur together in various combinations (e.g., task sequences) and that also have featural similarities (e.g., similar syntax of usage), then raters may base their judgments on different dimensions for different pairs of items, rather than weighing each pair on the same set of dimensions.

3.3.2 Context

This problem is a consequence of the aforementioned fact that it is not always clear what constitutes the set of items to be judged. In short, because estimates of relatedness may be affected by the context or frame supplied by the rating environment (Tversky, 1977; Murphy & Medin, 1985), the inclusion or omission of particular items may affect judgments of similarity for the other items. Although interface applications may provide a reasonably well-defined set of items, such applications are not exempt from this concern. For example, if only basic commands are included in the set of items to be rated, then higher-level concepts must be inferred from the scaling solutions or obtained from users' judgments (i.e., having subjects name groups or clusters of functions). Including these concepts along with the set of functions to be rated, however, may influence the ratings for the original items. Iterative cycles of rating, scaling, and expanding the set of concepts may be required.

3.4 Data Collection Methods

There are a number of ways of obtaining the estimates that comprise a proximity matrix. We will discuss several common techniques, although others (e.g., repertory grid) are also widely used. None of the methods discussed is ideal in that each has certain advantages and dis-advantages that may interact with particular scaling techniques.

3.4.1 Listing

Simply, subjects are asked to generate relevant domain concepts in a relatively unconstrained fashion. The assumption is that subjects will generate new concepts closely associated with those already produced. Because of their "free associational" nature, lists can also be used to obtain estimates of psychological distances, in addition to eliciting domain concepts. Distance can be computed in several ways, although we have most often calculated simple conditional probabilities (i.e., the probability that item B follows item A across subjects). If concept-elicitation times are obtained (i.e., inter-item intervals), they can be used to identify groups of items. Once groups of concepts are identified, proximity matrices can be constructed using techniques analogous to those for sorting.

Unfortunately, the listing procedure does not guarantee that estimates of distance will be obtained for all concepts from each subject. Further-more, because different sets of items are generally obtained from each subject, the process of combining individual lists into a composite proximity matrix may be complex. A final strength, at least for Pathfinder analysis, is that asymmetrical distance estimates are a natural con-sequence of using this technique.

3.4.2 Paired Comparison

In its simplest form, each subject is required to supply an estimate of similarity, or relatedness, for all $n(n-1)/2$ pairs of items (i.e., the combina-tion of n items taken two at a time). This technique offers several ad-vantages. First, all of the necessary distance estimates are obtained from each of the raters. Furthermore, the individual judgments required are relatively simple and do not require raters to introspect about the overall organization of the set of items. Therefore, it is possible to obtain relatively unbiased estimates of distances between pairs of items or, if the application requires it, to obtain estimates that are biased for specific dimensions (McDonald, Dayton, & McDonald, 1986). For example, general instructions to base judgments on relatedness may be useful for discovering important underlying dimensions, whereas instructions to base judgments on how often items co-occur may be useful for producing matrices that reflect procedural knowledge.

The major problem with this methodology is that it may not be suitable for real-world (large) applications, at least in its standard form. For example, in order to obtain distance estimates for 100 items (a relatively small, real-world set), each subject would have to rate 4,950 pairs. From experience we know that it takes subjects at least 5 seconds to rate a pair of items. Thus, rating this many pairs would take approximately 7 hours, if raters worked diligently at their task. The basic UNIX *man* system of 219 commands, discussed below, would require 39 hours per subject! Such times appear even more impractical when one considers that several valuable "experts" are usually required. This is a particularly troubling dilemma, because large systems are most likely to benefit from organization. One way of overcoming this problem is to have each subject rate only pairs from a subset of the items. Once again, however, judgments can be influenced by the context supplied by the set of items to be rated and raters may use different criteria for their judgments depending on the context. Thus, this procedure may introduce considerable noise into the combined proximity matrix and requires more raters.

A related concern is that the method of paired comparison is relatively inefficient, particularly for Pathfinder analysis. Within the context (or frame) of the items to be rated, most pairs are judged as "not related." Although raters are capable of making fine discriminations among related pairs, they are less able to do so for those that are unrelated. Unrelated items are simply unrelated, not more-or-less so. Because Pathfinder focuses on small distances and generally discounts large ones, fine discriminations between unrelated items would be of little value even if they could be obtained.

As mentioned above, even when judges rate all possible pairs of items, considerable error may be introduced into the ratings if the raters are not familiar with all of the items. It is important to remember that proximity matrices are comprised of distance *estimates*. These estimates (scores) form sampling distributions that may have high variability. Scaling analyses, particularly discrete methods (e.g., hierarchical clustering schemes and Pathfinder), are not equipped to handle variability and tend to treat all differences as meaningful. When combined proximity matrices are formed by averaging individual subjects' ratings, information about such variability is lost. As a consequence, the presence or absence of particular links (Pathfinder) or clusters (hierarchical cluster analysis) may be the result of error in the data, rather than meaningful differences. A potential solution to this problem is to establish confidence intervals for rating data and use these intervals, rather than means, in the scaling computations. Another possibility is to use the scaling solution to guide subsequent data collection, thereby empirically distinguishing true from artifactual results. We will describe this approach in more detail in the discussion of the UNIX *man* study.

3.4.3 Sorting

This method requires judges to sort items into piles based on logical relationships. It is a much more efficient technique than the method of paired comparison, thus particularly suitable for large sets of items. Furthermore, it is not as susceptible to shifts in the criteria (dimensions) used by raters, because all items must be considered as a set. However, it does require subjects to generate an overall organization for the set of items, and this task may not be as simple as making pair-wise judgments.

If the usual procedure is followed (i.e., items are not duplicated), then this method produces data matrices which individually satisfy the ultrametric and triangle inequalities (Miller, 1969). However, violations of these inequalities are common when individual matrices are combined to form a composite matrix. Furthermore, if duplicates are allowed, even individual proximity matrices may contain violations of the *triangle inequality*.

$D_{jk} \leq D_{ij} + D_{ik}$

or the more stringent *ultrametric inequality*:

$D_{jk} \leq \max[D_{ij}, D_{ik}]$.

The consequences of such violations are most clearly seen for hierarchical cluster analysis. As discussed in the section on psychometric scaling techniques, most hierarchical clustering schemes are of two types: the minimum methods (also referred to as "connectedness" or "single linkage" methods) that tend to emphasize smaller distances between clusters, and maximum methods (also referred to as "diameter" and "complete linkage" methods) that tend to suppress them. In the unlikely event that the ultrametric inequality holds without exception, both maximum and minimum hierarchical clustering schemes will produce the same results. However, if there are violations of the ultrametric inequality in the data, then the maximum and minimum methods will produce different solutions. Such differences may be relatively unimportant, although minimum and maximum solutions can be compared in order to assess the extent of the problem (Johnson, 1967). Substantial differences between the minimum and maximum hierarchical clustering solutions may indicate that the systems being represented are not hierarchical in nature.

The combination of the standard sorting procedure and hierarchical cluster analysis is particularly likely to suppress non-hierarchical relationships. Sorting imposes a "hierarchical filter" on the data acquisition process, limiting the extent to which nonhierarchical relationships can be expressed by judges. Because items must be partitioned into nonoverlapping sets, it is impossible for a subject to express the judgment that item x belongs in both groups *A* and *B* (let alone *A*, *B*, and *C*). By combining the judgments of several subjects, such nonhierarchical relationships may emerge (e.g., one subject might place item *x* in pile *A*, whereas another might place item *x* in pile *B*), although the strengths of these relationships may be artificially reduced. Furthermore, this result actually relies on judges having different, or ill-formed, conceptual models. Although it is theoretically possible to overcome the problem of hierarchical filtering by employing duplicates, thus allowing judges to directly express the belief that a particular item belongs in two different piles, it has been our experience that raters hesitate to use duplicates, probably because of the extra effort involved (see the UNIX sorting study).

3.4.4 Controlled Association

A promising alternative to paired comparison and sorting is the controlled association technique proposed by Miyamoto, Oi, Abe, Katsuya, and Nakayama (1986). In this technique, each of the n items is individually presented to the judge whose task it is to select the most associated concepts from the remaining $n-1$ items. Although not as efficient as sorting, it is potentially more efficient than paired comparison, because the number of comparisons does not necessarily increase as the square of the number of items. Furthermore, this technique produces considerably more information than sorting and allows judges to express asymmetrical as well as nonhierarchical relationships.

3.4.5 Event Recording

The event record technique is similar to listing, except that users are monitored while interacting with the system under investigation, or the actions of subjects are recorded while performing particular tasks, and the resulting event records, rather than lists, form the basis for distance estimation. As with lists, event records can be easily converted to conditional probability matrices. A major advantage of this technique is that the data are obtained automatically and judges, in the usual sense, are not required. Furthermore, event records contain task information that may not be obtainable from judgments.

The problems inherent in the listing procedure are also problems for the event-record technique. In particular, distance estimates for all pairs of items are not necessarily obtained. This shortcoming, however, may also be considered a strength, because estimates of command usage (i.e., frequency of occurrence) are automatically obtained, helping to define the concept set.

4. Applications of Psychometric Techniques

In the following section we describe several studies that take the general approach of acquiring users' task-related cognitive structures and reflecting them in the design of the user interface. One of the most obvious ways in which basing the system image on users' conceptual models can improve usability is by facilitating the process of locating necessary information. Simply put, the time users spend searching for information can be reduced by putting things where users expect them to be.

4.1 Menu Organization

McDonald, Stone, Liebelt, and Karat (1982) proposed a methodology for designing cognitive aspects of the human-computer interface which is roughly analogous to using anthropometric data (i.e., human body measurements) to design physical aspects of the interface. The method consists of obtaining measures of the cognitive characteristics of potential system users and using these data to organize information at the interface. McDonald et al. reported a study in which subjects learned to access word-processing (WP) terms organized in various ways. They measured performance on a standard paired-associate learning task in which subjects were required to associate a particular response (a sequence of menu selections) with a particular stimulus (the target word-processing function).

During the first phase of this study experienced WP operators were required to rate the similarity of thirty-four WP functions. The resulting proximity data were submitted to hierarchical cluster analysis, and the 16 functions that most strongly clustered in the hierarchical cluster analysis (four functions in each of four clusters) were selected to serve as the terminal nodes in a three-level hierarchy.

During the second phase of the experiment, McDonald et al. had a separate group of 24 subjects learn to access the subset of 16 WP functions selected during the knowledge acquisition phase. On each trial the subjects' task was to access a target word-processing function by selecting the correct menu options from among a series of alternatives. At the two highest levels of the hierarchy, subjects selected between two alternatives (e.g., *A* or *B* followed by *C* or *D*). At the lowest level of the hierarchy they selected among four alternatives (e.g., *E, F, G,* or *H*). Thus, as an example, the sequence of menu selection necessary to access a particular target (e.g., *Delete*) might be *ACF*. The intermediate nodes in the hierarchy were assigned arbitrarily selected consorants, rather than meaningful category labels, in an effort to assess the effects of organization independent of the goodness of category labels. The 16 WP functions were either assigned to terminal nodes in the hierarchy based on the results of the cluster analysis (categorically) or randomly. Subjects made fewer errors learning to access the WP functions when they were categorically organized compared to the random condition.

In an effort to further clarify the effects of menu organization on user performance, McDonald, Stone, and Liebelt (1983) compared categorical, alphabetical, and random organizations in a visual search task using a single-panel 64 item menu. Five different within-panel organizations were compared, from completely alphabetical to completely random. In three of the organizations the 64 items were organized by category (food, animals, minerals, and cities) into four columns of 16 items. Within these four categories the items were either organized categorically, alphabetically, or randomly. Similarity rating and cluster analysis were used to derive the categorical organizations.

This study also examined the effects that the *type* of target had on menu-selection performance by providing either explicit targets (e.g., "lemon") or single-line definitions (e.g., "a small, oblong, pale-yellow citrus fruit"). Presumably the task of locating targets based on vague definitions is more realistic and provides another measure of the effects of organization. "Real world" users seldom search for explicit targets in menus -- if they know exactly what they are looking for, then they probably know where it is. For example, if a user must search through a menu to find the command for removing a file, then it is unlikely that the name of the command is known (i.e., it might be *Delete, Remove, Erase, Drop,* etc.). If the user knows that the command is *Delete*, then searching the menu probably is not necessary at all. Learning that the name of the command for removing files is *Delete* usually involves using the system. Because there is ample evidence that the effects of menu organization disappear with practice (Card, 1982), using the explicit-target search task is a bit like having experienced users locate familiar items in rearranged menus. While this technique may be useful for assessing the degree to which a particular menu organization corresponds to the user's conceptual organization (a reasonable objective on occasion), it may not provide a valid measure of the effects of organization under realistic conditions.

The results of the McDonald et al. (1983) experiment showed a clear advantage for categorical menus over pure alphabetical and random organizations, especially when subjects were uncertain about the target. The advantage of the categorical-categorical organization (i.e., items clustered categorically within categorically organized columns) was especially pronounced during the first block of trials when subjects were shown definitions rather than explicit targets. As predicted, the effect of organization virtually disappeared by the last block of trials (block five, 64 trials/block), replicating the earlier results of Card (1982).

It is tempting to conclude from the preceding that interface organization only affects user performance during learning. In this regard, McDonald et al. (1983) argued that the structure of the interface may also influence the development of users' conceptual models and, consequently, there may be persistent effects of organization when users are required to perform complex tasks. Furthermore, there is some evidence for persistent effects of organization on relatively simple tasks, as shown by the following study.

McDonald, Dayton, and McDonald (1986) conducted a study in which the keys (menu items) on a simulated fast-food cash register keyboard were either organized according to MDS solutions or customized by individual users. During the scaling phase of this experiment, two groups of twelve subjects rated all 276 pairs of 24 fast-food items. One group rated the *similarity* of the pairs whereas the second group rated the pairs in terms of how likely they were to be ordered as part of a single customer's meal (judged *frequency of co-occurrence*). In the second phase of the experiment three groups of eight subjects used different keyboard layouts to enter one- to four-item food orders.

The Similar Keyboard (SK) group used a menu layout based on a nonmetric MDS analysis of the similarity ratings, whereas the Co-occurrence

Keyboard (CK) group used a keyboard layout based on an identical MDS analysis performed on the frequency of co-occurrence ratings. Because the purpose of the MDS analyses was to provide guidance in laying out the keyboards, two-dimensional solutions were used, and no effort was made to determine the optimal dimensionality for the MDS analyses. Thus, the average stress values (Kruskal's stress formula 1) for both solutions remained relatively high, although approximately equal (SK = .336, CK = .358). The keyboards were produced by mapping keys onto points in the MDS solution and reducing the inter-key spacing until all of the keys fit within the size limitations of the keyboard. Because of the nature of this procedure, only ordinal properties of the MDS solutions were retained[1]. Subjects in the Personalized Keyboard (PK) group were told to place the cash-register keys anywhere they wished, with the stipulation that they allow adequate spacing between them.

During the validation phase of this experiment, each subject participated in three, one hour sessions on consecutive days during which they were required to enter 24 single-item orders and 216 multiple-item food orders (72 each of the two-, three-, and four-item orders). Multiple-item food orders were classified as either complementary (e.g., *Hamburger, French Fries, Coke*), similar (e.g., *Cola, Root Beer, Iced Tea*), or odd (e.g., *Eggs, Sundae, Iced Tea*). The subjects' task was to select all of the items in a given food order by touching the corresponding keys on the keyboard. Each trial was terminated when the subject touched the *Total* key.

The results showed strong, early effects of organization which, as in the previous menu-selection studies, could largely be attributed to visual search. Subjects using the SK keyboard performed best with similar orders whereas subjects using the CK keyboard performed best with complementary orders. Contrary to expectations, subjects in the personalized keyboard group had the poorest performance on the first day. For purposes of this discussion, the most important finding was that the pattern of results for multiple-item orders in the SK and CK conditions remained essentially the same after practice. After the subjects learned

---

[1]We are currently investigating the use of a simulated annealing procedure for keyboard layout

the locations of the keys on the keyboards, thus eliminating the need for visual search, the effects of organization persisted. This persistence was probably due to the physical movement required in selecting items in multiple-item orders. Thus, visual search time was replaced by inter-item movement time as the source of the organization effect.

As mentioned above, subjects using personalized keyboards took more time to enter food orders than did subjects in the SK and CK conditions, particularly on the first day. Interestingly, by the third day of practice their performance approached that of subjects in the SK group, although subjects in the CK group remained superior. When the PK keyboards were compared with the SK and CK layouts, it became evident that the personalized keyboards were variations of the SK scheme. This obser-vation was supported by correlational analyses of inter-key distances; seven of the eight subjects' keyboards in the PK group resulted in sig-nificant positive correlations with the SK layout, whereas only two keyboards resulted in significant positive correlations with the CK layout (one subject's keyboard was positively correlated with both the SK and CK layouts). Furthermore, when asked to choose between the keyboard layout based on judged similarity or the layout based on frequency of co-occurrence, people generally preferred the similar keyboard. It is im-portant to note, however, that most fast-food orders are complementary, rather than similar or odd, and that a keyboard based on frequency of co-occurrence should be superior to one based on similarity and also better than keyboards based on individual preference.

In another application, Tullis (1985) described the development of a menu-based interface for an existing command-based operating system. He began by obtaining psychological distance estimates among existing system functions from individuals familiar with the command-based operating system. He had subjects sort function-labeled index cards into "logically related" groups. He then combined these data into a composite proximity matrix and then obtained a representation of the users' model of the system using hierarchical cluster analysis (maximum method).

Tullis was primarily interested in subjects' ability to access functions in "broad" vs. "deep" menu hierarchies. He selected two different cut-off levels in the same hierarchical cluster analysis for this comparison. The deep version of the menu-access system was restricted to 15 options per menu panel, arranged in a single column. In the broad version, the number of options on individual panels was extended by using two or three columns, up to a maximum of 45 options per panel. Subjects took essentially the same amount of time to accomplish tasks with both versions of the menu, but they made fewer errors with the broad hierarchy. He concluded that, in general, the better menu hierarchy is the one that requires the fewest steps (i.e., the "broader" menu).

The broad and deep organizations were both based on the results of the same hierarchical cluster analysis. Thus, the small effects reported for the depth/breadth manipulation should not be surprising, because all of the clusters corresponded to *potentially* meaningful categories. Earlier research into the depth versus breadth issue (Miller, 1981; Snowberry, Parkinson, & Sisson, 1983) largely ignored the question of category goodness by making the dubious assumption that a set of items can be assigned to the terminal nodes of different hierarchies with arbitrarily many intermediate nodes (category labels). However, a similar problem occurs when one assumes that all of the clusters in a hierarchical cluster analysis of composite data are meaningful.

Roske-Hofstrand and Paap (1986) showed that pilots could access the information pages of a Control-Display Unit (CDU) more efficiently when the menu structure was based on a Pathfinder network derived from judgments of pilots compared to a menu structure developed by a design team. The CDU is a menu-based system used by pilots to facilitate the planning and monitoring of flight activities. This study used the method of paired comparison to obtain similarity ratings for a subset of 34 of the CDU panels from four experienced pilots. The resulting proximity matrix was submitted to Pathfinder analysis to obtain a PFNET($r=\infty$, $q=n-1$) for ordinal data.

The Pathfinder network was used to determine the menu options that appeared at the bottom of each information panel. Two sets of "dominating nodes" (sets with the minimum number of nodes necessary to reach every other node in the network by traversing a single link) were selected to appear on the primary index page. These dominating-node sets differed in their level of redundancy, i.e., the number of extra links from the index pages to the lower-level pages. In the more redundant network, lower-level pages (nodes) could more often be reached from several of the index pages. Two other organizations were compared, a hierarchy and an organization described in the original specifications for the CDU.

The different organizations in the Roske-Hofstrand and Paap (1986) study can be thought of as consisting of three different kinds of panels. The primary index page, listing the "special" index pages corresponding to the dominating nodes, appeared at the highest level of each organization. The dominating-node panels, in turn, listed the lowest level panels that could be reached directly and, in the nonhierarchical organizations, other dominating node panels as well. The four organizations were compared in an experiment in which sixteen pilots were asked questions that could only be answered by accessing particular CDU panels. Four pilots were assigned to work with each of the four menu prototypes: high redundancy (22 extra links), low redundancy (10 extra links), hierarchical (0 extra links), and the organization based on the specifications of the original CDU design team. The results showed that the high-redundancy group had significantly faster task times than the other groups, supporting the use of cognitive networks for organizing menu panels. It is interesting to note that the advantage for the high-redundancy organization persisted with practice and that subjects in this group still performed faster than subjects in the other conditions during the last block of trials.

The studies discussed in this section have demonstrated that menus organized according to users' empirically-derived cognitive structures are superior to other alternatives (e.g., alphabetical, random, and subjective organizations). The general methodology used in these studies involves (1) obtaining judgments of relatedness for all pairs of menu items, (2) scaling the proximity matrix in order to obtain a representation of the set of items, and (3) mapping the obtained representation onto menu layout (logical or physical). When simple tasks requiring visual search have been used, the effects of organization generally disappear with practice, although persistent effects of organization have been obtained for more complex tasks, and other effects resulting from the development of conceptual models have not been assessed. In the following study we discuss an application in which facilitating the development of effective user models is of primary importance.

4.2 On-Line Documentation

The objective of our work on documentation is to provide structural descriptions of an existing command-based system (UNIX). These structures can be used to provide the kind of context-sensitive help facility typically available on menu-based systems. In addition, structural descriptions of systems might be made available to writers who are in the processes of writing system documentation. Such information should be useful for organizing information within as well as between information panels, and for insuring that important relationships between system elements are documented. Another goal is to allow users to efficiently develop accurate conceptual models of systems by interacting with the documentation.

As a component of the user-system interface, "help" poses a particularly difficult challenge for designers. Using help and documentation is, almost by definition, a problem solving activity. Users are confronted with the tasks of figuring out what they need to know, locating the required information (or discovering that it is not available), and inferring answers to their questions from the information provided. Some common techniques for providing help, such as context sensitivity, already rely on there being a close correspondence between the system and its documentation by assuming that when users request "help" they need help with whatever it is they are currently doing. However, context sensitive help has only been developed for moded systems, typically those with menu-based interfaces, and we propose to extend its application to modeless systems as well. Furthermore, context-sensitive help systems primarily aid users in selecting appropriate entry points into documentation and may be of little or no assistance when users commit a series of errors and are being led down a blind alley. In other words, the assumption underlying context-sensitive help systems is occasionally false, in that the error that eventually causes a user to request help may have occurred earlier in the transaction. Thus, our proposed organizing scheme will enhance the benefits provided by context-sensitive help by guiding users to relevant information after they enter the documentation system as well.

We are particularly interested in providing context sensitivity for command-based systems by developing network models, or state transition diagrams, and tracking user interactions (cf. Jackson & Lefrere, 1984). We hypothesize that when a user is in a particular state (i.e., location in the system network) and requests help, it should be possible to infer his or her goal and provide assistance in the form of suggested paths among help panels. Furthermore, a graphic representation of the system network (e.g., a map with a "you are here" marker) might encourage goal-directed, rather than procedural, behavior by allowing users to indicate where they want to go rather than how to get there (Newell & Simon, 1972). Allowing users to select goals, rather than the procedures necessary to accomplish them, should decrease the complexity of the user's task.

4.2.1 Superman

Sachania (1985) identified the need to improve access to information contained in the UNIX on-line manual system (*man*). He applied Pathfinder to the organization of this collection of information panels. Sachania converted the co-occurrence data inherent in the *man* system into a distance matrix. By summing the number of co-occurrences of commands in the "see also" references on each panel he was able to construct a matrix suitable for Pathfinder analysis. The resulting network solution [PFNET ($r=\infty$, $q=n-1$)] for over 200 UNIX commands formed the basis for his *Superman* system which guides users along paths of related topics. As a consequence of developing his system, Sachania discovered that 28 panels in the *man* system were not referenced by any others, a fact almost certain to be of interest to the designers of the system!

Although not empirically validated, *Superman* appears to be a step in the right direction. There are, however, a number of problems with this particular approach. The most questionable aspect of Sachania's methodology lies in his short-cut technique for constructing the distance matrix. Assuming that the algorithm he used for tallying "see also" references is optimal, the resulting network is, at best, a reflection of the impressions of a small set of documentation designers, rather than users. It is unclear what level of experience the developers of the UNIX *man* system had or what method they used in organizing the panels. The *man* system has evolved, along with UNIX, over a period of years and the backgrounds and qualifications of the developers undoubtedly vary, producing obvious inconsistencies. The 28 unreferenced panels are evidence that the procedure was flawed.

Superman only addresses a small set of the problems users have in locating information. If a user needs information about a command, and already knows the name of the command, then the unaugmented *man* system works reasonably well. If a user needs information about a command but does not know its name, then *Superman* may be of some assistance in locating the desired information (if the user knows the name of a related command). *Superman* is also useful for browsing, when the user is not searching for any particular information but simply exploring the system. However, indexing aids of this kind will most commonly be used to guide users to information via categorical entry points (e.g., editing, programming, filing, etc.). Thus, assistance is needed at a categorical level. A user should be able to request information about "printing" or "communication" functions and be guided to the appropriate subset of commands.

5. Superman II

Our approach to the UNIX interactive documentation guide (*Superman II*) is to develop a system that (1) is based on empirically derived representations of experienced users' conceptual models, (2) has several perspectives (e.g., functional and procedural), (3) has multiple levels of abstraction within each perspective, and (4) provides users who are familiar with other operating systems (e.g., DOS) a "bridge" for transferring their knowledge to UNIX. In order to achieve these objectives, we have employed both sorting and event recording techniques. We have also developed a procedure for eliciting the additional knowledge necessary to identify functional categories and task sequences from the basic representations. Furthermore, we are exploring ways of combining the separate analyses obtained from sorting and event recording to form a more complete coherence model of experienced UNIX users. We will then proceed to conduct a series of studies which will focus on the UNIX *man* system, *Superman*, and *Superman II*.

5.1 The Functional Perspective

Fifteen experienced UNIX users from New Mexico State University voluntarily participated in this phase of the project. A questionnaire administered to the subjects after participation characterized their varying degrees of UNIX experience. Seven were classified as expert or intermediate-to-expert users whereas eight were considered intermediate users (see Table 5-1).

Table 5-1: A summary of the UNIX sorting data showing the number of commands (CMDS) sorted, the number of piles, and the number of duplicates (extra cards) used by each subject

S#	EXPERTISE	PILES	CARDS	CMDS	EXTRA CARDS	PILE
1	I-E	34	139	139	0	4.09
2	I	36	141	137	4	3.92
3	I-E	15	138	138	0	9.20
4	I	54	224	204	20	4.15
5	I	32	116	116	0	3.63
6	I	47	140	135	5	2.98
7	I	34	149	134	15	4.38
8	I	39	113	113	0	2.90
9	E	15	154	154	0	10.27
10	I	22	94	94	0	4.27
11	E	18	220	219	1	12.22
12	E	9	199	199	0	22.11
13	E	32	125	125	0	3.91
14	I	41	190	160	30	4.63
15	I-E	31	125	125	0	4.03
	AVERAGE	30.60	151.13			6.45
	SD	12.64	39.40			5.18

A 5" by 7" index card was prepared for each of the 219 functions documented as part of the Berkeley 4.2 version of the UNIX *man* system running on SUN microsystems minicomputers. The name of each command was printed in large, boldface type on the face of the index card. The name of the command and a short command definition (up to four lines) were printed on the back.

Subjects participated individually in a single session of approximately one hour (range = 20 minutes to 2 hours). The sorting procedure took place in a large conference room with four adjoining tables. A file box containing the 219 printed cards, along with some blank index cards, was placed in front of the subject. Subjects were instructed to use functional criteria to sort commands which they knew how to use. After the initial sort, they sorted additional familiar commands by referring to the definitions on the back of the cards. Subjects were told not to sort any unfamiliar commands. To eliminate the "hierarchical filtering" associated with sorting, subjects were encouraged to use duplicate cards when they felt a particular command belonged in more than one pile.

A co-occurrence matrix was created for each subject by assigning values to all pairs of cards based on their membership in piles. If two cards were in the same pile they were assigned a distance of 0 in the co-occurrence matrix. If two cards were in different piles, they were assigned a distance of 1. A combined co-occurrence matrix was created by summing the individual matrices. This resulted in a "distance" matrix with values ranging from 0 (all fifteen raters placed the two commands in the same pile) to 15 (no rater placed the two commands in the same pile).

The number of unique commands sorted by individuals ranged from 94 to 219 (Table 5-1). All commands were sorted by at least one individual, but only 44 of the 219 commands were sorted by all 15 raters. Of these 44, 37 were identified as "core" UNIX commands by eliminating those commands not sorted in a pile with one or more of the other 43 by at least half of the raters. A hierarchical cluster analysis of these 37 commands is shown in Figure 5-1. Separate hierarchical cluster (using both the Maximum and Minimum methods) and Pathfinder analyses were performed on the "raw" co-occurrence matrix and a conditional probability matrix in order to determine the most appropriate representation. The conditional probability matrix was constructed by dividing each distance estimate in the co-occurrence matrix by the smaller of the two frequencies for that pair (i.e., the probability of the more frequent command given the less frequent command).

For example, the *cat* command (catenate one file to another file, often the display) was sorted by all fifteen raters. The *comm* command (merge two files and display), on the other hand, was sorted by only seven

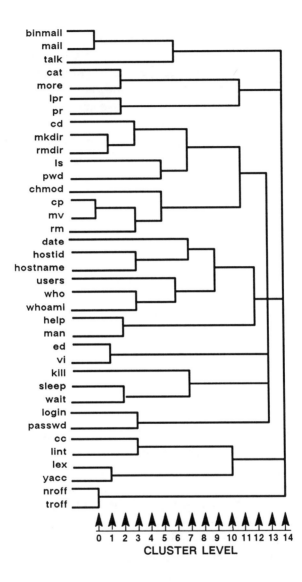

Figure 5-1: Hierarchical cluster analysis (Maximum Method) of the
37 'core' UNIX commands from the sorting study

raters. Of the seven raters who sorted both commands, only 3 put *cat*
and *comm* in the same pile. Thus, in the co-occurrence matrix this pair
had a distance of 4, whereas in the conditional probability matrix it was
assigned a distance of .57 (4/7), equivalent to approximately 8.6 in

co-occurrence units. As can be seen from this example, computing conditional probabilities in this way tends to increase the relative distances between pairs in which one or both items are not judged by all of the raters.

The preliminary Pathfinder analyses (all 219 nodes connected) resulted in a network with 655 links for the "raw" co-occurrence matrix and 417 links for the conditional probability matrix, PFNET($r=\infty$, $q=n-1$). The network derived from the conditional probability matrix was not only less complex, but also seemed to capture a more coherent organization as judged by experienced users. Accordingly, this network was used in the analyses to follow.

In *Superman II* we must graphically represent "subnets" (portions of a Pathfinder network) that correspond to high-level concepts. In Figure 5-2 we show one approach to representing subnets that involves the combined use of hierarchical cluster and MDS analyses. First, we obtained clusters using a minimum hierarchical cluster analysis (Johnson, 1967). We then subjected the appropriate subsets of distance estimates for each cluster to a 2-dimensional, nonmetric MDS. Finally, we used the MDS coordinates to guide node (command) layout and added the links specified by the Pathfinder solution. Comparing the hierarchical and network representations of these clusters is informative. In Figure 5-2, for example, not only are the two clusters consisting of directory-level and file-level commands evident in the PFNET, but the "bridge" between these two clusters, from *rmdir* (remove directory) to *rm* (remove file), can be seen as well. It is tempting to speculate that this connection represents more than the simple fact that both of these commands remove things. Most UNIX users will recognize that these commands have a more fundamental relationship as well; in order to remove a directory all of the files in the directory must be removed first.

A similar comparison of hierarchical cluster and Pathfinder analyses is shown in Figure 5-3. In this example we selected the subset of commands used in programming (e.g., compilers, interpreters, etc.). Rather than relying on an MDS analysis to help in laying out the network, we used the constraints inherent in the Pathfinder solution. This procedure is somewhat more subjective than the MDS approach, although many of

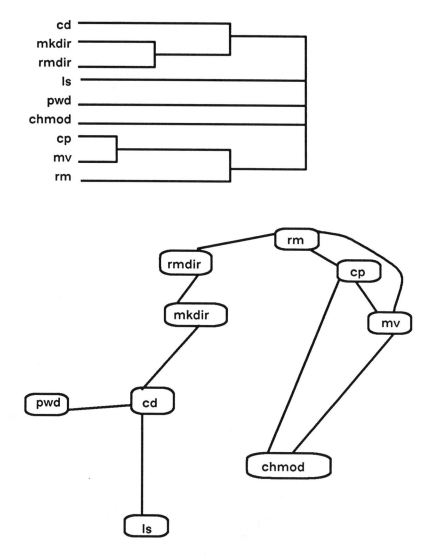

Figure 5-2: A comparison of hierarchical clustering (Minimum Method)
and network analysis [PFNET($r=\infty$, $q=n-1$)]
for UNIX directory commands

the layout rules, such as minimizing link crossings, are relatively unbiased. For those familiar with programming, but unfamiliar with UNIX,
the central role of the *C* compiler (*cc*) may seem a bit strange. An

experienced programmer might reasonably expect the assembler (*as*) to occupy such a role, but not a particular compiler. However, those familiar with UNIX will recognize the central importance of *C* to UNIX (e.g., UNIX is written in *C*). Other details in the Pathfinder representation can be observed in this comparison as well, such as the connections between the *C* utilities (*cb, cpp,* and *lint*) and the *C* compiler, and the particular way in which the Pascal functions (*pc, pi, pix,* and *px*) are linked. In both Figures 5-2 and 5-3, the PFNET provides more information than the corresponding hierarchical representation. Indeed, the minimum hierarchical cluster solution can be derived from the PFNET, but not vice versa.

The complete functional perspective requires not only valid categories, but appropriate category labels as well. As we have already discussed, judgments of relatedness contain error and the attempt to identify subnets, described above, is subject to the criticism that some of the clusters correspond to conceptual categories, whereas others are artifacts of the procedures employed. One approach to resolving such questions is to obtain more data. Therefore, we had four of the most experienced UNIX users from the original study judge the goodness of clusters obtained using hierarchical cluster analysis and name the better clusters.

For this phase of the procedure we selected the subset of 152 UNIX commands that were known by at least half of the 15 experienced users. We then performed a hierarchical cluster analyses on the 152 commands using the minimum method. The minimum method was selected because there is a direct correspondence between Pathfinder with $r=\infty$ and $q=n-1$ that guarantees our ability to map the resulting clusters onto subnets, and the minimum method tends to produce fewer distinct clusters, reducing the amount of rating required. The hierarchical cluster analyses produced a total of 83 distinct clusters, not including the highest-level cluster in which all 152 commands were grouped. Each judge was shown all 83 clusters in a random order and asked to rate the goodness of each cluster on a five point scale, ranging from 1 = Very Bad to 5 = Very Good, and to provide appropriate names for all but the Very Bad clusters. Judges were also allowed to enter a 0 if they did not know one or more of the commands in the cluster. The ratings of the judges were averaged for each of the 83 clusters. There was a general

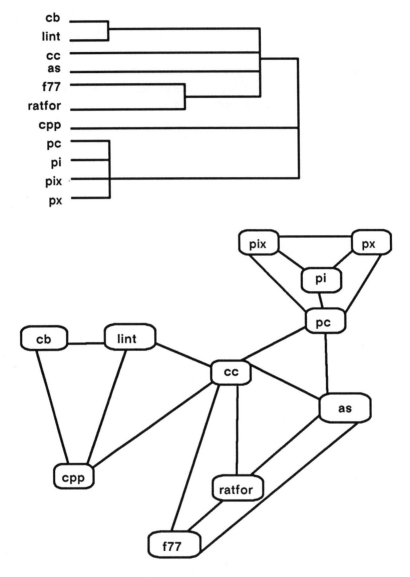

Figure 5-3: A comparison of hierarchical clustering (Minimum Method) and network analysis [PFNET($r=\infty$, $q=n-1$)] for UNIX programming functions

tendency for judgments of cluster goodness to decrease as cluster size increased ($r = -.50$). However, the ratings for clusters ranging in size from two to five commands averaged 4 or better (Good to Very Good).

In the next step, we used the ratings and names supplied by the judges to eliminate artifactual clusters. As an example, Figure 5-4 shows the cluster corresponding to communications functions, with the average ratings of the original nine clusters shown on the top and the reduced version with four categories shown on the bottom. Reduction was accomplished by comparing the names given by the judges for each of the smallest clusters with those given for the clusters above them in the hierarchy, and collapsing smaller clusters into larger ones when the names were the same. Although there is a certain amount of subjectivity involved in deciding that two sets of names are the same, in this case this procedure resulted in considerable simplification and produced very sensible categories. However, some anomalies are also evident, such as the *biff* command not being included in the *Electronic Mail* category, as one might expect, but only the more general *Communication* category. We are currently exploring the possibility of having judges indicate clusters, and name them, by referring directly to network representations, thereby eliminating such artifacts of the hierarchical clustering process.

5.2 The Procedural Perspective

Our approach to developing a procedural perspective was to obtain a number of protocols from nine of the UNIX users who participated in the sorting study. The technique we used required no special effort on the part of the participants. After obtaining permission, we modified users' *.login* files to increase the size of their *history* records so that all of the events that occurred during a session were automatically captured and, at the end of each session, mailed to us. A summary of the event-record data is shown in Table 5-2.

A total of 41,372 commands were obtained. Of these, approximately 61% came from section 1 of the *man* system. The number of unique commands used by individuals ranged from 42 to 133. Interestingly, as shown in Table 5-3, the top ten commands accounted for 66% of all commands issued -- the top three commands accounted for 32%! While these statistics would undoubtedly change somewhat from one group of users to another (e.g., *rsh* is only used when several machines are networked together), they are probably typical of commands usage.

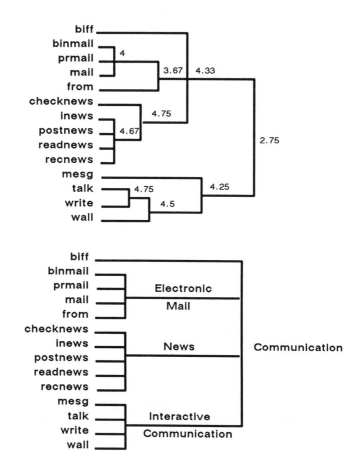

Figure 5-4: A hierarchical cluster analysis (Minimum Method) for Unix communication commands with average 'goodness' ratings (top) and after reduction based on naming (bottom)

The event records from all of the users were combined into a composite frequency of co-occurrence matrix by incrementing the appropriate cells each time a particular command followed another in an event record. Note that this is a relatively crude method for encoding the information in these data because only two-step sequences are considered. The data

Table 5-2: A summary of the UNIX event record data showing the number of commands recorded for each user and the number and percentage of these commands that come from Section 1 of the *man* system

| | ALL CMDS | | SECTION 1 CMDS | | |
USER	UNIQUE	TOTAL	UNIQUE	TOTAL	PERCENT
1	58	2,124	39	1,197	56%
2	72	1,139	41	685	60%
3	47	1,370	32	814	59%
4	97	2,786	57	1,728	62%
5	42	863	26	592	69%
6	84	9,499	51	4,994	53%
7	122	15,894	75	11,225	71%
8	49	2,196	27	771	35%
9	133	5,501	84	3,178	58%
TOTAL		41,372		25,184	
AVERAGE	78.22	4,597	48.00	2,798	58%

Table 5-3: The ten most frequently used commands from the UNIX event record study

RANK	CMD	FREQ	PERCENT
1	ls	4,719	11.41%
2	cd	4,420	10.68%
3	more	3,961	9.57%
4	|(pipe)	3,372	8.15%
5	mail	2,346	5.67%
6	emacs	2,078	5.02%
7	fg	2,060	4.98%
8	pwd	1,781	4.30%
9	rsh	1,588	3.84%
10	rm	815	1.97%
TOTAL		27,140	
ALL CMDS		41,372	65.60%

were then converted to conditional probabilities such that large conditional probabilities produced short distances in the matrix whereas small conditional probabilities produced large distances. This proximity matrix served as the basis for our subsequent analyses.

After converting the frequency of co-occurrence matrix into a conditional probability matrix, we submitted a subset of 49 commands to Pathfinder analysis ($r=\infty, q=n-1$). The network of commands selected consisted of those that occurred in the event records of at least half of the users. The purpose of this analysis was to identify task *sequences*. Figure 5-5 shows a portion of this network that includes all commands within two links (arcs) of *kill* . As an example of the type of information contained in the network, and its potential utility, suppose several programs were executing "simultaneously." Further, suppose that one of these programs was a particularly time-consuming analysis that had to be terminated for some reason (e.g., to reduce processor load). This is one of the few cases where the name of the appropriate UNIX command is fairly easy to remember (i.e., *kill*). However, in order to *kill* a program, you have to know its job number. The name of the command that returns job numbers is not so easy to remember. From the network in Figure 5-5 it is apparent that only one command, ps, frequently precedes *kill* (i.e., there is only one arc leading to *kill*). As you might anticipate from the fact that we are using this example, *ps* (program status) is the command that returns job numbers, along with some other useful information.

5.3 Future Directions

We are currently applying our techniques to other operating systems in an effort to establish a common level of abstraction. We hypothesize that operating systems quite similar to UNIX, such as DOS for the PC, as well as those that appear different, such as the graphic-based Mac system, can be described in terms of a prototypical operating-system model. The development of this model will facilitate the transfer of knowledge from one operating system to any other. Thus, in addition to simply establishing that two commands serve similar functions (e.g., *dir* in DOS and *ls* in UNIX), abstract categorical and task-level relationships can also be identified.

We plan to conduct a series of controlled experiments in which the three documentation systems will be compared (*man, Superman,* and *Superman II*). In the first of these studies, novice users of the UNIX system will be required to locate both specific information (information

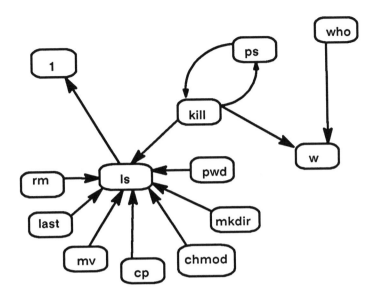

Figure 5-6: A Pathfinder analysis [PFNET($r=\infty$, $q=n-1$)] of UNIX
event-record data, including all commands
within two links (arc) of *kill*

contained on single panels) as well as information which will require
them to integrate information from several panels. In addition, once subjects are familiar with the documentation system, they will be given tasks
which require them to locate information previously not retrieved and,
finally, to provide an overall description of the UNIX system including all
of the commands they can recall and their interrelations. Success or
failure in completing tasks and task completion times will serve as the
general dependent measures, along with measures which will directly
assess the development of cognitive models.

6. Conclusions

In this paper we have presented a methodology for interface design.
The basic methodology consists of (1) selecting a set of items to be

analyzed (e.g., concepts, actions, objects), (2) obtaining estimates of distance between items in the set, (3) submitting the resulting proximity matrix to an appropriate scaling analysis (e.g., MDS, cluster analysis, Pathfinder), and (4) using the scaling solution as a "blueprint" for the system image. All of the scaling techniques suggested in this paper have been widely studied and are appropriate for different applications. Network scaling analyses seem particularly flexible and suitable for providing organization to complex systems.

Although a number of studies have employed the methodology we propose, some problems remain. More detailed guidance must be supplied if the methodology is to become widely applicable. In its present state, our methodology allows designers to acquire user knowledge to organize interface elements. Such user's models are potentially more useful, however, and may eventually form the basis for a comprehensive theory of user psychology.

Our main objective is to develop a theory of interface design. It is, of course, not possible to validate a theory. At best, one theory emerges as the most useful on a number of dimensions in comparison to competing theories. The best interface design theory will provide a useful framework for explaining what is known about human-computer interaction, make interesting predictions about what is not known, provide specific mechanisms for translating the theory's principles into design decisions, and have several successful applications to its credit.

We have discussed at some length the most obvious application of our methodology, menu organization, and the benefits one might expect. We are pursuing answers to the question of what other effects might be expected, specifically those that arise from the development of conceptual models. In the process, we are constructing models of users and tasks that can be applied in a variety of ways. By extending the basic knowledge acquisition methodology, it is also possible to use these results to construct data-bases suitable for expert-system development (Butler & Corter, in press; Cooke & McDonald, 1986).

Acknowledgements

The content and presentation of this chapter have benefited substantially from reviews by authors of other chapters of this volume, and from comments by Nancy Cooke and Ken Paap.

References

Butler, K. A., & Corter, J. E. (in press). Use of psychometric tools for knowledge acquisition: A case study. In W. Gale (Ed.), *Artificial intelligence and statistics.* Reading, Mass.: Addison-Wesley.

Card, S. K. (1982). User perceptual mechanisms in the search of computer command menus. *Proceedings of Human Factors in Computer Systems, CHI'82,* 190-196.

Carre, B. (1979). *Graphs and networks.* Oxford: Clarendon Press.

Christofides, N. (1975). *Graph theory: An algorithmic approach.* New York: Academic Press.

Collins, A. M., & Loftus, E. F. (1975). A spreading activation theory of semantic processing. *Psychological Review, 82,* 407-428.

Constantine, A. G., & Gower, J. C. (1978). Graphical representation of asymmetric matrices. *Applied Statistics, 27,* 297-304.

Cooke, N. M. (1983). *Memory structures of expert and novice computer programmers: Recall order vs. similarity ratings.* Unpublished M. A. thesis, New Mexico State University.

Cooke, N. M. (1987). *The elicitation of units of knowledge and relations: Enhancing empirically-derived semantic networks.* Unpublished Ph.D. dissertation, New Mexico State University.

Cooke, N. M., Durso, F. T., & Schvaneveldt, R. W. (1986). Recall and measures of memory organization. *Journal of Experimental Psychology: Learning, Memory, and Cognition, 12,* 538-549.

Cooke, N. M., & McDonald, J. E. (1986). A formal methodology for acquiring and representing expert knowledge. *Proceedings of the IEEE, 74, 10,* 1422-1430.

Cunningham, J. P. (1978). Free trees and bidirectional trees as representations of psychological distance. *Journal of Mathematical Psychology, 17,* 165-188.

Dearholt, D. W., Schvaneveldt, R. W., & Durso, F. T. (1985). *Properties of networks derived from proximities* (Memorandum in Computer and Cognitive Science, MCCS-85-14). New Mexico State University, Computing Research Laboratory.

Feger, H., & Bien, W. (1982). Network unfolding. *Social Networks, 4,* 257-283.

Gibbons, A. (1985). *Algorithmic graph theory*. Cambridge: Cambridge University Press.

Halasz, F., & Moran, T. P. (1982). Analogy considered harmful. *Proceedings of Human Factors in Computer Systems, CHI '82*, 383-386.

Harary, F. (1969). *Graph theory*. Reading, Mass.: Addison-Wesley.

Harshman, R. A., Green, P. E., Wind, Y., & Lundy, M. E. (1982). A model for the analysis of asymmetric data in marketing research. *Marketing Science, 1*, 205-242.

Hutchinson, J. W. (1981). *Network representations of psychological relations*. Unpublished Ph.D. dissertation, Stanford University.

Jackson, P., & Lefrere, P. (1984). On the application of rule-based techniques to the design of advice-giving systems. *International Journal of Man-Machine Studies, 20*, 63-86.

Johnson, S. C. (1967). Hierarchical clustering schemes. *Psychometrika, 32*, 241-254.

Krumhansl, C. L. (1978). Concerning the applicability of geometric models to similarity data: The interrelationship between similarity and spatial density. *Psychological Review, 85*, 445-463.

Kruskal, J. B. (1956). On the shortest spanning subtree of a graph and the traveling salesman problem. *Proceedings of the American Mathematical Society, 7*, 48-50.

Kruskal, J. B. (1964). Nonmetric multidimensional scaling: A numerical method. *Psychometrika, 29,* 115-129.

Kruskal, J. B. (1977). Multidimensional scaling and other methods for discovering structure. In Enslein, Ralston, and Wilf (Eds.), *Statistical methods for digital computers*. New York: Wiley.

Manheimer, J., Stone, J. D., & McDonald, J. E. (1983). *A multidimensional scaling analysis of copier-function similarity rated by copier engineers and office workers* (IBM Technical Report No. TR77.0129).

McDonald, J. E., Dayton, J. T., & McDonald, D. R. (1986). *Adapting menu layout to tasks* (Memorandum in Computer and Cognitive Science, MCCS-86-78). New Mexico State University, Computing Research Laboratory.

McDonald, J. E., Stone, J. D., & Liebelt, L. S. (1983). Searching for items in menus: The effects of organization and type of target. *Proceedings of the 27th Annual Meeting of the Human Factors Society*, 834-837.

McDonald, J. E., Stone, J. D., Liebelt, L. S., & Karat, J. (1982). Evaluating a method for structuring the user-system interface. *Proceedings of the 26th Annual Meeting of the Human Factors Society,* 551-555.

Miller, D. P. (1981). The depth/breadth tradeoff in hierarchical computer menus. *Proceedings of the 25th Annual Meeting of the Human Factors Society, 296-300.*

Miller, G. A. (1969). A psychological method to investigate verbal concepts. *Journal of Mathematical Psychology, 6,* 169-191.

Miyamoto, S., Oi, K., Abe, O., Katsuya, A., & Nakayama, K. (1986). Directed graph representations of association structures: A systematic approach. *IEEE Transactions on Systems, Man and Cybernetics, 16,* 53-61.

Moran, T. P. (1981). An applied psychology of the user. *Computing Surveys, 13,* 1, 1-11.

Murphy, G. L., & Medin, D. L. (1985). The role of theories in conceptual coherence. *Psychological Review, 92,* 289-316.

Newell, A., & Simon, H. A. (1972). *Human Problem Solving.* Englewood Cliffs, N.J.: Prentice-Hall.

Norman, D. A. (1982). Steps toward a cognitive engineering: Design rules based on analyses of human error. *Proceedings of Human Factors in Computer Systems, CHI'82,* 378-382.

Norman, D. A. (1986). Cognitive engineering. In D. Norman and S. Draper (Eds.), *User centered system design.* New Jersey: Lawrence Erlbaum Associates.

Rosch, E., & Mervis, C. B. (1975). Family resemblances: Studies in the internal structure of categories. *Cognitive Psychology, 7,* 573-605.

Roske-Hofstrand, R. J., & Paap, K. R. (1986). Cognitive networks as a guide to menu organization: An application in the automated cockpit. *Ergonomics, 29,* 1301-1311.

Sachania, V. (1985). *Link weighted networks and contextual navigation through a database.* Unpublished M. S. thesis, New Mexico State University.

Sattath, S., & Tversky, A. (1977). Additive similarity trees. *Psychometrika, 42,* 319-345.

Schvaneveldt, R. W., & Durso, F. T. (1981). *Generalized semantic networks.* Paper presented at the meeting of the Psychonomic Society, Philadelphia.

Schvaneveldt, R. W., Durso, F. T., & Dearholt, D. W. (1985). *Pathfinder: Scaling with network structures* (Memorandum in Computer and Cognitive Science, MCCS-85-9). New Mexico State University, Computing Research Laboratory.

Schvaneveldt, R. W., Durso, F. T., Goldsmith, T. E., Breen, T. J., Cooke, N. M., Tucker, R. G., & DeMaio, J. C. (1985). Measuring the structure of expertise. *International Journal of Man-Machine Studies, 23,* 699-728.

Schvaneveldt, R. W., McDonald, J. E., & Cooke, N. M. (1985). *The user interface in computer systems: A research program* (Memorandum in Computer and Cognitive Science, MCCS-85-10). New Mexico State University, Computing Research Laboratory.

Shepard, R. N. (1962a). Analysis of proximities: Multi-dimensional scaling with an unknown distance function. I. *Psychometrika, 27*, 125-140.

Shepard, R. N. (1962b). Analysis of proximities: Multi-dimensional scaling with an unknown distance function. II. *Psychometrika, 27*, 219-246.

Shepard, R. N. (1963). Analysis of proximities as a technique for the study of information processing in man. *Human Factors, 5*, 33-48.

Shepard, R. N. (1974). Representation of structure in similarity data: Problems and prospects. *Psychometrika, 39*, 373-421.

Shepard, R. N., & Arabie, P. (1979). Additive clustering: Representation of similarities as combinations of discrete overlapping properties. *Psychological Review, 86*, 87-123.

Snowberry, K., Parkinson, S. R., & Sisson, N. (1983). Computer display menus. *Ergonomics, 26*, 7, 699-712.

Tullis, T. S. (1985). Designing a menu-based interface to an operating system. *Proceedings of Human Factors in Computing Systems (CHI'85) Conference.*

Tversky, A. (1977). Features of similarity. *Psychological Review, 84*, 327-352.

Tversky, A., & Hutchinson, J. W. (1986). Nearest neighbor analysis of psychological spaces. *Psychological Review, 91*, 3-22.

Young, R. M. (1983). Surrogates and mappings: Two kinds of conceptual models for interactive devices. In D. Gentner & A. Stevens (Eds.), *Mental models.* New Jersey: Lawrence Erlbaum Associates, pp. 35-52.

Index

Author Index

Subject Index